almanac on the nuclear balance, taking the reader through the chemistry and physics of nuclear explosives systems of aircraft and air and sea de sues for controllers, strategic arm is precise, co

—Walter C Jr., *Perspective*

"This is an excellent book. . . . The authors clearly demonstrate that they have a thorough grasp of the complex technological and political issues treated. At times gripping to the point of mesmerization. . . ."

—*Science Books* (AAAS)

"A carefully documented and well-written analysis of the nuclear arsenals of the world. . . . The clarity and comprehensiveness of this volume commend it." —*Library Journal*

ALBERT LEGAULT is Professor of Political Science and Director General, Centre québécois de relations internationales, at Laval University, Quebec. A graduate of the University of Montreal, he received his M.A. degree from the University of Chicago and his Ph.D. degree from the Graduate Institute of International Studies, Geneva.

GEORGE LINDSEY is Chief of the Operational Research and Analysis Establishment in the Canadian Department of National Defence, which he joined in 1950. He holds a B.A. degree from Toronto University, an M.A. degree from Queen's University, and a Ph.D. degree from Cambridge University.

D0915597

THE DYNAMICS of the NUCLEAR BALANCE

REVISED EDITION

THE DYNAMICS of the NUCLEAR BALANCE

by ALBERT LEGAULT
and GEORGE LINDSEY

REVISED EDITION

CORNELL UNIVERSITY PRESS | Ithaca and London

Copyright © 1974, 1976 by Cornell University

All rights reserved. Except for brief quotations in a review, this book, or parts thereof, must not be reproduced in any form without permission in writing from the publisher.
For information address Cornell University Press, 124 Roberts Place, Ithaca, New York 14850.

First published 1974 by Cornell University Press.
Published in the United Kingdom by Cornell University Press Ltd,
2-4 Brook Street, London W1Y 1AA.
Second printing 1975
Revised edition 1976

International Standard Book Number 0-8014-1007-x
Library of Congress Catalog Card Number 75-36367
Printed in the United States of America

355.02
L49

Preface

125771

Our modern society is rightly concerned about the presence of nuclear weapons and the state of the strategic balance. However, most persons interested enough to wish to think the issues through for themselves, but not able to devote months of study to the subject, are likely to be discouraged by the nature of the reading matter at their disposal.

It is not that there is a shortage of writing. There is a surfeit of material, scattered through many articles, pamphlets, and books of uneven quality. The problem has so many aspects—of technology, of military strategy, of international relations, and of morality—that if one began reading and analyzing any of them, all too likely one's investigations would be confined to a single point of view. This temptation is particularly enticing for university students, immersed in the atmosphere of their own faculty. Political scientists may not have the time or the inclination to prepare themselves to follow the arguments of engineers, and vice versa. The writings of both groups provide striking examples of what C. P. Snow has called "the two cultures."

The authors of this book have different backgrounds, one having spent more than two decades in defense research and the other nearly a decade teaching students of political science about contemporary strategic problems. Our aim here is to outline in the first few chapters, in a manner easily comprehensible to a reader without a background in the physical sciences, the salient features of nuclear energy and strategic weapon systems, and to follow this with a strategic analysis of deterrence and arms control, including the basic information which may be unfamiliar to those not well read in international affairs. The treatments are necessarily brief, but references are given to aid those wishing to read further. We emphasize facts and realities and do not attempt to treat moral issues.

We would like to thank the International Institute for Strategic Studies, which has kindly allowed us to use a chart from *Strategic Survey 1969* and numerous references from various issues of *The Military Balance*, *Survival*, and *Adelphi Papers*. And we would like to acknowledge permission from the Stockholm International Peace Research Institute to quote material from several issues of the *SIPRI Yearbook of World Armaments and Disarmament*.

One of us (G. L.) wishes to acknowledge the opportunity to study in Quebec afforded by the Defence Research Board of Canada and the Public Service Commission. However, the opinions do not represent the official views of any government body or of Laval University, where the authors did the work.

ALBERT LEGAULT
GEORGE LINDSEY

Quebec

Preface to the Revised Edition

In the two years since the writing of the first edition the most important developments have been in the SALT negotiations. Chapter IX has been extended to cover these changes, and numerous other small changes have been added in the earlier chapters to update numerical and technical data and to cite recent useful references.

A.L./G.L.

Quebec and Ottawa, June 1975

Contents

THE DYNAMICS of the NUCLEAR BALANCE

REVISED EDITION

CHAPTER I

Nuclear Explosives

Introduction

Although the first discoveries of nuclear physics date back to the beginning of the twentieth century, most of humanity received its first dramatic introduction to this immense new power when two nuclear weapons were used against Japan in August 1945. Since that date mankind has not ceased to debate the true significance of nuclear energy, the possible consequences of the use of nuclear weapons, and the menace which they pose for humanity.

This book is not about nuclear physics. But in order to discuss and understand the significance of nuclear weapons and the possibilities of controlling their dissemination or of defending against them, it is necessary to know certain rudimentary facts concerning the phenomena of nuclear fission and fusion, the steps necessary to prepare nuclear explosives, and the effects of nuclear explosions on people and on structures. Such information regarding nuclear explosives is presented in a very condensed form in this chapter.

A complete nuclear weapon or weapon system must include the vehicles to deliver the explosive and the means of their direction and control. A political scientist or strategist need not be able to design a weapon, but he will not be able to comprehend the significant factors determining the dynamics of the nuclear balance without a certain minimum knowledge of the fundamental characteristics of the weapon systems. Chapters II to V offer the necessary material with a minimum of technical detail.

From Chemistry to Nuclear Physics

If a pure substance is divided into portions of a size that can be seen, weighed, and handled in the laboratory, each portion exhibits the same chemical properties. In principle, this process can be continued to the level of a single *molecule*. Molecules can be subdivided into *atoms*, but once a molecule is broken, its parts become substances whose chemical properties are quite different from those of the parent molecule. Chemistry concerns itself with the process of the assembly and disintegration of molecules, and with the ways in which atoms associate to form new molecules.

For example, the burning of carbon in air is a chemical reaction described by the following equation:

$$\underset{\text{(carbon atom)}}{C} + \underset{\text{(oxygen molecule)}}{O_2} \rightarrow \underset{\text{(carbon dioxide molecule)}}{CO_2} + \underset{\text{(heat)}}{\text{energy}}$$

This reaction yields a product (molecules of carbon dioxide) that is more stable than the ingredients, and it also releases energy (in the form of heat). However, the reaction will not begin of its own accord at room temperature; it requires a stimulus, such as heat. But because heat is produced, once the reaction has been started it sustains itself as long as there is a continuing supply of both ingredients.

The atoms which make up the molecules contain a central *nucleus* surrounded by one or more shells of *electrons*. Chemical energy, the interactions among atoms and molecules, and the formation of molecules all are due to interactions among these electrons. The nuclei take no part at all in chemical reactions. Figure 1 illustrates these points.

The carbon atom has its central nucleus C, an inner shell of two electrons, and an outer shell of four. Two oxygen atoms each have their nuclei O and an inner shell of two electrons, but the two atoms have combined to form a molecule O_2 by partially merging their outer electron shells. The combustion produces a single molecule CO_2 in which the three nuclei (and their inner electron shells) remain inviolate but the outer electrons are shared. The CO_2 molecule is

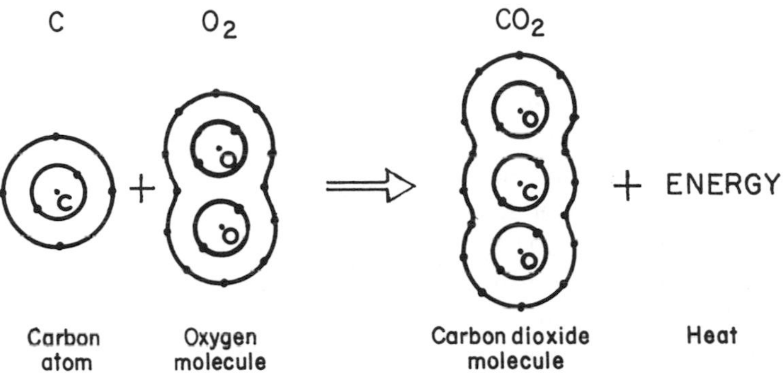

Figure 1. Combustion of carbon in air

more stable than the two ingredient particles C and O_2, in the sense that it would require energy to dissociate the CO_2 and reverse the reaction.

All chemical reactions follow this general type of behavior, including the most energetic, such as the combustion of gasoline, the detonation of explosives, or the burning of a rocket's propellant. It is most unlikely that new chemical reactions will be discovered that will yield substantially greater energy than do those already known. One of the most energetic chemical explosives is trinitrotoluene, or TNT. A common standard for the measurement of the energy released in an explosion is the quantity produced by one ton of TNT[1].

Until the early years of the twentieth century it was possible to build a deep and practical knowledge of chemistry on the assumption that atomic nuclei would always remain as permanent and indivisible units of matter. The dreams of the ancient alchemists to transmute base materials into precious metals were abandoned as impossible.

Nuclear physics began with the study of the heaviest nuclei, such as radium and uranium. Certain of these were found to emit radia-

[1] The explosion of 2000 lb of TNT produces 10^9 calories.

tions, at which times the nuclei altered their structures. This phenomenon became known as *natural radioactivity*. Measurement of the radiations indicated releases of energy far greater than anything ever found in the case of chemical reactions. However, these radioactive disintegrations occurred spontaneously, and there seemed to be no way to induce or prevent them.

It became possible to estimate the sizes of atoms and molecules, and it was learned that the nucleus was extremely small in comparison to the dimensions of the electronic shells. The outer shells had diameters between 10,000 and 100,000 times the diameter of the nuclei. Since the electrons themselves are even smaller than the nuclei, it can be seen that matter resembles astronomical space, in that the centers of mass are separated by empty spaces very large in comparison to the size of the masses.

Although these facts were proved only after centuries of experimental research, some of them had been foreseen by the Greek philosophers. In 450 B.C. Leucippus advanced the theory that matter was not infinitely divisible; he postulated that the constituent atoms were attached to one another by hooks. Thirty years later one of his disciples, Democritus, described matter as a collection in empty space of atoms which were indivisible, indestructible, and eternal. Reached by inductive reasoning and imagination, their conclusions bear close comparison to the modern concept of the atom, maintained in equilibrium by electrostatic forces between the nucleus and its surrounding electrons, and with the tiny dimensions of the particles dwarfed by the spaces between them.

Eventually, by using the energetic radiations from naturally radioactive nuclei, physicists succeeded in producing reactions in light nuclei. Researches later were greatly aided by the construction of high-voltage accelerators, cyclotrons, and other devices that could produce bombarding particles with energies very high in comparison to those associated with chemical reactions.

Little by little the secrets of nuclear structure have been discovered, certain steps having to await the construction of even more energetic accelerators. According to the current theories, nuclei are composed of elementary particles called *nucleons*. There are two types of nucleon: *protons*, which carry a positive electric charge, and *neutrons*, carrying no charge. Because like charges repel, it follows that protons experience a mutual electrostatic force of repulsion. However, should two nucleons (whether two protons, two neutrons, or a proton and a neutron) approach to close range, they are subjected to a very strong nuclear force of attraction, different in quality from the electrostatic force. In many cases the attractive forces are sufficient to overcome the repulsive forces and thus to retain an assembly of nucleons together as a stable nucleus. But the electrostatic repulsion, though weaker than the nuclear force at short range, decreases with increasing distance more gradually than does the nuclear force.

Because the protons are positive and the neutrons neutral, the nucleus always carries a positive charge. The electrons which make up the outer layers of the atom carry negative charges, and the electrostatic force of attraction between the positive nucleus and the negative electrons binds the atom together.

The electrons, the electronic shells of atoms, and their interactions form the subject of study of chemistry and of atomic physics. The concern of nuclear physics is with the properties of the nuclei of atoms.

Isotopes

Since the chemical characteristics depend on the electronic shells, and the number of electrons in a neutral atom (one with no net electric charge) must equal the number of positive charges in the nucleus, it follows that the chemical nature of an element is determined by the number of protons in the nucleus. If two nuclei contain the same number of protons, their atoms will have the same chemical properties, and they will carry the same name (the name of their element). But should the number of neutrons be different, the two nuclei belong to what we call different *isotopes* of the same element.

The simplest atom is that of light hydrogen. Its nucleus has a single proton, and its outer structure is a shell containing a single electron. Its symbol is H^1, where the index indicates the number of nucleons. Of all the hydrogen found in nature, 99.985 percent is of this type. However, the remaining 0.015 percent is another isotope, *deuterium*, or heavy hydrogen, whose nuclei contain one proton and one neutron, and whose symbol is H^2. The deuterium atom has only one electron and exhibits the same chemical behavior as does light hydrogen. Consequently, compounds of deuterium (such as heavy water) are chemically indistinguishable from those of light hydrogen (such as ordinary water).

To obtain deuterium in commercial quantities, we must separate the two hydrogen isotopes. Because the chemical properties are identical, the process is long, difficult, and very expensive.

A third isotope of hydrogen, known as *tritium* (H^3), has one proton and two neutrons in its nucleus. Tritium is not found in nature, but it can be created in a nuclear reactor.

The other isotopes to be encountered in this chapter are those of uranium. There are several isotopes, but we will be primarily concerned with two: uranium-235 and uranium-238. Each has 92 protons in its nucleus and 92 electrons in seven shells. The nucleus of U^{235} has 143 neutrons, while U^{238} has 146. Of the uranium found in nature 99.3 percent is the heavier isotope U^{238}, only 0.7 percent being U^{235}.

Some of the characteristics of the isotopes of hydrogen and of uranium are summarized on Figure 2.

Natural Radioactivity

Each of the 235 nucleons in a nucleus of U^{235} will be sufficiently close to a few of the others to experience the strongly attractive nuclear forces. But each of the 92 protons will be subject to the electrostatic force of repulsion from all of the other 91 protons. The net result is close to a balance: U^{235} is only just stable. In fact, after a lapse of time which may be long or short, nucleons escape spontaneously and leave behind a lighter nucleus. This is the phenomenon of natural radioactivity. Practically all of the nuclei which exhibit

Symbol	Name of isotope	Number of protons	Number of neutrons	Number of nucleons	Natural proportion	Nucleus	Atom
H^1	Light hydrogen	1	0	1	99.985%		
H^2 (or D^2)	Deuterium	1	1	2	0.015%		
H^3 (or T^3)	Tritium	1	2	3			
U^{235}	Uranium-235	92	143	235	0.7%		
U^{238}	Uranium-238	92	146	238	99.3%		

Figure 2. Table describing certain isotopes

natural radioactivity are heavy ones, containing more than 120 neutrons and 80 protons. The main cause of the instability producing the natural radioactivity is the mutual repulsion between the protons.

The radioactive disintegration can result in the emission of α or β particles, or of γ rays. α particles are nuclei of helium 4, β particles are electrons, and γ rays are similar to X rays, although more penetrating. For all three the energy can be measured, and it is invariably very large in comparison to the energy produced in chemical reactions. However, as previously indicated, the process is spontaneous and does not appear to have practical application for the production of energy.

Nuclear Fission

Fission Chain Reactions

Since the nucleus of uranium -235 is just on the point of instability, and since very large release of energy is associated with its disintegration, it appears to be a promising material to investigate for controlled production of energy. Is there some way in which U^{235} can be stimulated or excited so that it disintegrates at the wanted moment? Would the introduction of an additional nucleon provoke a disintegration? It would be very difficult to make a proton penetrate into the nucleus, since it would have to overcome the combined electrostatic repulsion of the 92 protons already present. On the other hand, a neutron would meet no such opposition.

A neutron can in fact be inserted into a U^{235} nucleus, but the probability of its absorption depends on its velocity. If it is moving slowly, there is a much greater probability that it will be captured. Once captured, the new nucleus, now U^{236}, is extremely unstable and quickly disintegrates. However, its mode of disintegration, known as *fission*, is very different from that of natural radioactivity, in which a small particle was emitted. In this case, the unstable U^{236} breaks into two large fission fragments, each containing approximately half of the 236 nucleons, and, most important, two or three neutrons. Moreoever, there is a very large release of energy, appearing in the velocity of the fission fragments and neutrons and in γ rays also emitted at the moment of disintegration, amounting in all to about forty times the energy released by a naturally occurring radioactive disintegration of U^{235}.

Since the reaction, which was started by a neutron provoking the fission of one U^{235} nucleus, produces two or three neutrons, there exists the possibility that further fission of additional U^{235} nuclei can be provoked and that a self-sustaining *chain reaction* can be produced by these newly liberated neutrons.

The following equation summarizes the fission reaction, in which the two fission fragments happen to be nuclei of xenon and strontium. The symbol n^1 indicates a neutron.

$$U^{235} + n^1 \longrightarrow \underset{\text{(unstable)}}{U^{236}} \xrightarrow[\text{fission}]{\text{instantaneous}} \underbrace{Xe^{140} + Sr^{94}}_{\text{radioactive fission products}} + n^1 + n^1 + \text{energy}$$

can cause the fission of other U^{235} nuclei

The way in which the chain reaction can spread is illustrated on Figure 3.

For a chain reaction to be sustained, several conditions must be met, however. It is by no means certain that a neutron produced by fission will be captured by a U^{235} nucleus and hence produce another fission. Remembering the small size of the nucleus and the comparatively enormous spacings between adjacent nuclei, a neutron can pass through millions of uranium atoms before coming close enough to a nucleus to be captured. Instead, the neutron may escape from the mass of uranium and be lost without provoking a fission. The arrows on Figure 3 illustrate such escaping neutrons.

If the mass of fissile material is too small, most of the neutrons will escape before they are captured by fissile nuclei. The ratio of neutrons which escape to neutrons which are captured can be reduced by making the mass of fissile material large, since the average path of a neutron will then pass through more material before it comes to the outer surface. It may be possible to cause some of the escaped neutrons to return to the fissile material by surrounding it with a substance capable of reflecting neutrons. If nuclei of a type which do not fission are present, they may nevertheless compete for capture of the neutrons.

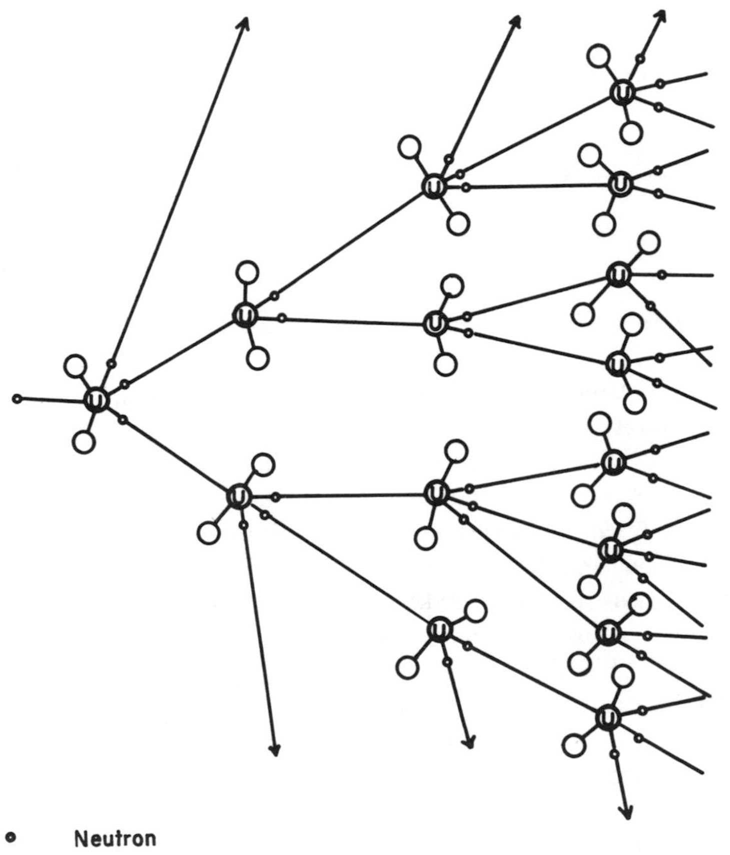

Figure 3. Fission chain reaction

Taking all these factors into account, the requirement for the chain reaction to be sustained is that the number of neutrons produced must be equal to or greater than the number of neutrons which disappear.

So far we have discussed only the isotope U^{235}. The more abundant U^{238} behaves differently. If irradiated by slow neutrons, U^{238} nuclei can capture the neutron to form U^{239}, but this new nucleus is not sufficiently unstable for instantaneous fission. However, it is unstable enough for radioactive disintegration over a longer time-span, following these equations:

$$U^{238} + n^1 \longrightarrow U^{239} \xrightarrow[\text{disintegration (23 min)}]{\text{radioactive}} Np^{239} + e^0$$

$$Np^{239} \xrightarrow{\text{radioactive disintegration (2.3 days)}} Pu^{239} + e^0$$

Np^{239} represents neptunium and Pu^{239} plutonium; neither is found in nature[2]. The symbol e^0 designates an electron or β particle. U^{238} cannot be used as the basic fuel for a self-sustaining chain reaction; however, the artificially created element Pu^{239} is fissile and can sustain a chain reaction according to the following plan:

$$Pu^{239} + n^1 \longrightarrow \underset{\text{(unstable)}}{Pu^{240}} \xrightarrow[\text{fission}]{\text{instantaneous}} \begin{pmatrix}\text{radioactive}\\ \text{fission}\\ \text{products}\end{pmatrix} + (\text{neutrons}) + \text{energy}$$

(neutrons) → can cause the fission of other Pu^{239} nuclei → n^1

The third substance capable of sustaining a fission chain reaction is U^{233}.

[2] Discovery of tiny traces of Pu^{244} in naturally occurring rare earth mixtures has been announced by Seaborg, *Le Monde*, September 11, 1971, p. 5.

Fission Reactors

There are two quite different practical methods of producing energy through nuclear fission. One is to maintain a chain reaction at a steady controlled rate over a long period in a nuclear reactor. The other is to produce an enormous sudden release of energy in an explosion.

The cheapest fuel for a fission reactor is natural uranium, containing both U^{235} and U^{238}. The reactions occurring will be as follows:

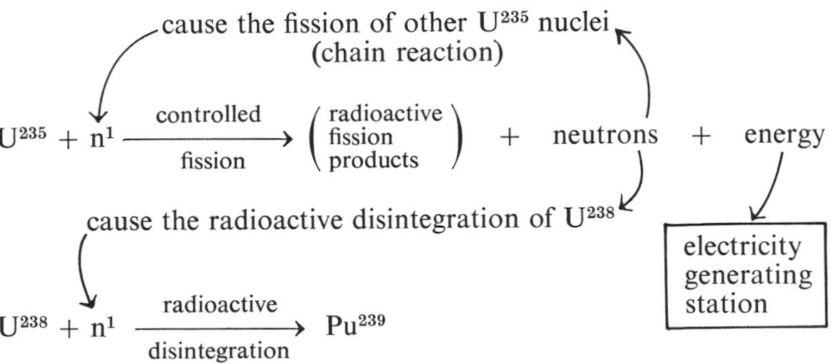

Note that the chain reaction is sustained by the isotope U^{235}, present in the small proportion of 0.7 percent. U^{238}, 140 times more abundant, presents severe competition for the capture of the fast neutrons resulting from fission. However, since the probability of fission capture by U^{235} is greater for slow than for fast neutrons, the proportions of neutrons which produce fission can be increased by slowing them down in a "moderator" such as heavy water or graphite.[3] In a power reactor, the heat is removed from the fissioning material and used for the generation of electricity. The power level is governed by the movement of control bars made from a substance which captures neutrons, such as cadmium.

A fission reactor can be made more efficient, and can be operated

[3] The presence of a moderator lengthens the time between successive fissions by a factor as large as 10,000.

without the need for a moderator, if the proportion of U^{235} is greater than the 0.7 percent found in the natural mixture. But the presence of U^{238} will ensure that plutonium is created as long as the reactor is operated, a fact of considerable significance for the control of materials capable of being made into nuclear weapons.

The design objective of a fission reactor is to operate at a constant controlled level for long periods of time, with the purpose of producing commercial power, plutonium for nuclear explosives, or neutrons for research or for the manufacture of artificial isotopes.

Fission Bombs

The design objective of a bomb is to release a very large amount of energy in a very short time, and at the precise moment desired, for the purpose of destruction. One result of the explosion will be to blow the reacting material apart and to stop its reacting. As a consequence, the energy yield of the bomb depends in a very sensitive way on the speed with which the fission reactions can be completed. The material will begin to separate within about one-half of one-millionth of a second after the fission reaction has started, but 99.9 percent of the energy released will be produced during the last seven one-hundredths of a millionth of a second that the reaction continues.[4] It is not possible to indulge the preference of U^{235} for slow neutrons, and, since U^{238} would capture the majority of fast neutrons if it were present in the proportion of 140:1, natural uranium cannot be used for a fission bomb. It is necessary to enrich the proportions of U^{235} to 90 or 95 percent or to use plutonium-239 instead of uranium.

It was explained earlier that if the block of fissile material is too small, too many neutrons will escape before causing fission and a chain reaction cannot be sustained. The mass which is just large enough to allow a chain reaction to be maintained is called *the critical mass*. This crucial importance of size is used for the initiation of the nuclear explosion. The fissile material (U^{235} or Pu^{239}) is formed into

[4] Samuel Glasstone, ed., *The Effects of Nuclear Weapons* (rev. ed.; U.S. Department of Defense and U.S. Atomic Energy Commission, 1964), pp. 14–16.

two or more subcritical masses. To detonate the bomb, the subcritical masses are suddenly brought together by the detonation of a conventional explosive, to form one supercritical mass. Alternatively, a subcritical mass of fissile material can be surrounded by a sphere of conventional explosive and compressed into a supercritical mass by the inward shock wave (or *implosion*).[5]

The Energy Released by Fission

In the case of the two nuclear bombs used against Japan in 1945, it is estimated that about two and a half pounds of uranium or of plutonium underwent fission. The power of each explosion was approximately equivalent to the energy released by the detonation of 20,000 tons of TNT[6]—that is to say, 40,000,000 pounds of TNT. It follows that one pound of fissile material yields as much energy as about 16,000,000 pounds of TNT, so that the ratio of the energy yields of the nuclear and of the chemical reactions is about sixteen million.

This enormous factor is a measure of the differences in the energies involved in the outer electronic shells of atoms, which govern chemical processes, and in the interactions between nucleons.

As a final illustration of the immense gulf between chemical and nuclear energy, the fission of one ounce of uranium-235 produces as much energy as the burning of nearly eighty tons of coal, which also requires about 1100 tons of air.

Production of the Explosive Material for Fission Bombs

We have seen that the isotope U^{235} is needed in a greater concentration than the 0.7 percent with which it is found in natural uranium. And, because the chemical behavior of U^{235} and U^{238} is identical,

[5] Glasstone, ed., *op. cit.*, pp. 18–19.

[6] A weapon with a yield of 20,000 tons of TNT, or 20 kilotons, is commonly referred to as "a nominal bomb." More accurate measurements have fixed the yield at 14 KT for the Hiroshima bomb and 21 KT for the one exploded at Nagasaki. See page 50 of Stockholm International Peace Research Institute, *SIPRI Yearbook of World Armaments and Disarmament, 1969/70*; afterwards cited in the abridged form *SIPRI, 1969/70*.

separation of the two isotopes is very difficult. It is necessary to use the small difference in mass, which produces a small difference in the rate at which the two will diffuse through a porous membrane.

Separation by diffusion is best performed with gases, and for this purpose the gaseous compound uranium hexafluoride is used. The gas is forced under pressure through a series of porous membranes, and at each membrane the proportion of lighter isotope U^{235} in the gas which penetrates is very slightly greater.[7] The gas must be cycled through thousands of membranes if a large concentration of U^{235} is desired; the scale of the necessary plant is very large indeed and the process consumes a great deal of energy. To give an idea of the enormous quantities of electricity involved, the separation of U^{235} in the United States about ten years ago was using as much electric power as generated in the whole of France.[8] And the three great American separation plants in Oak Ridge, Paducah, and Portsmouth, operating at full capacity, need as much power as does the whole of Australia.

The cost of these separation plants is correspondingly huge. The first American gaseous diffusion plant is said to have cost a billion dollars,[9] as is the French installation at Pierrelatte. It is not surprising that uranium-235 enriched to 95 percent is priced at more than $7000 per pound.[10]

The other fission explosive, plutonium-239, must be manufactured in nuclear reactors. As explained earlier, it is a necessary product of the fission of natural uranium, or of uranium fuel in which the proportion of U^{235} has been enriched to a few percent. The extraction

[7] The factor is about 1.0043 in the early stages.

[8] Yves Chelet, *L'énergie nucléaire* (Paris: Editions du Seuil, 1968), p. 31.

[9] Leonard Beaton, "Capabilities of Non-Nuclear Powers," in Alastair Buchan, ed., *A World of Nuclear Powers* (Englewood Cliffs, N.J.: Prentice-Hall for the American Assembly, 1966), p. 14.

[10] Chelet, *op. cit.*, p. 31. A figure of $5000–$5500 per pound is quoted by the *Report of the Secretary-General on the Effects of the Possible Use of Nuclear Weapons and on the Security and Economic Implications for States of the Acquisition and Further Development of These Weapons* (United Nations Publication E.68.IX.1, A/6858), p. 23; hereafter this document will be cited under the abridged title *Report of the U.N. Secretary-General, 1967.*

of the plutonium from the used uranium fuel rods is not a simple process, and handling is complicated by the fact that the rods are highly radioactive because of the fission products. However, since plutonium has 94 protons in its nucleus and 94 electrons in its atomic shells, its chemistry is different from that of all the other materials and it can be separated by chemical means. A reactor and a chemical separation plant for the production of moderate quantities of plutonium would cost only about one-twentieth as much as a gaseous diffusion plant[9] for the separation of U^{235}. Moreover, the former would produce electric power while the latter would consume it. In a few years power will be produced by "fast breeder" reactors using Pu^{239} as fuel, but creating more Pu^{239} than they consume.[11]

There is a conflict of policy to be faced by the operators of reactors intended for both power and weapons-grade plutonium. For the most economical power generation, the fuel rods should be left in the reactor until a considerable proportion of the U^{235} has been depleted by fission. However, in this case, a significant fraction of the Pu^{239} nuclei will absorb a neutron and become Pu^{240}, which is not fissile. For the most efficient weapons, it is necessary to use Pu^{239} with no more than a few percent of nonfissionable isotopes, and hence to remove the rods early.

High enrichment is necessary for weapons and for compact power plants, as used in nuclear-powered submarines, but much lower factors are adequate for static reactors generating electricity.

The first nuclear bomb, exploded in a test at Alamogordo in the United States in July 1945, was a plutonium fission device. The one burst over Hiroshima used U^{235}, with two subcritical masses being brought together by a conventional explosive. The Nagasaki bomb used Pu^{239}, with detonation by implosion.[12] The first French test, in 1960, used plutonium.

[11] Glenn Seaborg and Justin Bloom, "Fast Breeder Reactors," *Scientific American* 223 (November 1970), 13–21.

[12] R. E. Lapp, "Nuclear Weapons: Past and Present," *Bulletin of the Atomic Scientists* 26 (June 1970), 103–106.

It was a great surprise to the Western world when the first Chinese test, in 1964, proved to be a bomb based on U^{235}. It had been assumed that a country newly embarking on the construction of nuclear weapons would have begun with the cheaper and easier plutonium, before undertaking the much more expensive and difficult process of the separation of uranium isotopes.

Nuclear Fusion

Once the practicality of nuclear fission bombs had been demonstrated, technical improvements were made towards more powerful bombs and also toward smaller, more efficient weapons. It required a large bomber to carry the first nuclear bomb, but as the yield-to-weight ratio was increased, it became possible to place powerful nuclear warheads on long-range rocket vehicles, and to propel smaller warheads from artillery pieces or other mobile tactical launchers or to drop them from comparatively small aircraft.

However, there is a practical upper limit to the yield which can be obtained from the explosion of a fission bomb, probably in the vicinity of a few hundred kilotons. Beyond this limit, additional fissile material will be dispersed by the explosion before it can fission. Also, fissile material is extremely expensive, so that there were economic as well as technical reasons to seek another method of obtaining very high energy yields, whether for weapons or for the production of power.

We have seen that fission was possible because very heavy nuclei are less stable than those of middle weight. At the other end of the scale, the assembly of nucleons making up certain very light nuclei can be made more stable if they merge or fuse into larger units. The opportunity for the strong nuclear forces of attraction to act among an increased number of nucleons will increase stability and result in a large release of energy. However, owing to the electrostatic repulsion between protons, the same difficulty which prevented protons from being a means of sustaining a fission chain reaction with heavy nuclei will arise in the attempt to make two light nuclei approach sufficiently closely for the powerful short-range nuclear forces to act. It is possible to use an accelerator to give light nuclei enough energy to overcome the electrostatic repulsion and fuse with certain other nuclei, but a chain reaction cannot be sustained in this manner. There is, however, another method. If the fusible material could be raised to a very high temperature, of the order of tens of millions of degrees, the intense thermal agitations would permit a certain fraction of the nuclei to enter into contact sufficiently close to permit fusion. And, since the result of the fusion would be to liberate thermal energy, there is the possibility of a self-sustaining chain reaction.

Temperatures of tens of millions of degrees are not normally reached on Earth, but they exist in the centers of stars, including the sun. This is no coincidence, because the heat of the sun and the light from the stars have their origin in a series of *thermonuclear* reactions.

To this date, it has not been found possible to sustain a continuous and controlled thermonuclear reaction for the production of power. However, the necessary temperatures can be attained (momentarily) in the vicinity of an exploding fission bomb. If material containing light fusible nuclei is placed around a fission bomb, detonation of the bomb can raise the temperature sufficiently to trigger the fusion process, which can then sustain itself.

The main fusible nuclei are the heavy isotopes of hydrogen: deuterium (H^2) and tritium (H^3). However, for a practical weapon, it is common to commence with deuterium and the isotope Li^6 of lithium.[13] On capturing a neutron, Li^6 divides into He^4 (a helium nucleus, or α particle, which is particularly stable) and H^3. At temperatures of tens of millions of degrees H^2 and H^3 will fuse, liberating a very fast neutron and a great amount of energy. The neutron can react with another Li^6 nucleus, to produce a new tritium nucleus, and the energy can maintain the high temperature which will allow the tritium to fuse with deuterium. One has a self-sustaining thermonuclear chain reaction.

[13] Chelet, *op. cit.*, p. 136, and Lapp, *op. cit.*, p. 104.

Such a bomb is called a thermonuclear weapon, fusion bomb, or H-bomb (because of its dependence on isotopes of hydrogen). There is a certain analogy to the chemical reaction of the burning of carbon in air, which is a self-sustaining thermal reaction once it has been lighted by bringing some of the material to a high temperature. The match which lights the thermonuclear reaction is the fission bomb.

Fission bombs are sometimes called atomic bombs, or A-bombs, in contrast to thermonuclear or H-bombs. Atomic bomb is an inaccurate term, since both types of bomb depend on nuclear rather than atomic reactions.

Since the matter of critical size does not arise, there is no limit to the amount of fusible material that can be placed in fusion bombs, and they produce so much more energy than fission bombs that their yields are commonly measured in megatons (millions of tons of TNT) rather than kilotons (thousands of tons of TNT).

To be precise, a thermonuclear bomb triggered by a fission reaction should be labeled a "fission-fusion bomb." However, it is possible to take advantage of the yield of very fast neutrons from the fusion process to obtain even more energy in a three-stage *fission-fusion-fission*, *F-F-F*, or "*doped*" bomb.[14] To do this, the fission-fusion bomb is surrounded by a thick shell of natural uranium, which is much cheaper than the separated isotopes of U^{235}, H^2, or Li^6. Although U^{238} cannot be induced to fission by neutrons with the energy produced in the fission of U^{235}, the neutrons produced by the fusion reaction are much more energetic, and are able to excite the U^{238} nucleus to the energy level at which it will fission. The added energy due to these fissions adds considerably to the total yield of the three-stage weapon.[15]

[14] There are also doped fission bombs, containing fusible material which augments the yield without sustaining a fusion chain reaction. See *Le Monde*, August 27, 1968, p. 11.

[15] According to Glasstone, ed., *op. cit.*, p. 6, roughly equal amounts of energy [illegible]t from fission and from fusion.

The reactions in an F-F-F bomb are summarized below:

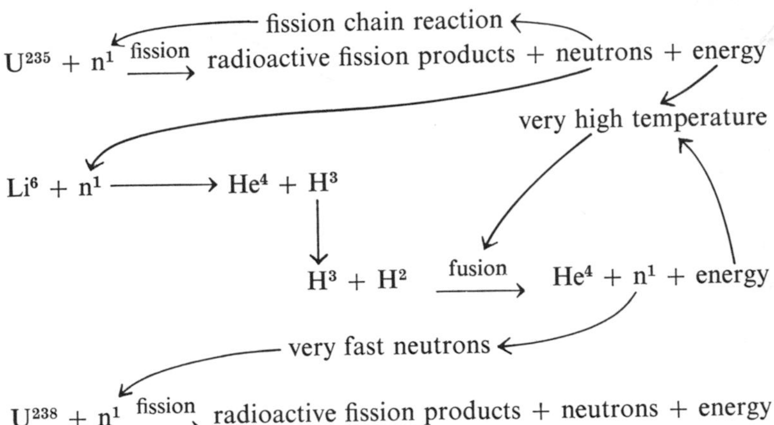

There does not appear to be any theoretical limit to the energy yield attainable by an F-F-F bomb. The Soviet Union exploded one which released 58 megatons. It has been estimated[12] that a 100-megaton three-stage bomb could be carried by a heavy strategic bomber, but that the maximum payload of the largest operational ballistic missiles would not be adequate for such a weapon.

It appears that the fission bomb to ignite the thermonuclear reaction should be based on U^{235} rather than plutonium.[16] Consequently, a country intending to arm itself with fusion weapons will need to build the enormously expensive plants for the separation of uranium isotopes. All five members of the "nuclear club"—the United States, the Soviet Union, Great Britain, France, and China (listed in order of entry)—have produced both fission and fusion weapons. However, unless a cheaper method can be found to separate U^{235}, depending on smaller installations,[17] it seems that a

[16] *Report of the U.N. Secretary-General, 1967*, p. 23. See also John Maddox, "The Nuclear Club," *Survival* 11 (September 1969), 274–278, and the subsequer correspondence with Van Voorhis in *Survival* 12 (February 1970), 66.

[17] Such possibilities have been suggested, based on gas centrifuges of mode size. See, for example, pp. 373–374 of *SIPRI, 1972*.

small country attempting the clandestine manufacture of nuclear weapons would almost certainly choose fission bombs based on plutonium.[18]

Although the power of nuclear weapons to destroy structures depends on their energy yield, it will be explained in the final section of this chapter that there is an additional hazard to living beings from the nuclear radiation. Designers of nuclear weapons could attempt to maximize the radiation, using a "dirty" bomb to contaminate a large region, or they might wish to minimize it, using a "clean" bomb to diminish hazard to life and to avoid contamination. The most serious hazard from radiation originates in the fission products, which are almost all strongly radioactive. It is impossible to have fission without producing fission products, and therefore prolonged radiation. The cleanest bomb would be a fission-fusion bomb with the minimum amount of fission necessary to trigger the thermonuclear reaction.[19] A three-stage bomb will be fairly dirty because of the large amount of fission in the third stage. But it is possible to make a bomb very dirty by surrounding it with a material which will be rendered highly radioactive by the absorption of neutrons.[20] Cobalt is such a material. A "cobalt bomb" can be a dirty nuclear weapon. Unfortunately, the same term is used for cobalt irradiated by neutrons in a reactor and used to irradiate malignant tumors. To protect handlers from its radiation, the cobalt is kept in a thick metal container known as a "bomb."

It will be seen in the last section of this chapter that the amount of radiation caused by a nuclear weapon depends in great measure on the altitude at which it is burst.

[18] *Report of the U.N. Secretary-General, 1967*, p. 23.

[19] If it were possible to attain the high temperature by some other means, such as by concentration of energy in a laser beam, fusion could be triggered without fission. See William R. Van Cleave, "NPT and Fission-free Research," *Orbis*, Winter, 1968, reprinted in *Survival* 10 (October 1968), 327–333.

[20] This is called "induced radioactivity."

The Number of Nuclear Weapons Already Manufactured

The total power of the nuclear explosives already manufactured by the five nuclear powers has been estimated at 50,000 megatons.[21] It is very difficult to say into how many weapons this may have been placed. The number of nuclear warheads in the U.S. strategic forces is about 8500,[22] and the number with the NATO forces in Europe is about 7000, all except a very few being held under American custody.[23] If one adds to these published figures the nuclear antiaircraft and antisubmarine weapons, the nuclear demolition mines, and the reserve stocks, the United States could have over 50,000 nuclear warheads. The Soviet Union must have some tens of thousands, of which about 2800, including the largest ones, are mounted on their strategic weapons.[24] The International Institute for Strategic Studies estimates that there may be 3500 Soviet tactical nuclear warheads in the European theater. Britain may have 1500 nuclear warheads, France some hundreds, and China two or three hundred.[25]

Effects of Nuclear Explosions

General Characteristics[26]

If a nuclear weapon is exploded in the air at an altitude below 100,000 feet, about 50 percent of the energy is transmitted in the form of blast and shock, about 35 percent as radiated heat, and 15 percent

[21] *SIPRI, 1969/70,* p. 381.

[22] The U.S. Secretary of Defense J. R. Schlesinger gave 8500 as the force loadings for mid-1975. *Annual Defense Department Report for FY 1976 and FY 197T* (Washington, February 1975), p. II–19. In subsequent citations this document will be entitled *Statement of Secretary Schlesinger, 1975.*

[23] According to *The Military Balance, 1975–76* (London: The International Institute for Strategic Studies, 1975), p. 16, the average yield of the bombs stockpiled in Europe for the use of NATO tactical aircraft is about 100 KT, while the missile warheads average 20 KT.

[24] Dr. Schlesinger's report gave 2800 for mid-1975, but the number will rise as new large submarines are built and multiple warheads fitted to missiles.

[25] Figures from *SIPRI, 1969/70,* pp. 378–381, and *The Military Balance, 1975/76,* pp. 48, 101.

[26] Glasstone, ed., *op. cit.,* chap. I.

as nuclear radiation. But at higher altitudes, where there is too little air to transmit shock waves, more of the energy will be radiated as heat. On the other hand, all of the energy of an underground or underwater explosion will be transmitted as shock.

Blast and shock transmitted through the air can be extremely destructive to exposed structures on the surface of the earth, and buried structures can be destroyed by underground shock waves.

Transmission of heat radiation from a source at high altitude to the ground depends on atmospheric conditions, as illustrated by the example of heat from the sun. On a clear day nearly all of the energy in the visible light spectrum penetrates, and exposed skin is vulnerable to sunburn. But on a cloudy or rainy day most of the light is absorbed or scattered before reaching the earth. In the case of a nuclear explosion, the pulse of heat radiation is intense but of short duration. On a clear day it could set flammable materials alight and inflict severe or fatal burns to exposed human skin. As with sunburn, a very light protection will very greatly reduce the damage done to the skin.

Of the 15 percent of the total energy transmitted as nuclear radiation, perhaps 5 percent is emitted within a minute of the explosion and is called *initial nuclear radiation* (or "prompt" nuclear radiation). It is largely composed of γ rays and neutrons, both of which are penetrating and damaging to living tissue. Also, neutrons can induce radioactivity in various substances. As far as its practical consequences are concerned, initial nuclear radiation is the least important of the effects, since persons close enough to the burst and with slight enough protection to be endangered by these radiations would be subject to a greater hazard from blast.

The other 10 percent of the energy appears in the form of *residual nuclear radiation*, which is due almost entirely to the radioactive fission products, and is emitted over a long period of time. The radiations are in the form of β and γ rays. The mixture of fission products is extremely complex, involving two hundred isotopes with radioactive half-lives ranging from a small fraction of a second to a million years. The activity is intense during the hours immediately following the explosion but slowly decreases with time, so that two days after the explosion it will have dropped to 1 percent of its strength at one hour.

The dissemination of the fission products depends on the location of the burst and the meteorological conditions. If the explosion occurs at or close to ground level, fission products may fuse with particles of earth and fall to the ground fairly close to the explosion, causing severe contamination in the area immediately downwind. But an explosion at high altitude will scatter the fission products widely through the stratosphere, and the subsequent *radioactive fall-out* will be very widely distributed in time and space and correspondingly much less intense. As a result of about four hundred nuclear test explosions performed in the atmosphere since 1951, a slight but measurable level of radioactive fallout is constantly descending to the earth.

The effects on the human body of nuclear radiations are much more harmful than their quantity of energy would suggest. β rays will cause surface burns. But γ rays and neutrons penetrate deep into the body and can cause somatic damage and *radiation sickness*, which can be fatal. Moreover, these radiations can produce genetic injury to the hereditary mechanisms of the body, causing defects to succeeding generations.

One of the most dangerous of the radioactive products is strontium-90, which has a chemical resemblance to calcium and consequently fixes itself in the bones. It has a radioactive half-life of 28 years. Other isotopes from the fallout may enter the ecological cycle of plants and animals. Cow's milk, for example, may contain several of the radioactive elements which have fallen on the pasture land.

A full discussion of the effects of nuclear weapons would need to cover not only the effects on individual men and structures but a detailed description of their use against various types of targets, such as, for example, tactical targets on the battlefield, strategic military targets (for example, missile sites or airfields), or cities. This chapter will terminate with a few examples of the effects of nuclear attack on cities; the vulnerability of strategic targets will be discussed in Chapter II.

Effects on Cities[27]

A nuclear weapon burst above a large city can destroy life and structures over an area of many square miles, owing mainly to the effects of blast and of heat. The loss of life would be greatest in a surprise attack during working hours on a clear summer day, with a large concentration of people in the central area and many exposed outside with a minimum of protective clothing. The fire hazard depends on the type of buildings and the weather; the damage from blast depends on the type of construction.

In general, persons or structures close to *ground zero*, the point directly beneath the detonation, are likely to be destroyed in spite of any feasible protection, while persons and structures many miles away will escape the effects of blast and heat. It is in the intermediate ring-shaped zone that many can save their lives by taking shelter before the moment of detonation. However, if the weapon is burst at a low altitude, the area exposed to radioactive fallout may extend far away from the attacked city.

In the case of Hiroshima, the 14-kiloton fission bomb was burst at a height of 1850 feet during a clear summer day. Of the 300,000 inhabitants, 78,000 were killed and 84,000 injured.[28] Sixty thousand buildings were completely or partially destroyed. Within a mile and a half of ground zero, wooden buildings were carried away and brick buildings collapsed. Severe damage to houses occurred as far out as five miles. However, there were no casualties due to fallout.

The radius of the blast effects does not vary in direct proportion to the energy yield of the explosion.[29] If, for example, an attacker wished

[27] *Report of the U.N. Secretary-General, 1967*, chap. I.

[28] Glasstone, ed., *op. cit.*, p. 550, gives 256,300 inhabitants, 68,000 killed, and 76,000 injured.

[29] The radius of the blast effect varies as the cube root of the weapon yield, *ibid.*, pp. 127–133.

to maximize the area on the ground subjected to a level of 4 pounds per square inch (4 psi) of blast peak overpressure, and had a weapon of 100-KT yield, he would explode it at a height of 4650 feet. The overpressure would then exceed 4 psi out to a distance of about 2 nm, and over an area of about 12 square nm. If the attacker used a weapon of ten times the yield (that is, 1 MT), he would maximize the area subject to the 4-psi overpressure by bursting his weapon at 10,000 feet but the radius of the desired effect would only extend to 4.3 nm and over an area of 58 square nm. The factor of 10 in yield produces factors of 2.15 in range and 4.64 in area.

The U.N. report[27] calculated the results of a one-megaton ground burst in a city of over a million inhabitants spread over an area of five or six miles. The outcome was as follows:

Killed by blast and heat	270,000
Killed by radioactive fallout	90,000
Injured	90,000
Uninjured	710,000

These figures can be compared with the 305,000 civilians killed by the aerial bombardments of Germany in World War II.[30] However, since the large weapon was supposed to have been burst on the ground, there could have been heavy radioactive fallout over considerable areas up to hundreds of miles downwind from the location of the burst.

If the one-megaton weapon were exploded at a height of 10,000 feet above the city, there would be negligible local fallout, but the damage due to blast and heat would be greater. The U.N. report estimates that for a city of a million inhabitants distributed over 120 square nm such a weapon would destroy all the buildings and kill or seriously injure

[30] The total weight of bombs dropped on Germany was in the vicinity of 1.3 megatons, composed of conventional explosives and incendiary bombs. The total weight of bombs used by all combatants for both strategic and tactical purposes in World War II and Korea combined is estimated at 3.1 megatons, while the total weight dropped on Indochina between 1965 and 1973 by the U.S. Air Force was 6.5 megatons.

90 percent of the people within a radius of about $1\frac{1}{2}$ nm. At distances between $1\frac{1}{2}$ and 3 nm, buildings would be partially or completely damaged, with 50 percent human casualties. And in the ring distant from ground zero between 3 and $4\frac{1}{2}$ nm, buildings would be severely damaged and about 35 percent of the people injured.

The U.N. study also considered the effect of a 20-megaton explosion over Manhattan. Unless the population were evacuated or in shelters, it was estimated that between six and eight million inhabitants would be killed, in addition to another million outside New York.

Figures such as these demonstrate the frightful consequences for humanity should an all-out war ever involve the use of nuclear weapons against unprepared cities.

CHAPTER II

Offensive Strategic Missiles

The proudest long-range weapons in military arsenals have included, in their time, javelins, bows and arrows, heavy artillery, and the bomber aircraft.

Heavy artillery reached its practical limit with the Paris Gun, popularly known as "Big Bertha," with which the Germans bombarded Paris in 1918 from a range of 65 nm. Weighing 129 tons and with a barrel 100 feet long, Big Bertha was so unwieldy and suffered so many technical difficulties that it was of more psychological than military value.

The heavy bomber offered far more range, mobility, and concentrated firepower than artillery. It was the supreme strategic weapon from 1940 to 1960. But it is very vulnerable on its base, is vulnerable in flight, and is likely to be detected in its approach.

The latest long-range weapon to appear, and without doubt the most effective for strategic use, is the Intercontinental Ballistic Missile (ICBM) armed with a thermonuclear warhead. The increase in speed by a factor of ten over the bomber represents the second great jump in the capabilities of modern weapons, second only to the gigantic jump from chemical to nuclear explosives, which has allowed a ten-ton "high-explosive" bomb to be replaced by an H-bomb with the power of ten million tons of "high-explosive." The ICBM, with a thermonuclear payload, combines both of these remarkable developments.

The Ballistic Rocket

The principle of rocket propulsion has been known for a long time. It depends on Newton's third law: "action is equal and opposite to reaction." If, from any free body, matter is ejected with momentum in a certain direction, then the body gains equal momentum in the opposite direction. The presence of air around the body is not necessary (and is in fact a hindrance), so that rocket propulsion can be achieved outside the atmosphere.

To achieve a high velocity by the time it leaves the muzzle of the gun, a projectile must be able to withstand an enormous acceleration (many thousand times the acceleration of gravity), and as a consequence it must be very strongly constructed. On the other hand, a rocket motor can apply a modest acceleration over a period of seconds or minutes and achieve very high velocity without the need for particularly rugged construction.

In the past, the usefulness of long-range rockets was limited by their poor accuracy. But this difficulty has been overcome by modern electronic control techniques and by the method of *inertial guidance*. And the improvement of rocket motors and rocket fuels has allowed the ranges and the payloads to be increased.

To obtain intercontinental ranges or space flight, it is necessary to accelerate to very high velocities not only the payload but also the rocket motors and the as yet unburned fuel. To reduce the expenditure of energy in accelerating mass other than the payload, the rockets are built in several stages. The first stage contains the heaviest and most powerful motors. Once its fuel has been expended, the first stage is separated. The second-stage rockets are then ignited, and they need accelerate only themselves and the higher stages. As each stage is burnt out, it is left behind, so that fuel need not be spent in accelerating a mass that is no longer useful. The separation of the burnt-out stages and the ignition of the succeeding stages must, of course, function properly.

There are two principal phases in the trajectory of a rocket. The *propulsion phase* lasts while the motors are burning to accelerate the rocket. It may represent a comparatively short part of the entire trajectory, but during it we can most easily apply guidance and control by altering the direction of thrust of the motors and selecting the moment to shut them down. Once the thrust of the motors ceases, the rocket proceeds on the *ballistic phase* of its trajectory, which is determined by the velocity and direction of motion at the end of the propulsion phase and is affected only by the acceleration of gravity (due to the attraction of the earth) and, if it is in the atmosphere, by the deceleration due to air resistance. In the absence of air resistance, a ballistic trajectory which eventually returns to earth is an ellipse. During the ballistic phase the rocket acts the same as a projectile from a gun, offering no opportunity for guidance or control.

For a missile which reenters the atmosphere at the end of its trajectory there is the *terminal phase*. During this phase the resistance of the atmosphere may affect the trajectory, and it is possible that some form of terminal guidance may be applied, possibly through the use of aerodynamic surfaces on the missile.

Intercontinental Ballistic Missiles

The ballistic trajectory of a missile is determined by the velocity and direction at the moment propulsion ceases. For a given range between burnout and impact, there is a direct relationship between the payload[1] and the thrust delivered by the motors. The greater the thrust, or the longer it is sustained, the more payload can be delivered. Alternatively, for a given total impulse from the motors, it is possible to obtain an increased range by reducing the payload (or vice versa). However, the trajectories do not depend on the mass of the objects or on the means by which they were accelerated to their velocities.

To illustrate the effect of burnout velocity on range, Figure 4 shows

[1] More precisely, the total weight which can be put into the ballistic trajectory, sometimes called the *throw-weight*.

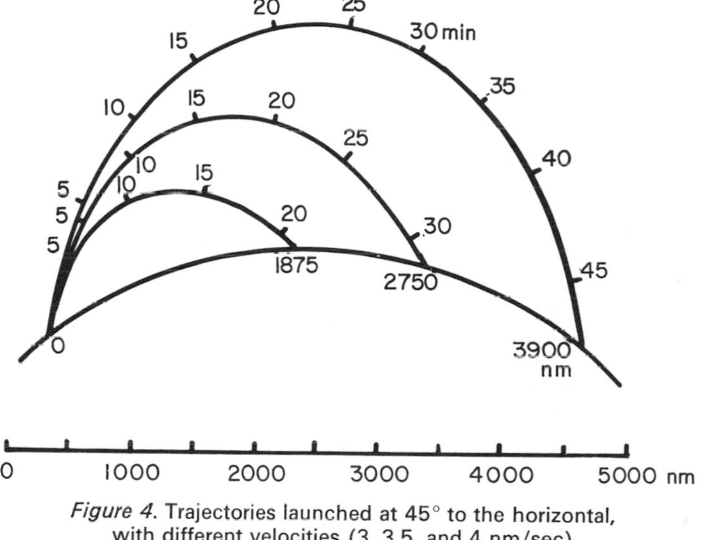

Figure 4. Trajectories launched at 45° to the horizontal, with different velocities (3, 3.5, and 4 nm/sec)

three trajectories with the same launching angle, 45° above the horizontal, but different velocities, 3, 3.5, and 4 nautical miles per second (nm/sec). In this and subsequent diagrams it will be supposed that the missile begins its flight from the ground with the stated burnout velocity (V_0) and launching angle. In fact, of course, the missile completes the propulsion phase of its trajectory before attaining the burnout velocity and angle, and it is already a certain distance from the launching point. A missile of intercontinental range could move several hundred miles during a propulsion phase lasting a few minutes.

The numbered marks on the trajectories show minutes from launch, and the numbers at the ends of the trajectories show range to impact (measured along the earth's surface). For the ranges shown here the curvature of the earth is quite significant. Note that the ranges and the times of flight increase in greater proportion than the launching

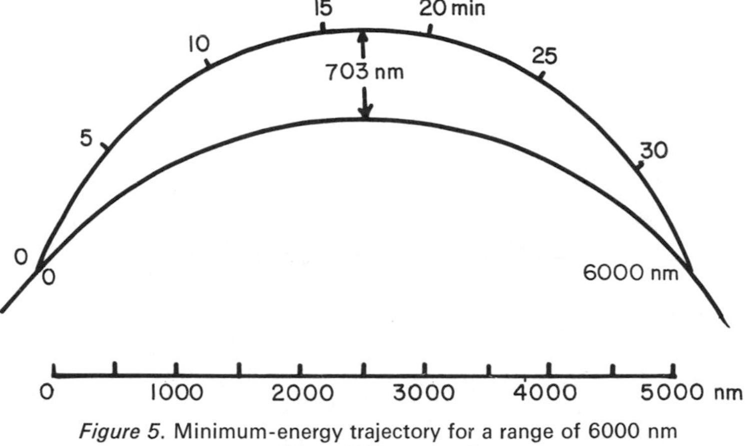

Figure 5. Minimum-energy trajectory for a range of 6000 nm (V_0 = 3.98 nm/sec)

velocity. Longer ranges could be obtained for the same velocities by employing launching angles lower than 45°.

When the launching angle is selected to give the longest possible range for a given launch velocity, the resulting path is called the *maximum-range trajectory* or *minimum-energy trajectory*. The latter term indicates that the least possible launching velocity has been employed which could reach the given range. Figure 5 shows the minimum-energy trajectory for a range of 6000 nm. It requires a launching velocity of 3.98 nm/sec and a launching angle of 20°. The flight lasts for 34 minutes, and the *apogee* (or highest point from the center of the earth) is at an altitude of 703 nm.

Figure 6 illustrates the result of altering the launching angle but leaving the velocity fixed, in this case at 4 nm/sec. The maximum-range trajectory is obtained for a launching angle of 19⅓°, the flight lasts 35 minutes, and the range is 6160 nm. The other two trajectories on Figure 6 each attain a range of 4000 nm, still with a launching velocity of 4 nm/sec. The high trajectory is launched at an angle of

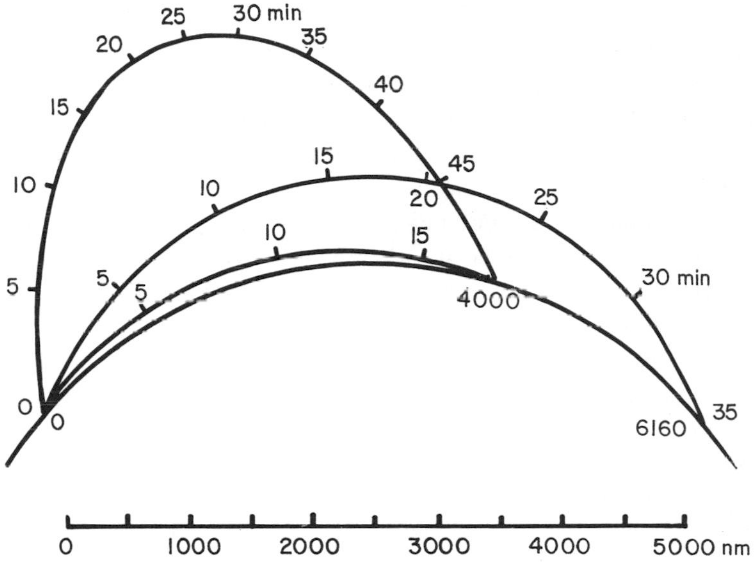

Figure 6. Trajectories with the same velocity (4 nm/sec) but different directions

51°, and the time of flight is 49 minutes, much longer than for the maximum-range trajectory. More easily seen on this trajectory than the lower ones is the fact that the marks indicating five-minute time intervals are not equally spaced. The missile is slowed down by gravity during the ascending portion of its flight and speeded up again as it descends. The low trajectory to 4000-nm range is launched at an angle of less than 6° and completes the flight in only $17\frac{1}{2}$ minutes.

All of the trajectories illustrated in this chapter have been calculated without allowance for air resistance. Since this has very little effect above an altitude of 100 nm, and most of the trajectories spend most of their time at greater altitudes, the error will be very small. However, for the low trajectory of Figure 6, which is almost entirely below 100 nm altitude, air drag would decelerate the missile considerably, and the true low trajectory to 4000 nm would require a higher launching angle and a longer time of flight. However, the principle is generally true that for a given launching velocity there is a maximum attainable range, which can be reached only by using the maximum-range trajectory, and that any range shorter than this can be attained by two different trajectories, one higher and one lower than the maximum-range trajectory, with time of flight respectively longer and shorter than the time of flight of the maximum-range trajectory.

One sees on Figure 4 that the curvature of the trajectories decreases as the launching velocity increases. The trajectory on Figure 5, launched at 3.98 nm/sec, is hardly more curved than is the spherical surface of the earth. What would happen if the launching velocity were increased until the curvature of the trajectory became less than the curvature of the earth?

Figure 7 shows the spherical earth and a point marked V_0, 500 nm above its surface. Vehicles traveling in a horizontal direction with velocities of $V_0 = 3$, 4, 5, and 5.64 nm/sec at this point would follow the four trajectories shown. The slowest would fall back to earth in an elliptical path. But for a velocity of 4 nm/sec the vehicle would "fall" in a path whose curvature is that of a circle passing 500 nm above the earth. It would orbit the earth, completing a revolution in 1 hour 43 minutes. The path of the vehicle moving horizontally at V_0 with a velocity of 5 nm/sec would be less curved than the circular orbit; it would orbit the earth in an elliptical trajectory, completing a circuit in 6 hours 4 minutes. However, for a velocity of 5.64 nm/sec at V_0 the vehicle will not be drawn into an orbit but will depart from the earth on a parabolic path, never to return. This represents the *escape velocity*. A velocity higher than this will produce a hyperbolic path, less curved than the parabola.

In order to place a vehicle at V_0 with a horizontal velocity of 4 nm/sec or more, it would be necessary to launch it from the surface of the earth and to steer it into the proper path by directing the thrust of the rocket motors. All of this would be accomplished during

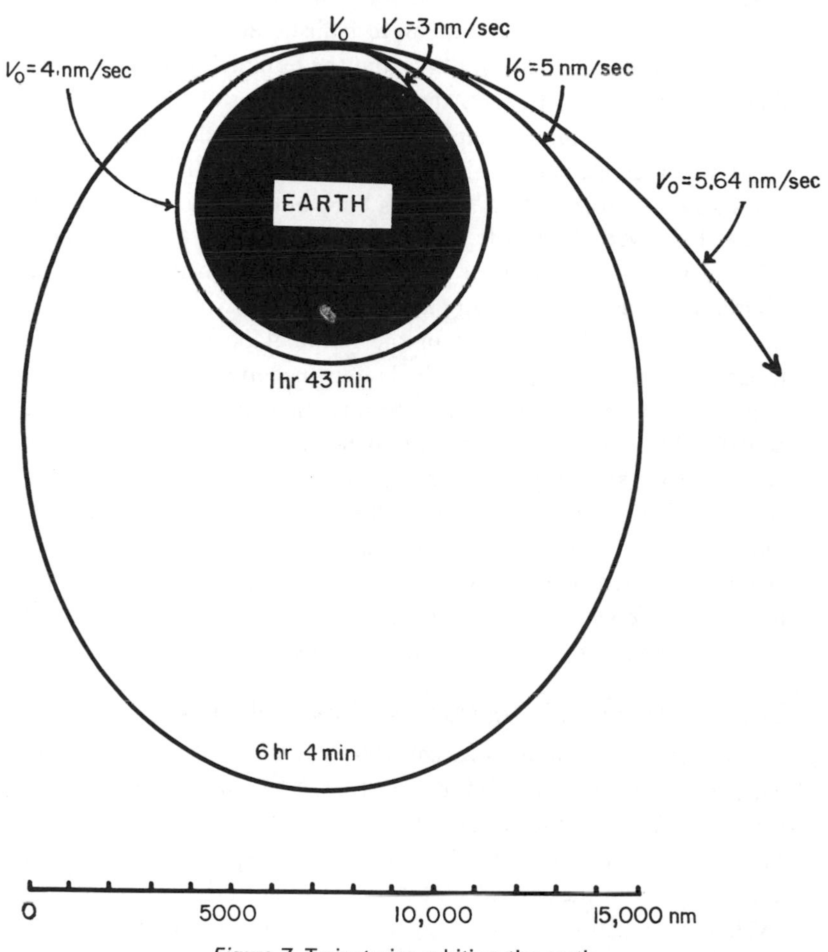

Figure 7. Trajectories orbiting the earth

the propulsion phase of the trajectory. It is assumed in Figure 7 that propulsion has ceased; consequently, all the paths shown are ballistic trajectories.

As has been mentioned, the illustrated trajectories have been calculated as if the entire path were ballistic and in a vacuum. In other words, the propulsion phase and the terminal phase have been compressed to zero. In fact, the precise plotting of the propulsion phase would be quite complicated, since the acceleration of each stage will increase as fuel is burned, but there will be sharp discontinuities in acceleration as stages burn out and succeeding stages ignite. However, the whole process is completed in a few minutes. Air resistance will not affect the trajectory much in the propulsion phase, since high velocity is not attained until the rocket has ascended into air of low density. But in the terminal phase of a missile's trajectory, when the re-entry vehicle must penetrate the dense lower atmosphere with a velocity close to 4 nm/sec, air resistance will be considerable and will produce rapid heating of the surface of the vehicle. It is usual to place a protective heat shield around the nose cone, which absorbs the heat by melting or *ablation*. The same technique is used for the reentry of manned space vehicles. The final velocity with which the nose cone of a ballistic missile impacts on the ground depends on its *ballistic coefficient*, which is determined by its weight-to-drag ratio and therefore its shape.

The Accuracy and Destructive Power of Missiles

All intercontinental missiles carry nuclear warheads, in most cases with energy yields measured in megatons. Used against city targets, we have seen that the radius of destruction is measured in miles. Most important cities extend for miles. Consequently, an error of a mile or two in the arrival of a missile will not greatly degrade the level of destruction wreaked by its thermonuclear warhead. And, though the secret figures concerning missile accuracy are jealously guarded, it is generally believed that present-day missiles have accuracies of the order of half a mile, if not better.

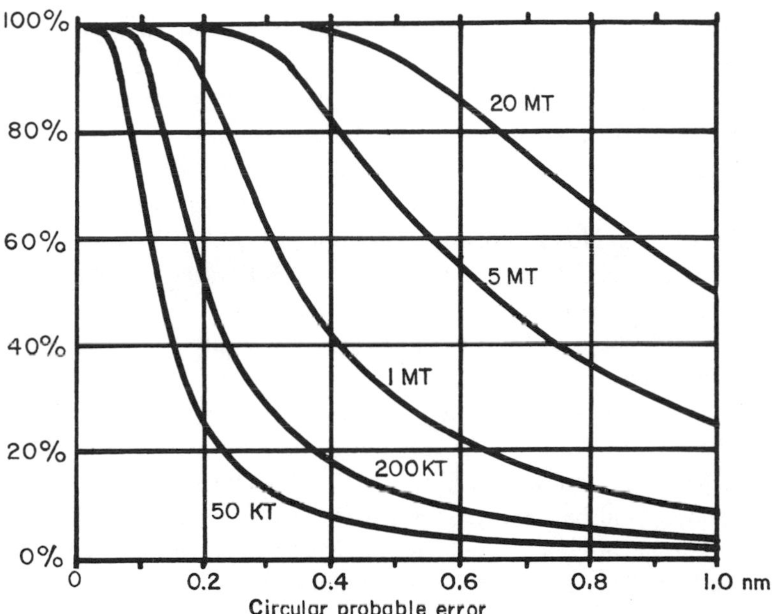

Figure 8. Probability of destruction of a 300-psi silo as a function of the accuracy and yield of the attacking warhead. Adapted from *Strategic Survey, 1969*, p. 33, with the kind permission of The International Institute for Strategic Studies, London.

The accuracy of missiles can be ascertained only by actual test firings (with dummy warheads). It is measured by the *circular probable error* (abbreviated CEP). If the CEP is one mile, this signifies that if a large number of missiles were fired at a target point, 50 percent of the shots would land within a distance of one mile from the point.

Although a CEP of one mile would be adequate for effective attack upon almost any large city, it would not suffice against a hardened point target such as a missile silo or underground command post. The Minuteman missiles are encased in a heavily protected underground shield, able to withstand a shock wave of 300 psi. Even for a one-megaton warhead, impact must be within about 2100 feet of the silo in order to deliver the necessary shock. Therefore, if the CEP of the missile were 2100 feet (0.35 nm), one shot would have a 50 percent probability of destroying the silo. The distance by which the missile can miss the target, but still destroy it, is called the *lethal radius*. The *lethal diameter* is twice the lethal radius.

Figure 8 shows the probability that a target hardened to 300 psi will be destroyed by a single missile, for various warhead sizes and various CEPs. Note, for example, that a probability of destruction of 80 percent could be obtained with a 200-KT warhead and a CEP of 0.15 nm, or with a 20-MT warhead and a CEP of 0.66 nm. Thus, a factor of 100 in weapon yield can be compensated by a factor of $4\frac{1}{2}$ in accuracy.

From Figure 8 one can deduce the result of an attack by 1000 missiles, each with a yield of one megaton, against 1000 silos, each hardened to 300 psi. If the CEP of the attacking missiles were 0.5 nm, 300 silos would be destroyed. For 0.25 nm the figure would be 760, while a CEP of 0.1 nm would be sufficient to demolish virtually all of the 1000. This demonstrates the dominant importance of accuracy for the attack on small hard targets.

Progress has been rapid in the improvement of missile accuracy. Between 1954 and 1970 the CEP of missiles of intercontinental range has been reduced by a factor of twenty. A further reduction by a factor of two to four would threaten the destruction of the great majority of silos attacked.[2]

During the propulsion phase the guidance is normally effected by

[2] U.S. Senate, Committee on Foreign Relations, *ABM, MIRV, SALT and the Nuclear Arms Race: Hearings before the Subcommittee on Arms Control, International Law and Organization,* March–June 1970; hereafter cited under the abridged title U.S. Senate *Hearings on ABM, MIRV, SALT, and the Nuclear Arms Race,* 1970, p. 61. *Strategic Survey, 1974* (London: The International Institute for Strategic Studies, 1975), pp. 46–47, believes the most accurate strategic missile to be Minuteman 3, with a CEP of 0.21 nm, and foresees reductions to 0.1 nm or better. Kosta Tsipis, in "The Accuracy of Strategic Missiles," *Scientific American* 233 (July 1975), 14–23, suggests 0.1 nm for land-based and 0.2 nm for submarine-based ballistic missiles of the most advanced types.

an inertial system independent of any external control. During the long ballistic phase there is no guidance. But it may be possible to add some corrective guidance toward the end of the flight, applied by small auxiliary rockets or by aerodynamic surfaces, and perhaps depending on matching of a precalculated image of the ground with direct observation of clearly recognizable landmarks. Although improved accuracy is extremely important for the attack of strategic military targets, it may be attainable only at a considerable cost in payload.

The Various Types of Strategic Missiles

Up to now we have spoken only of surface-to-surface strategic missiles. There are many other types of strategic missiles, both offensive and defensive, as well as "tactical" weapon systems which are not always readily distinguished from "strategic."

This book is about strategic rather than tactical weapons, and this chapter is about offensive strategic missiles. Defense against ICBMs is discussed in Chapter III, while the offensive and defensive aspects of strategic submarine and aerial warfare, including the use of missiles, are the subjects of Chapters IV and V, respectively.

Table 1 lists the various combinations of the element from which a missile is launched and the element in which its target rests. If there are strategic missiles for a particular pair of elements, an entry appears in the table—O if the missile is considered offensive and D if defensive. A blank indicates that the missiles are considered tactical or have not been built.

Table 1. Types of strategic missiles

	Target			
Firing location	Land	Air	Under water	Sea surface
Land	O	D		
Air	O	D	D	
Under water	O		D	
Sea surface			D	

O = offensive; D = defensive.

Present Deployment of Surface-to-Surface Strategic Missiles

The only countries possessing ICBMs are the United States and the Soviet Union. The numbers and main characteristics of their ICBMs are listed in Table 2.

Still in the category of strategic offensive missiles, it is necessary to include Intermediate Range Ballistic Missiles (IRBM), with ranges between 1300 and 3500 nm, and Medium Range Ballistic Missiles (MRBM), with ranges from 450 to 1300 nm. Short Range Ballistic Missiles (SRBM), with ranges less than 450 nm are considered as tactical rather than strategic weapons. The Soviets possess about 100 IRBMs of the type SS-5, with a maximum range of 2000 nm. Its launching velocity must be about 2.9 nm/sec and its time of flight about 16 minutes. And they have about 500 MRBMs, known as SS-4, with a maximum range of 1050 nm.[3] For this capability, SS-4 would need a launching velocity of about 2.2 nm/sec, and a time of flight of about 11 minutes. France has installed 18 SSBS S-2 IRBMs, with a range of 1600 nm and a warhead yield of 150 KT.[3] China is believed to have deployed MRBMs and IRBMs, and to have developed a multistage IRBM with a range of as much as 3000 nm.[4]

Submarine-launched Ballistic Missiles

The first submarine-borne missiles had wings and breathed air. They were pilotless aircraft rather than rockets. Such *cruise missiles*[5] are still in service, but they are intended primarily for use against ships and may be considered as tactical rather than strategic weapons. The submarine must come to the surface in order to launch them.

The underwater-to-land missile of fundamental significance as an

[3] *The Military Balance, 1975–76,* pp. 71, 73–74.

[4] *The Military Balance, 1975–76,* p. 48.

[5] Cruise missiles on Soviet submarines intended for use against a NATO nuclear strike fleet could be considered as defensive strategic missiles. The U.S. are developing a submarine-launched cruise missile for both strategic and tactical use. *Statement of Secretary Schlesinger, 1975,* pp. II, 39–40.

Table 2. Intercontinental ballistic missiles

Number[a,b] 1975	Missiles	Category[c]	Nuclear warhead[b]
		United States	
54	Titan 2	OH	5–10 MT
450	Minuteman 2	L	1–2 MT
550	Minuteman 3	L	3 MIRV × 170 KT
1054			
		Soviet Union	
209	SS-7, SS-8	OH[d]	5MT
288[e]	SS-9	H	18–25 MT[f]
991[g]	SS-11	L	1–2 MT or 3 MRV[c]
60	SS-13	L	1 MT
	SS-X-16		1[a]
10	SS-17	[h]	4 MIRV[a]
10	SS-18	H	5–8 MIRV[a] or 18–25 MT
50	SS-19	[h]	6 MIRV[a]
1618[i]			

[a] *Statement of Secretary Schlesinger, 1975,* pp. II–12–21; *United States Military Posture for FY 1976,* by Chairman of the Joint Chief of Staff, General G. S. Brown (Washington, 1975), hereafter cited as *Statement of General Brown, 1975,* pp. 9–20; Pentagon news conference, June 20, 1975.

[b] *The Military Balance, 1975–76* (London: The International Institute for Strategic Studies, 1975), pp. 3–5, 8, 71. The numbers are for July 1975.

[c] O = Old (pre-1964); H = Heavy; L = Light.

[d] The old, heavy ICBMs are being phased out to allow more SLBMs.

[e] Some of these "heavy launcher" silos are being converted for more advanced missiles.

[f] Alternatives are 3 MRV of 4–5 MT, a depressed trajectory missile (DICBM) with a smaller payload, or a fractional orbital bombardment system (FOBS). *Statement of General Brown, 1975,* pp. 11, 12.

[g] About 100 of the SS-11 missiles are sited in IRBM/MRBM fields.

[h] These appear to be larger than SS-11, in which case the U.S. will consider them to be "heavy," but the U.S.S.R. has not agreed to a definition. They are being deployed in modified SS-11 silos.

[i] In February 1975, Secretary Schlesinger estimated that 1590 would be operational by the middle of the year. However, the announcement in June that 70 of the new missiles were now deployed may require the estimate to be increased.

offensive strategic weapon is the Submarine-Launched Ballistic Missile (SLBM). The present day SLBMs are launched when the submarine is submerged. Because of the space limitations in a submarine, today's SLBMs do not have the range or payload of ICBMs, but the larger SLBMs are comparable with IRBMs. SLBMs are also likely to be less accurate than ICBMs, since the launching platform is constantly on the move, and its instantaneous position cannot be determined as accurately as that of a surveyed permanent location on land. The motion of the submarine makes it necessary to calculate the trajectory to the assigned target on a continuous basis, keeping the electronic "memory" of each missile supplied with the necessary data for guidance. Once a missile is launched, all contact with the submarine is lost, and the missile proceeds on its self-contained inertial guidance system.

American SLBMs have undergone considerable development since their first launching in 1970. Polaris A1, with a maximum range of 1200 nm, was followed by Polaris A2 and A3, with ranges of 1500 and 2500 nm.[6] Poseidon has twice the weight of Polaris A3, with the added size being used for an increased payload of multiple warheads and penetration aids, and the two types of Trident will be more powerful still. See page 121. All of the U.S. ballistic missile submarines carry sixteen missiles, which can be launched from a submerged position, in succession, at very short intervals, perhaps 15 to 20 seconds.

The Soviets have closed the considerable gap, at least in numbers if not in quality, by which they had lagged the United States in SLBMs.[7] The SALT I agreement of May 26, 1972, confirmed that building programs then underway would carry the number of Soviet SLBMs beyond the American total in 1974.

The largest Soviet deployment is in Y-class nuclear-powered sub-

[6] *SIPRI, 1968/69*, pp. 96–111.

[7] *Statement of Secretary of Defense Melvin R. Laird before the U.S. Senate Armed Services Committee on the Fiscal Year 1973 Defense Budget and Fiscal Years 1973–77 Program*, February 15, 1972 (Washington: USGPO, 1972); hereafter cited with the abridged title *Statement of Secretary Laird, 1972*, pp. 30–39.

Table 3. Submarine-launched ballistic missiles

Number of missiles 1975[a]	Number of missiles 1977[b]	Missiles	Maximum range	Nuclear warhead
		United States		
256	160	Polaris A3	2500 nm	3 MRV × 200 KT
400	496	Poseidon (B3)	2500	10–14 MIRV × 50 KT
	[c]	Trident I (C4)	4000	MIRV, MARV
	[d]	Trident II (D5)	6000	
656	[e]			
		Soviet Union		
27		SS-N-4	305 nm	Abour 1 MT
57		SS-N-5	650	About 1 MT
544[b]		SS-N-6	1600[f]	About 1 MT[f]
156		SS-N-8	4200	About 1 MT
784[g]	[h]			
		Great Britain		
64		Polaris A3	2500 nm	3 MRV × 200 KT
		France		
32		MSBS M-1	1350 nm	0.5 MT
16		MSBS M-2	1650	0.5 MT

[a] *The Military Balance, 1975–76* (London: The International Institute for Strategic Studies, 1975), pp. 3–4, 71, 74. The numbers are for July 1975.

[b] *Statement of Secretary Schlesinger, 1975,* pp. II–19, II–30–31; *Statement of General Brown, 1975,* pp. 20–28.

[c] Initial Operational Capability may be later than 1977.

[d] A missile for the 1980s.

[e] Interim SALT I agreement allows U.S. to havė 710 SLBMs if Titan ICBMs are dismantled.

[f] *Statement of General Brown, 1975*, pp. 22–23. Has been tested with MRV.

[g] Protocol to Interim SALT I agreement suggested that U.S.S.R. had 740 SLBMs operational or under construction in July 1972. Secretary Schlesinger estimated 700 for mid-1975 exclusive of those in SSB boats, thus implying a total of 760.

[h] Interim SALT I agreement allows U.S.S.R. to have 950 SLBMs in nuclear-powered submarines if older ICBMs (SS-7, SS-8) are dismantled.

marines, carrying 16 SS-N-6 missiles, whose range of 1500 nm is much inferior to that of Polaris A3 and Poseidon. However, the Delta class submarines carry 12 SS-N-8 missiles with a range of 4200 nm, and longer versions of the Delta may be able to take more than 12 missiles.[8]

Great Britain has four nuclear-powered ballistic missile submarines, carrying a total of 64 Polaris A3 missiles. France has undertaken a program to construct five, which will accommodate a total of 80 SLBMs with ranges of more than 1300 nm.

Table 3 shows the deployment of SLBMs.

Air-to-Surface Missiles

There is a whole collection of Air-to-Surface Missiles (ASM), starting with the free-falling aerial bomb and extending all the way to the Air-Launched Ballistic Missile (ALBM), for which one could say that the aircraft provided the first stage. A heavy bomber aircraft can be used in strategic or tactical roles, whether its armament consists of simple bombs or sophisticated guided missiles. The full discussion of the strategic role of the bomber will be left until Chapter V, but this is an appropriate place to say a few words about the ALBM.

Several technical and economic reasons suggest an aircraft as first stage for the launching of a long-range ballistic missile or a space vehicle. The first stage of an intercontinental rocket is very expensive, and it can be used only once. A significant fraction of its fuel is expended in accelerating the body and motor of the first stage, which then becomes a dead weight to be discarded. And the air resistance is, of course, most serious at low altitudes. But an aircraft can be used many times. Especially if refueled in the air, it has very long range. Once it is off the ground, its vulnerability is low until it crosses hostile territory, and the range of the ASM should enable it to be launched outside the perimeter of the air defenses.

[8] *Statement of Secretary Schlesinger, 1975,* p. II–14.

These were the advantages sought by the American "Skybolt," an ALBM with a range of 1000 nm, intended for the USAF B-52 and for the British Vulcan bombers. However, considerable technical difficulties were encountered, the costs of the program soared, and it became evident that Skybolt was not competitive with alternative strategic systems for the attack of weapon sites or of cities.[9] The program was canceled in 1962.

It should be made clear that modern bomber aircraft do carry ASMs, some with ranges of hundreds of miles. They are likely to be particularly important for the suppression of air defenses. But they are not ballistic missiles, and they are best considered as adjuncts to the bomber and discussed in Chapter V.

Evasive Trajectories

In the absence of any defense, the attacker can select his trajectories to maximize payload and accuracy, probably by using minimum-energy trajectories. But if the attacker wishes to avoid or delay detection or to foil interception by the defender, he may elect to sacrifice payload and accuracy in exchange for increased probability of penetration. There are a number of means available to him, but this section will be confined to the various feasible trajectories which might be employed as a countermeasure to antimissile defenses.

Figure 9 shows two points L and T located 6160 nm apart. The attacker wishes to launch a missile from L to impact on target T. As we saw in Figure 6, a minimum-energy trajectory can span this

[9] In *How Much Is Enough?* (New York: Harper & Row, 1971), Alain C. Enthoven and K. Wayne Smith remark that the Skybolt system combined the disadvantages of the bomber with those of the missile, bearing the bomber's vulnerability on the ground and its slow overall time to target as well as the poor accuracy and reliability and relatively low payload of the missile (p. 258). Nevertheless, the United States is reintroducing consideration of an air-mobile ICBM and has launched Minuteman from C-5A aircraft. See *Statement of Secretary Schlesinger, 1975*, pp. II–27–29. The U.S. is also developing an air-launched cruise missile. *Ibid.*, pp. II–39–40.

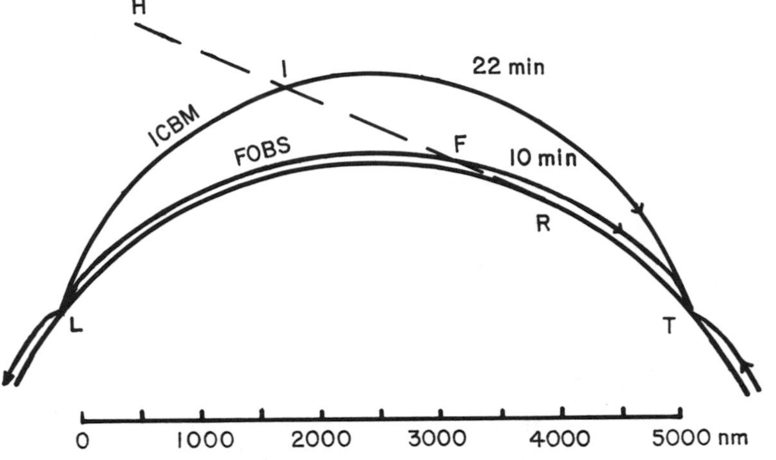

Figure 9. Missiles using different trajectories of attack

distance in 35 minutes, provided that the attacker has a rocket able to achieve a burnout velocity of 4.0 nm/sec. To defend himself against such an attack, the opponent may place a powerful radar at R, as far forward from T as his territory (or that of his allies) will permit. In Figure 9, R is advanced 1500 nm from T in the direction of L. The beam of the radar may skim the horizon, but it cannot "see" beyond the horizontal line HR. It will, then, be able to detect the approaching missile no earlier than point I. The time of flight from I to T is 22 minutes ; hence the maximum warning could not exceed 22 minutes.

Suppose that the attacker were prepared to use additional propulsion and/or sacrifice payload in order to reduce the warning time. Instead of projecting the missile with a burnout velocity of 4.0 nm/sec at a launch angle of $19\frac{1}{3}°$ to the horizontal, in order to achieve the minimum-energy trajectory, he could accelerate it to a velocity of 4.2 nm/sec in a horizontal direction 100 nm above the earth. In this case the missile would be in a circular earth orbit and would pass over T in about 25 minutes. A decelerating rocket could be added, however, to reduce the velocity and cause the missile to descend onto T. Such a weapon is called a Fractional Orbital Bombardment System (FOBS); its trajectory is shown on Figure 9. Note that the point F at which it crosses HR, the horizon of the radar at R, is much closer to T than was the point I. The time of flight from F to T is only about 10 minutes. Consequently, FOBS would give a much shorter warning time than would an ICBM on a higher trajectory.

An attacker able to employ FOBS on the direct trajectory LFT with the range of 6160 nm has two further options. He can launch in the opposite direction, leave the missile to orbit two-thirds of the earth's circumference, and use the retro rockets to descend on T from the rear (as T faces towards L). This will cost no more in rocket fuel than the direct path, since an object once placed in a circular orbit continues without further propulsion. It could, however, reduce the accuracy because of the longer distance and time of flight (about 63 minutes). But if all of the detection systems for T were sited to intercept only trajectories along the direct path, T would receive no warning at all of the attack from the rear.

Instead of bringing the vehicle down on its first crossing of T, the attacker could leave it to make a number of orbits of the earth, possibly serving only as a threat. This Multiple Orbital Bombardment System (MOBS) has several considerable disadvantages as compared to FOBS or ICBM. As the earth rotates beneath the MOBS orbit, any given target will pass beneath it only twice a day, and unless the orbiting body is provided with considerable propulsive power for lateral maneuver, there will be only a very few instants per day during which it could commence its descent on T. The accuracy is likely to be poor, and the missile in orbit will be easy to detect and indeed to intercept if the defense can choose the appropriate moment. It seems that MOBS could be more a psychological than a strategic weapon.

The Outer Space Treaty, whose signatories agree to refrain from placing in orbit any objects carrying nuclear weapons, would forbid MOBS but not FOBS.

A further possibility for an evasive trajectory, intermediate between the minimum-energy trajectory ICBM and the direct-trajectory FOBS, is to use one of the low ballistic trajectories, such as illustrated on Figure 6. These "Depressed Trajectories"[10] cannot attain the maximum range possible for the burnout velocity and may encounter difficulties due to air resistance. However, in the case of the SLBM they are, for several reasons, very likely to be employed. It is probable that all the SLBMs in a submarine will be capable of the same burnout velocity, but it is very likely that the movement of the submarine will take it much closer to some of its targets than the maximum possible range. And one of the chief advantages of the SLBM is its capability for surprise regarding direction and time of attack. It would be logical to exploit this further by making as difficult as possible the early detection of the missile in flight.

Figure 10 shows two SLBM trajectories. The upper one, from L to T, represents a maximum-range trajectory for 1300 nm. The necessary launching velocity is 2.4 nm/sec, and the time of flight is 13 minutes. If the radar is near the target (which may be close to the seacoast), then its horizon HT will intercept the trajectory about $2\frac{1}{2}$ minutes after the missile has been launched.[11] Consequently, the longest possible warning time is $10\frac{1}{2}$ minutes. But if the submarine can move to S, where the range ST is only 600 nm, the same launching velocity of 2.4 nm/sec permits the very low trajectory shown on Figure 10, with a time of flight of only $4\frac{1}{2}$ minutes. And of this short time, the first $1\frac{1}{2}$ minutes will be below the horizon, so that the maximum warning time is a mere 3 minutes.

FOBS and MOBS required rocket propulsion (in the reverse direction) in order to decelerate the reentry vehicle and make it descend to earth. This is a form of vertical maneuver away from the

[10] DICBM stands for "Depressed Trajectory ICBM."

[11] As before, the propulsion phase has been compressed to zero. However, this will hardly affect the estimate of the remaining time to target.

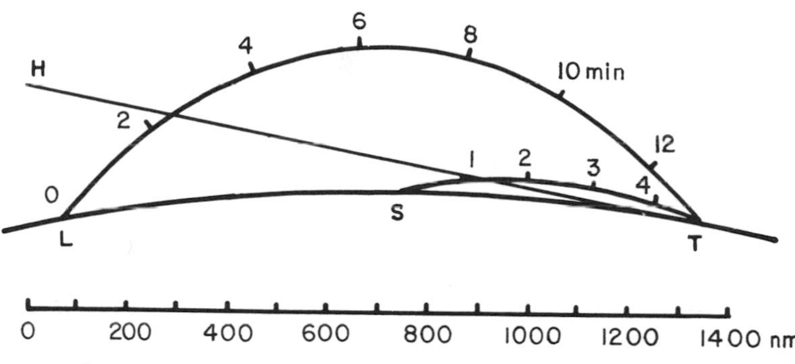

Figure 10. Effect of different SLBM trajectories on detection

ballistic path. If he can accommodate the necessary throw weight (or by sacrifice of payload), the attacker can deflect the reentry vehicle from its ballistic path by a rocket thrust at any point. Since the defense will probably plan interception on the assumption that the attacking missile will follow a predictable ballistic path, this tactic may cause the interception to fail, especially if the maneuver is executed just after the interceptor has been launched. If a maneuver is desired after reentry into the atmosphere (possibly for evasion of a short-range interceptor, or possibly to apply final correction to the trajectory in order to achieve better accuracy), this may be accomplished by the use of aerodynamic control surfaces rather than rockets.[12]

One common factor among all evasive trajectories is that the attacker is obliged to use more propulsion or to achieve less payload than would be required for the minimum-energy trajectory.

Penetration Aids

In addition to evasive trajectories, just described, and multiple warheads, to be discussed in the next section, an attacker may use a number of measures to increase the probability that his missiles will

[12] Another acronym is MARV, "Maneuverable Reentry Vehicle."

succeed in penetrating the opposing defenses. These are commonly labeled as *penetration aids*.

In addition to the technical measures about to be described, successful penetration may depend on the selection of targets and the timing of the launchings. Destruction of indispensible elements of the defense system (for example, the control radars) could precede uncontested attack on the targets. Or simultaneous arrival of several missiles in the same area might overload the capacity of the defense for simultaneous interception.

In the next chapter, it will be explained that the effectiveness of antiballistic missile interception depends to a very large degree on the radius of destruction of the interceptor's nuclear warhead. The most vulnerable part of the attacking reentry vehicle is the firing mechanism of its nuclear bomb. It may be possible to reduce this vulnerability by placing a suitable protective shield around the bomb.[13] This is sometimes known as "hardening" the warhead.

Many of the penetration aids are intended to deceive the defensive radar system. One simple measure exploits the fact that the final rocket stage necessarily travels on the same trajectory as the nose cone. Once its fuel has been expended and it has been separated from the nose cone, it is a simple matter to blow the empty fuel tank into a swarm of irregular fragments by a small explosive charge. Each fragment will return an echo to the radar, which must now try to distinguish the echo from the nose cone amidst a confusing background.

If the attacker believes that the defending radars will be able to discriminate tank fragments from nose cones, he may construct sophisticated decoys designed to give radar echoes identical to that of the real nose cone. For example, it is possible to make a balloon

[13] Hans Bethe, "Countermeasures to ABM Systems," in Abram Chayes and Jerome B. Wiesner, eds., *ABM: An Evaluation of the Decision to Deploy an Anti-Ballistic Missile System* (New York: New American Library, 1969; paperback edition), pp. 130–132. See also Hans Bethe, "Hard Point versus City Defense," *Bulletin of the Atomic Scientists* 25 (June 1969), 25–26.

with a thin metallic coating, which can be inflated after release to assume the shape of the nose cone.

Once the cloud of objects reenters the atmosphere, those with low weight-to-drag ratios, such as irregular tank fragments or balloons, will be decelerated by air resistance much more than a heavy streamlined nose cone. A high-resolution radar and a computer should be able to reject the fragments and light decoys. But the offense can include heavier decoys resembling the nose cone in both radar-reflecting and ballistic properties. However, if a satisfactory decoy has a weight comparable to that of a warhead, it may be more effective to load the missile with genuine multiple warheads.

Another countermeasure against radar detection is to use large quantities of fine metallic wires (or "chaff") of a size calculated to produce a large diffuse echo likely to conceal the signal from the nose cone.

Finally, if the attacker is prepared to devote a few ICBMs to the purpose, he can create an "electromagnetic blackout" over a considerable area of the upper atmosphere. The initial nuclear radiation and the intense heat of a large nuclear explosion produce immediate ionization[14] of the surrounding air in the general vicinity of the burst; in the case of explosions at very high altitudes, β radiation from fission products causes ionization at great distances, mainly at altitudes of about forty miles. Radar rays encountering a patch of ionized air may be deflected or absorbed, especially if the radio frequency is low. The extent of the ionized zone and the duration of the radar blackout depend on the energy yield and altitude of the explosion as well as on the radar frequency. Bethe estimates that the explosion of a bomb of several megatons at high altitude could produce blackout over an area more than 100 nm in diameter, whose effects would last perhaps ten minutes for long-range radars.[15] An attacker could employ several "precursor bursts" at high altitude to blind the defenses, then follow them by a salvo of missiles aimed at the targets.

[14] Ionization is the electrification due to removal or addition of electrons.

[15] Bethe, "Countermeasures to ABM Systems," *op. cit.*, pp. 135–142. See also ... ed., *op. cit.*, chap. 10.

Multiple Warheads[16]

The most important recent development in the technology of intercontinental ballistic missiles is the placing of multiple warheads in the nose cone of a single missile. One objective could be to require the defense to control several interceptions from the same ABM battery at the same time. For this purpose, the multiple warheads would need to be too far apart to allow their simultaneous destruction by a single interception.

A second objective could be to increase the damage to a large city. If it were possible to replace one large warhead by several small ones with the same total weight and also the same total energy yield, the damage to a large city would be considerably increased.[17] However because each small warhead needs its own bomb mechanism, casing and heat shield, there will be an inevitable sacrifice in weight of explosive material and in total energy yield. The reduction in yield has been estimated at 40 to 80 percent.[18,19] Thus is it not certain that multiple warheads would produce more damage to a single city than would a single large warhead, especially for a small city.

A third objective for the employment of multiple warheads could be the destruction of several separate targets with one missile. For this purpose, a considerable separation of the individual trajectories might be necessary.

Figure 11 shows a missile launched from L which propels four

[16] Ian Smart, "Advanced Strategic Missiles: A Short Guide," *Adelphi Paper No. 63* (London: The International Institute for Strategic Studies, 1969), pp. 11–13 and 22–24.

[17] Eight small warheads would subject to a given peak overpressure a total area twice as great as would one large warhead with eight times the yield, assuming that none of the eight small areas overlapped. And if the shape of the city was far from circular, it could be covered more effectively by the proper placing of several small circles than by one large one.

[18] Smart, *op. cit.*, p. 11.

[19] For the example in footnote 17 the area destroyed by the eight small heads would surpass that of the one large one only if the total reduction were less than 65 percent.

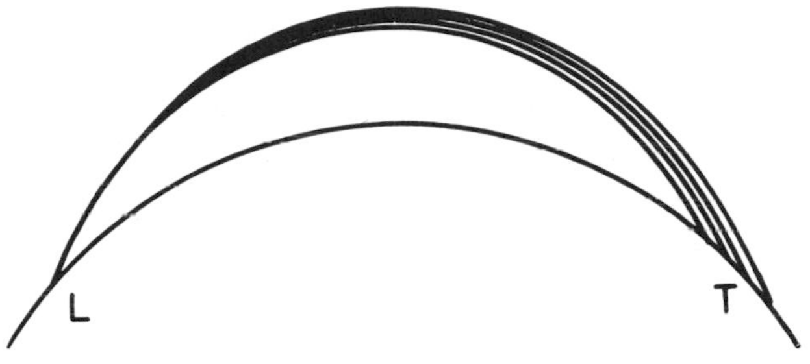

Figure 11. Trajectories of multiple warheads (MRV)

separate reentry vehicles into slightly different paths. The vehicles are separated from one another soon after the completion of the acceleration of the main rockets in the propulsion phase. All four remain fairly close together and impact around the same target T at about the same time. If no individual propulsion or guidance is given to the separate vehicles, they are labeled as Multiple-Reentry Vehicles (MRV). Polaris A3 is fitted with 3 MRV warheads,[20] each of 200 KT, instead of the previous single warhead of 1 MT.

A more sophisticated method is to provide individual guidance to each of several warheads. These can be carried by a "bus" boosted toward the target area by the main rocket stages, then separated from the boosters, and finally using vernier rockets to make small adjustments to its trajectory as it releases individual warheads one at a time. Such an arrangement is called a Multiple Independently Targeted Reentry Vehicle (MIRV).[21] Smart remarks that the terms are not completely satisfactory, because it is not clear whether they are distinguishing the distance separating the points of impact, the intention to

[20] *SIPRI, 1969/70,* p. 50.

[21] Smart, *op. cit.,* pp. 22–23. Herbert F. York, "Multiple Warhead Missiles," *Scientific American* 229 (November 1973), 18–27. *The Origins of MIRV* (Stockholm: SIPRI, 1973). Tsipis, *op. cit.*

attack several as opposed to a single target, or the intention to face the defender with the need for simultaneous interception by several defensive missiles.[22] A further difficulty (encountered while preparing this manuscript in French) is that it is not clear whether the term MIRV (or MRV) refers to the collection of reentry vehicles in the nose cone or to each separate vehicle. In this text we shall use the term MIRV for a single rocket containing several reentry vehicles, each of which can be individually guided toward a different target. Their individual trajectories could look like those on Figure 11, or they could commence their separate paths at different points and impact at more widely separated targets.

The United States has fitted MIRV on both Minuteman 3 and Poseidon. Minuteman 3 carries three warheads, each of about 170 KT,[23] while Poseidon has ten, each of 50 KT.[24] In addition to the version of SS-9 with 3 MIRV already deployed, the U.S.S.R. has been testing SS-17 with 4 MIRV, SS-18 with 6–8 MIRV, and SS-19 with 6 MIRV. All are expected to become operational in 1975.[25]

It seems inevitable that the added complexity of MIRV will require a greater penalty in weapon yield (for the same gross rocket weight) than will MRV. However, if the objective is to attack a number of small hard targets, such as missile silos or underground command posts, it is probably worth a considerable sacrifice in yield in order to improve the accuracy of the invididual warheads.[26]

The problem of attacking many small hard targets is illustrated on Figure 12. The solid black circles represent buried missile silos, distributed in an irregular pattern but always spaced farther apart

[22] *Op. cit.*, pp. 12–13. Smart also points out that logically MIRV should be a subset of MRV, whereas the terms are usually employed as mutually exclusive.

[23] *SIPRI, 1974* says 160 KT (p. 107).

[24] The number can be increased to fourteen, with a consequent range penalty. *SIPRI, 1974* gives 40 KT for each.

[25] *Statement of Secretary Schlesinger, 1975,* II–12–15. See also *Statement of General Brown, 1975,* pp. 15–16.

[26] Refer to the discussion of the accuracy and destructive power of missiles earlier in this chapter.

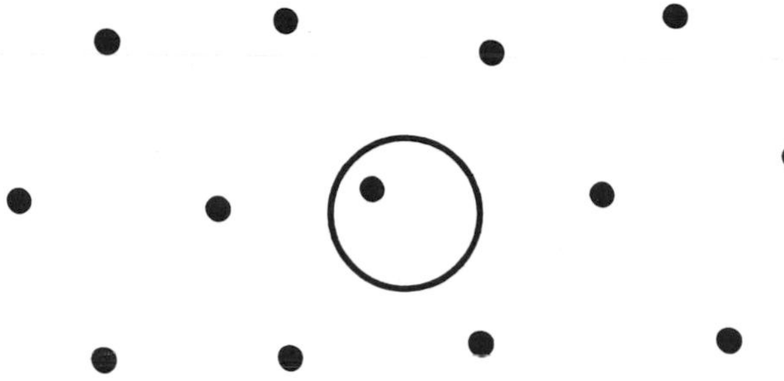

One powerful and accurate warhead One silo hit

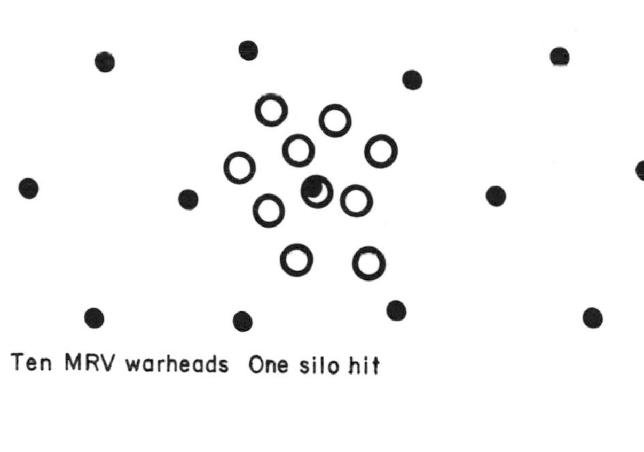

Ten MRV warheads One silo hit

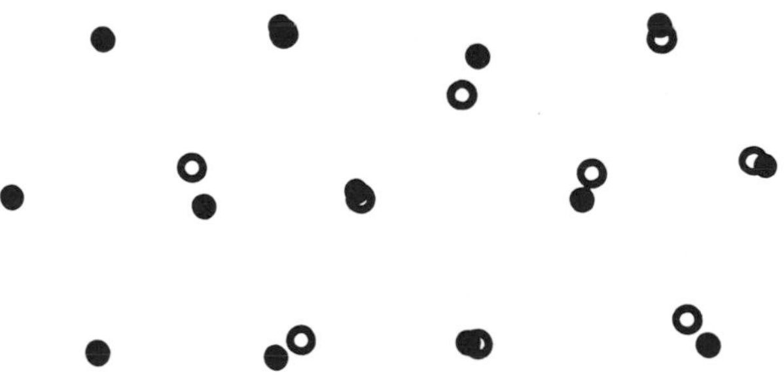

Ten MIRV warheads Five silos hit

Figure 12. Attack by one missile on ten silos

than the lethal diameter of a very large nuclear warhead.[27] In the top diagram, the attacking missile is fitted with one large warhead. Therefore, its lethal diameter is large, and even with moderate accuracy it has a very high probability (say 98–99 percent) of destroying the silo at which it is aimed.

In the middle diagram of Figure 12, the nose cone has been fitted with MRV, and ten warheads with yields considerably less than one-tenth of that of the single large warhead are delivered in a random cluster into the middle of the field of silos. The lethal diameter of each small warhead is much less than for the large warhead. Under plausible assumptions concerning yields and CEPs, each warhead may have a probability in the neighborhood of 10 percent of destroying a silo. Successive firings might result in the destruction of 0, 1, 2, or 3 silos by each group of ten small warheads, but the most probable outcome would be that one silo was destroyed (as illustrated), and in a large attack the numbers of silos destroyed would be approximately equal to the number of missiles launched—the same result as for the single large warheads, except, of course, that the defense would be faced with a much more difficult problem of interception.

The bottom diagram of Figure 12 shows an attack by ten individually guided MIRV warheads. The weight of the guidance mechanisms has obliged a further reduction in yield, and consequently in the lethal diameter of the small warheads. But each of the ten small warheads is aimed at a different silo, and with a small CEP, assumed in this case to be about the same as the lethal radius. Therefore, about 50 percent of the small warheads will destroy a silo. The group of ten warheads from one missile might destroy 3, 4, 5, 6, or 7 silos, but the most probable number destroyed would be five (as

[27] A map of the sites at Malmstrom, near Great Falls, Montana, shows a few silos separated by less than five miles, and few whose nearest neighbor is as far as ten. See Herbert F. York, "Military Technology and National Security," *Scientific American* 221 (August 1969), 26. Smart (*op. cit.*, p. 24) states that the average distance between Minuteman silos is ten miles. R. T. Pretty and D. H. R. Archer, eds., *Jane's Weapon Systems, 1971–72* (New York: McGraw-Hill, 1971), p. 4, state that each site is at least 5½ miles from any other launch site.

illustrated), and an attacker launching several missiles could expect to destroy five silos for each missile launched (assuming no defense).[28]

To summarize the significance of multiple reentry vehicles, the ability to attack widely separated targets, even with only moderate accuracy, would increase the effectiveness of ICBMs and SLBMs against cities, while for the attack of small hard targets such as missile silos, the crucial requirement is high accuracy of the individual reentry vehicles. We shall see in Chapter VII that these two possibilities could result in fundamental alterations of the stability of the strategic balance, and in opposite directions.

Future ICBMs and SLBMs[29]

Future ballistic missiles will exploit technical improvements in propulsion, accuracy, warhead arming and fuzing, efficiency of warhead energy release, technology of multiple warheads, and penetration aids. Terminally guided maneuvering reentry vehicles will be developed. However, there may also be changes in other major respects, especially with the objective of reducing the vulnerability of land-based ICBMs to attack by highly accurate MIRVs. ICBMs could be made mobile and moved among a number of hardened shelters, or launched from aircraft kept on airborne alert.

The United States is designing a new ICBM called MX, to fit into Minuteman silos, but also with the possibility of mobile operation. And, as mentioned earlier, the two new Trident SLBMs will have ranges far in excess of Poseidon.

The Soviet SS-17 and SS-18 are "cold-launched," that is, boosted out of their very hard silos by compressed gas, before the rocket motors are ignited. SS-X-16 may be land-mobile.

[28] The calculation becomes more complicated if the attack is of sufficient magnitude that silos are targeted more than once. This is taken into account in Chapter VII and Appendix A.

[29] *Statement of Secretary Schlesinger, 1975*, pp. II–20–33.

CHAPTER III

Ballistic-Missile Defense

In recent years, Ballistic-Missile Defense (BMD), often referred to as the Anti-Ballistic Missile (ABM), has been the subject of heated debate in the United States and elsewhere. It is a complex subject, both technically and from the points of view of strategic implications and of international affairs generally. Most of the participants in the debate are relatively misinformed either on the technical aspects or on the implications for international relations (or on both). And yet it is impossible to comprehend the problem without some knowledge of both the technical and the engineering aspects.

In this chapter we shall attempt to outline the main technical problems connected with BMD, and to show briefly the limits, the difficulties, the possibilities, and the demands. We leave until later chapters the discussion of the implications of BMD for the strategic balance.

Ballistic-Missile Detection and Information Systems

Early Warning

There are many reasons why a country would need warning of the impending arrival of ballistic missiles. Active defenses would be impotent without some system of detection, and they would be used more efficiently with better knowledge of the scale and targets of the attack. Some retaliatory weapons (such as bomber aircraft) could be saved from destruction with a few minutes of warning. Certain measures of civil defense can be taken on comparatively short warning. But perhaps most important for the prevention of a nuclear war is the question of immediate retaliation. If the attacked country has a weak and vulnerable retaliatory force, it may be faced with the choice of launching its retaliation instantly on receipt of warning, or having its weapons destroyed. This is an undesirable state of affairs from two points of view: the opponent is tempted to catch the defender by surprise, hoping to disarm him, and in the event of an accidental launching of one or a few missiles, perhaps by a country not considered to be the main opponent, or of an erroneous report of attack by a faulty detection system, the defender is tempted to launch what he believes to be retaliation but would, in fact, be the initiation of nuclear war by mistake. The basic cause, as will be discussed in Chapter VII, would be the weak and vulnerable state of the retaliatory force, but in both cases (contemplation of an attack by the aggressor, and mistaken retaliation by the defender against an imagined attack) the probability of the disaster could be reduced by the existence of a reliable and comprehensive warning system.

Even if the defender were not so weak as to be obliged to adopt a "fire on warning" strategy, there would always be the danger that his reaction to an attack by mistake, or to a mistaken report of an attack, would be to make some bellicose reaction which would precipitate hostilities. The stable and desirable condition is that no country should believe that it can disarm an opponent in a surprise attack, that no country need set its forces on a hair-trigger for instant response, and that all countries should feel confident that if threatening reports should come in from their detection system, they could rely on the information as being both correct and complete.

Present day warning systems depend on one of four signals:[1]

(*a*) radar energy reflected from the nose cone in ballistic flight;

[1] Useful descriptions of systems able to detect the launching of ballistic missiles are to be found in Ted Greenwood, "Reconnaissance, Surveillance and Arms Control," *Adelphi Paper No. 84* (London: The International Institute for Strategic Studies, 1972).

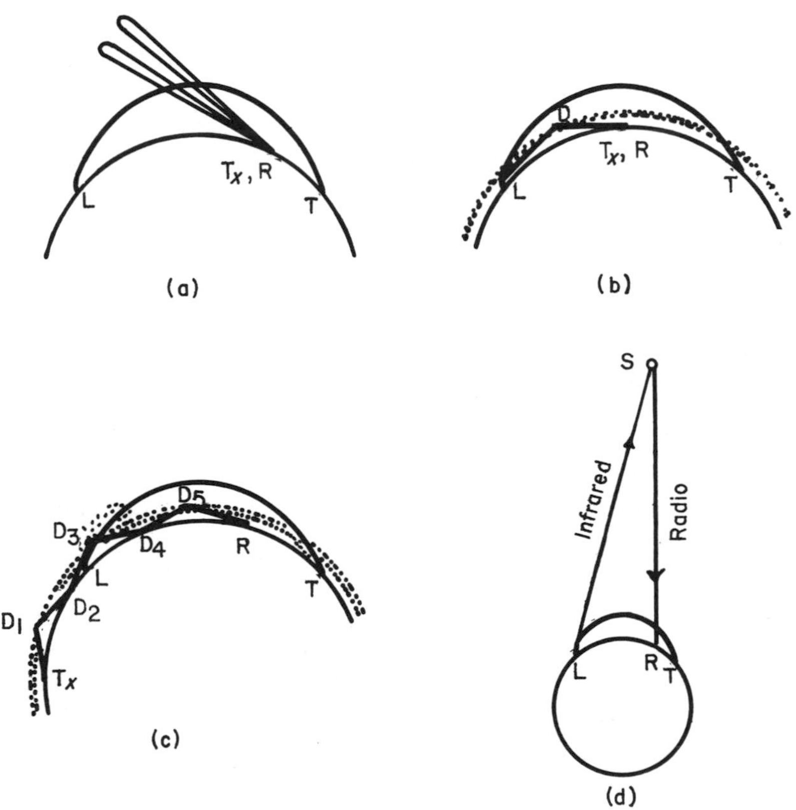

Figure 13. Main antimissile warning systems: (a) radar detection by direct path, (b) over-the-horizon backscatter radar, (c) over-the-horizon forward-scatter radar, (d) satellite

(*b*) radar energy reflected from ionized gas in the rocket exhaust, during the propulsion phase;

(*c*) disturbance of radio signals reflected by the ionosphere which is perturbed by passage of a rocket; and

(*d*) infrared energy radiated by the hot rocket exhaust.

Four such systems are illustrated on Figure 13. In each case the trajectory of the missile starts at the launch point L and finishes at the target T. Unlike the drawings of Chapter II, these show the propulsion phase, beginning with vertical liftoff and rotating into the ultimate launching angle for ballistic flight.

In Figure 13(a) a powerful radar, with a transmitter T_x and a receiver R, sharing the same antenna, directs beams just above the horizon in the direction of L. Although the nose cone is small and distant, there is no other reflecting matter in its vicinity, and the radar echo can be detected at very long range. If there are two or more beams, or if the beam is capable of tracking the nose cone, its position and velocity can be determined and a rough prediction of its future trajectory computed. Space vehicles and the burned-out later stages of rockets used to place satellites in orbit will be detected by such a system, but the computer should be able to distinguish them from missiles on attacking trajectories. Detection cannot occur until the nose cone rises above the horizon of the radar, so that the warning time will be of the order of fifteen to twenty minutes.

The Americans have had a system of this type operating throughout the 1960s. It is called BMEWS (for Ballistic Missile Early Warning System) and has radars located in Alaska, Greenland, and England.

A second type of warning system used Over-the-Horizon Backscatter Radar (OTHB). It has already been mentioned that ionized gas can scatter or reflect radio waves of low frequency. At various heights above the earth, extending from about 40 to above 300 nm, there are layers of ionized gas forming the ionosphere. It is possible to reflect or scatter radar energy off the ionosphere in order to project it beyond the horizon. Some of the energy reaching the path of an ascending rocket will be reflected backwards, not only from the metallic body of the rocket casing but also from the ionization produced by the hot gases in the rocket exhaust. Energy reflected straight backwards will retrace the path, with reflection in the ionosphere, back to the radar. In Figure 13(b) the radio pulse travels from the transmitter at T_x via the ionosphere at D to the rocket exhaust above L, and then back again via D to the radar receiver at R. This type of detection will give warning of the launching of a rocket soon after it leaves the ground. It will not, however, be able to distinguish between the launchings of a missile and a space vehicle.

Ionospheric reflection or scattering can be used in another manner in the system known as Over-the-Horizon Forward Scatter (OTHF). This makes use of the phenomenon well known to radio amateurs, who can receive signals from the Antipodes which come halfway around the earth by a series of reflections from the ionosphere and the ground.[2] Figure 13(c) shows a signal proceeding from a transmitter at T_x and experiencing reflections at D1, D2, D3, D4, and D5 before arriving at a receiver R. At the points D1, D3, and D5 the ionosphere is acting as a mirror. If, now, a large rocket is launched and penetrates the ionosphere close to D3, the ionization produced by its hot exhaust gas will disturb the ionosphere and alter the reflecting properties of the mirror. The receiver at R will receive a changed signal and will know that something has disturbed the ionosphere (at D1, D3, or D5). Detection will occur early in the trajectory, but it will not be able to distinguish a missile from a space vehicle.

The fourth system, depicted on Figure 13(d), depends on a satellite that is making a 24-hour orbit of the earth and consequently hovering over a point on the equator.[3] A very sensitive infrared detector can identify the heat radiated from the rocket of a missile in the propulsion phase, especially once the rocket has risen above the dense layers of the atmosphere. The information can be relayed by radio to a receiver in friendly territory. Again, detection will be early in the flight but probably cannot distinguish between a missile and a space launching.

[2] It is usual for reception to be much better at night. The ionosphere is much affected by the radiation from the sun.

[3] This requires a circular orbit 22,800 nm, or 19,400 nm above the surface of the earth. A satellite cannot be made to "hover" above a fixed point on the earth at a lower altitude.

The most reliable warning requires the combination of information from several systems in a single data center, including all known statistics regarding space vehicles and weapon tests. The Satellite Early Warning System has proven to be the most useful of the four.

Decision Making and Control

Although of fundamental strategic importance, simple warning that a missile attack is imminent must be supplemented by more detailed information if interceptions are to be efficiently performed. The detection system must be able to discriminate real warheads from fragments, chaff, and decoys. The defense must commit its interceptors with full knowledge of the targets and timing of the attacking missiles, perhaps having to leave some missiles unopposed if the capacity of the defensive system is overtaxed.

The collection and display of the information, its evaluation, the making of decisions regarding interception, the calculation of precise guidance instructions for the intercepting missiles, and the modification of tactics as further information is acquired must all be performed with a minimum of delay if not in "real time." Intercepting as well as attacking missiles must be detected and tracked. All of this requires a reliable and widespread communication system and very large and fast computers, both of high capacity. Nearly all of the operations must be automatic. Where human interventions are necessary, the only way to make them sufficiently rapid may be to have a number of alternative "options" already programmed in the computer, so that the commander need only select among a limited number of possible courses of action. In fact, a practical antimissile interception system could not be contemplated without the use of modern high-speed computers.

Kinematic Requirements for Interception

The interception of an object moving at a speed of 4 nm/sec is no simple matter. And, as we have already seen, the problem is likely

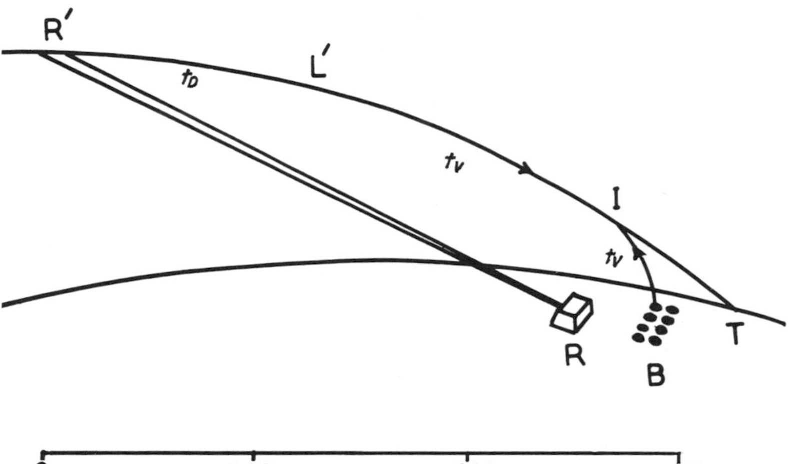

Figure 14. Kinematic requirements of interception

to be made more difficult by the use of various tactics to delay detection of the attack, to supply confusing signals to conceal the position of the attacking warheads, and to present the defense with the necessity of conducting several interceptions at the same time.

The kinematic[4] demands of the problem are illustrated on Figure 14. The curve R′L′IT represents the last part of the trajectory of an intercontinental ballistic missile aimed at a target T. Defensive installations include a radar at R and a battery of interceptor missiles at B.

Suppose that T, or other vulnerable locations on the ground, will be damaged if the attacking warhead (or the defensive warhead, if it is more powerful) explodes below the altitude marked by the point I on the trajectory. Thus, the objective of the defense is to intercept the ICBM before it passes the point I.

[4] Kinematics deals with motion, taking account of distances but not forces. When forces are considered as well, the proper term is "dynamics."

There are several stages in the process of interception—namely, detection, discrimination, deciding to launch an interceptor, launching the interceptor, the flight of the interceptor, and the detonation of the defensive warhead.

Suppose that the radar makes its first detection of incoming objects when the real nose cone is at R′. It will be necessary to track the objects for some time before it is possible to determine that some of them are likely to impact on T. If the real warhead can be distinguished on a trajectory aimed at T, or if it decided to intercept the swarm (or a certain part of the swarm) of objects, it will be necessary to send the firing order to the selected antimissile battery at B. A further short delay will ensue before the chosen interceptor is launched. Suppose that all these actions take t_D seconds. During this interval, the nose cone will have advanced to L′. When the nose cone is at L′, the interceptor is launched from B, and both proceed towards the point of interception I. If the interception is perfectly directed, the time for the nose cone to cover the distance L′I will be exactly equal to the time of flight of the interceptor from B to I, say t_V seconds.

To obtain a long range of first detection RR′, it is necessary to have a radar with a large antenna, a powerful transmitter, and a sensitive receiver. It is also necessary that no object intervene in the direct path RR′,[5] so that nearby hills or the distant horizon will limit the attainable range. The range of such a radar can reach about 1200 to 1500 nm.[6] First detection can be made earlier if the radar can be sited ahead of the target. If we suppose that R′ is 1500 nm from I, and that the nose cone is approaching with a velocity of 4 nm/sec, it

[5] The path RR′ will, in fact, be very slightly curved downwards because of refraction in the atmosphere.

[6] In testimony before a senatorial committee Daniel J. Fink quoted a range of 1500 nm, and Deputy Secretary of Defense David Packard "well in excess of 1000 miles." See U.S. Senate, Committee on Foreign Relations, *Strategic and Foreign Policy Implications of ABM Systems: Hearings before the Subcommittee on International Organization and Disarmament Affairs*, Part 1, March 1969, pp. 25 and 264; hereafter cited under the abridged title *Hearings on the Strategic and Foreign Policy Implications of ABM Systems*, 1969.

follows that the time taken to cover the distance R′I is 375 seconds, or a little more than 6 minutes. Thus the sum of the two intervals $t_D + t_V$—for detection, discrimination, decision to launch an interceptor, launching the interceptor, and time of flight of the interceptor—must be no more than about 6 minutes.

If it were not for the evasive trajectories and penetration aids described in the preceding chapter, t_D would be quite short, and 6 minutes would be quite long enough to accomplish these tasks with an interceptor rocket of relatively modest design. But with low trajectories and electromagnetic blackout, the range of detection (and hence $t_D + t_V$) will be reduced, while with tank fragments, chaff, and decoys, the time necessary for discrimination, and hence t_D, will be increased, especially if it becomes necessary to await reentry into the atmosphere in order to discriminate light decoys by the action of air drag. If $(t_D + t_V)$ is reduced, but t_D is increased, the only hope for an interception is to reduce t_V, the time of flight of the intercepting missile. This will require a missile of high acceleration, and hence of robust construction and able to withstand considerable aerodynamic heating.

The interceptor missile will need to be able to accept corrections to its trajectory as more accurate predictions of the ICBM path are made, especially if the attacking vehicle can maneuver. The interceptor may require small rockets, capable of being ignited and shut down for several brief periods, for maneuvering; or, if all of its flight is to be within the atmosphere, it may be able to maneuver by aerodynamic control.

The Antimissile Warhead

Even with the best modern guidance and control technology it would be extremely difficult to intercept an ICBM in the sense that the interceptor missile would literally collide with the attacking nose cone. This task has been likened to hitting a bullet with a bullet, although the ICBM is going about ten times as fast as a rifle bullet. If it had been necessary to physically strike the nose cone with the interceptor, ballistic missile defense would probably not have been attempted at all.

What has made BMD possible is the same force which made the ICBM worth developing: the destructive power of nuclear energy. The attacking weapon is vulnerable to three effects of a nuclear explosion: X rays, neutrons, and shock.[7]

If a nuclear explosion occurs at high altitude, a considerable fraction of the energy which would be transmitted as a shock wave in the atmosphere appears instead in the form of soft X rays.[8] In the absence of any absorbing material these X rays are propagated away from the explosion until they encounter some form of matter. If they strike the reentry vehicle, the soft X rays will be absorbed in its outer surface and the energy will be propagated into the weapon in the form of a shock wave, likely to damage the outer heat shield or the delicately fitting mechanism of the bomb. In addition, it is probable that balloons, chaff, and light decoys will be vaporized by intense X radiation. Therefore, the "X-ray kill" should be extremely effective, but only at the high altitudes where there is very little air. And at high altitudes it is possible to employ a defensive warhead of high energy yield without provoking damage on the ground.

Neutrons are more penetrating than X rays and will, therefore, enter into the fissile material which is the heart of the nuclear weapon inside the attacking nose cone. Although a chain reaction will not develop, there will be energy released by the fission reactions following the absorption of neutrons, and the resulting heat may be enough to melt or at least distort the blocks of fissile material, so that the nuclear explosion cannot occur. An interception depending on "neutron kill" can be attempted at a much lower altitude than X-ray kill, and if the energy yield of the defensive warhead is small, there will be a minimum of danger to persons or structures on the ground.

[7] Bethe, "Countermeasures to ABM Systems," *op. cit.*, pp. 130–132.

[8] Soft X rays carry more energy than visible light but less than hard X rays. They are less penetrating than hard X rays. The soft X rays produced in an explosion within the atmosphere are absorbed by the surrounding air; the energy is then propagated through the air as a shock wave and thermal radiation.

The damaging effects of shock have already been described as regards structures on the ground. A reentry vehicle needs to be of rugged construction and must have a heat shield, which will also provide a degree of protection against shock. The effect of shock becomes greater at lower altitudes, since air is the medium through which the energy is transmitted.

The contest between measure and countermeasure is being pursued in this domain as in many others, and it is probable that the purpose of many of the underground nuclear tests being conducted by the United States and the Soviet Union is to improve the kill mechanisms of their defensive warheads and the shielding of their offensive warheads.

Components of the Safeguard System

The United States has been developing antimissile interception systems since 1956.[9] They were soon able to demonstrate the technical feasibility of intercepting an ICBM at high altitude, but they realized that this early system would be unable to deal with simultaneous interceptions or with decoys. It would be necessary to make substantial improvements to the radar and to the interceptors.

The radars of the 1950s depended on large antennae, mechanically rotating at a few rpm to scan 360°, or else mechanically tracking the movement of a single target. But the first did not renew its information at intervals sufficiently short to allow adequate tracking and data processing for the calculation of interceptions, while the second could deal with only one target at a time. The solution was found with the *phased-array radar*. This radar has no moving parts; it directs its beam of energy from a large fixed array of many small antennae by controlling the phase of the energy pulse sent to each. Freed from the inertia of large moving structures, the beam can be

[9] See Daniel J. Fink's testimony in *Hearings on the Strategic and Foreign Policy Implications of ABM Systems*, 1969, pp. 22–30. The first program was called "Nike Zeus." An extensive account of the developing policy and programs is given in Benson Adams, *Ballistic Missile Defense* (New York: Elsevier, 1971).

darted in any direction for very brief intervals and can, therefore, give frequent reports on each of many targets. Another advantage of the fixed phased array is that it is considerably less vulnerable to damage by blast. A large phased-array radar is, however, an expensive proposition, especially if it has several faces covering different sectors.

If the acceleration and burnout velocity of the interceptor missile are low, then t_V, the time of flight to intercept, will be long (except in the fortuitous case where the attacking missile passes very close to the antimissile battery). Since $(t_D + t_V)$ is limited by the high speed of the ICBM, t_D, the time for detection, discrimination, and decision, is necessarily short. In particular, the interceptor must be launched before the swarm of decoys has entered the atmosphere, so that the decelerating effect of air drag on the lighter objects cannot be observed before the interceptor has been committed.

The American solution to this problem was to design two radically improved interceptors with different characteristics. The first, named *Spartan*, is designed to make its interception at long range and high altitude. Its range is in the vicinity of 300 to 400 nm,[10] and it is equipped with a nuclear warhead with a yield of several megatons.[11] The large warhead, burst above the atmosphere, will have a long radius of X-ray kill for the attacking weapon and will be able to completely destroy light decoys throughout a large volume. Inevitably, the defensive bursts will produce a degree of electromagnetic blackout, but there may be some latitude to choose the height of burst to minimize this effect.

For those nose cones or heavy decoys which survive interception attempts above the atmosphere by Spartan, a second interceptor, *Sprint*, is designed for use within the atmosphere. Its range is about

[10] *Hearings on the Strategic and Foreign Policy Implications of ABM Systems*, 1969 (testimony of Deputy Secretary of Defense David Packard), p. 268. Smart, *op. cit.*, p. 20, quotes about 400 miles.

[11] A warhead of about 4 MT for the Spartan missile was tested in an underground explosion of Amchitka in November 1971. See *SIPRI, 1972*, p. 21.

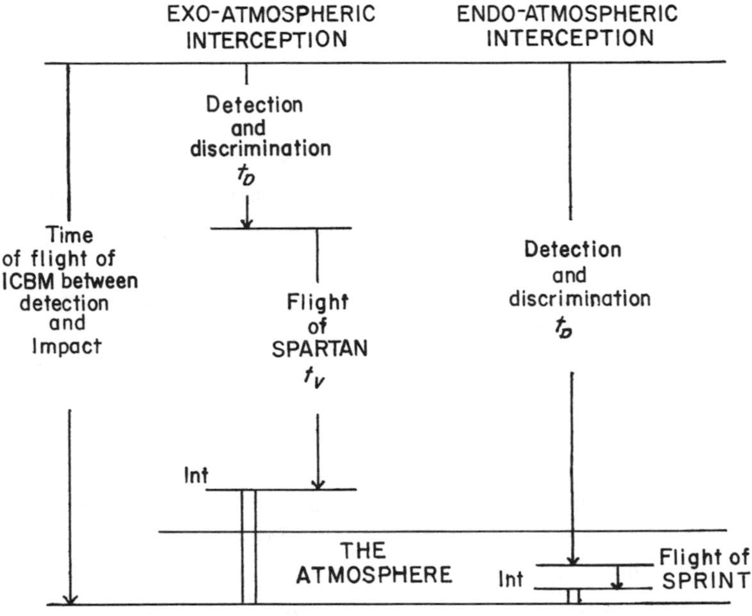

Figure 15. Subdivision of the time available for interception

25 miles and its nuclear warhead "a few kilotons."[12] The kill radius, depending on neutrons and blast at low altitude, will be much less than that of Spartan at high altitude. Because Sprint is fired late, and t_V cannot be long, the interceptor must have extremely high acceleration.

Figure 15 portrays the very different time scales for exo-atmospheric and endo-atmospheric interceptions. Note that Spartan is fired early, before there has been a long time for discrimination, has a long time of flight, and intercepts above the atmosphere. But Sprint

[12] Deputy Secretary Packard quotes "20, 30 miles" (*Hearings on the Strategic and Foreign Policy Implications of ABM Systems*, 1969, p. 209). Chayes and Wiesner, eds., *op. cit.*, p. 7, gave 25 miles; so does Smart, *op. cit.*, p. 20.

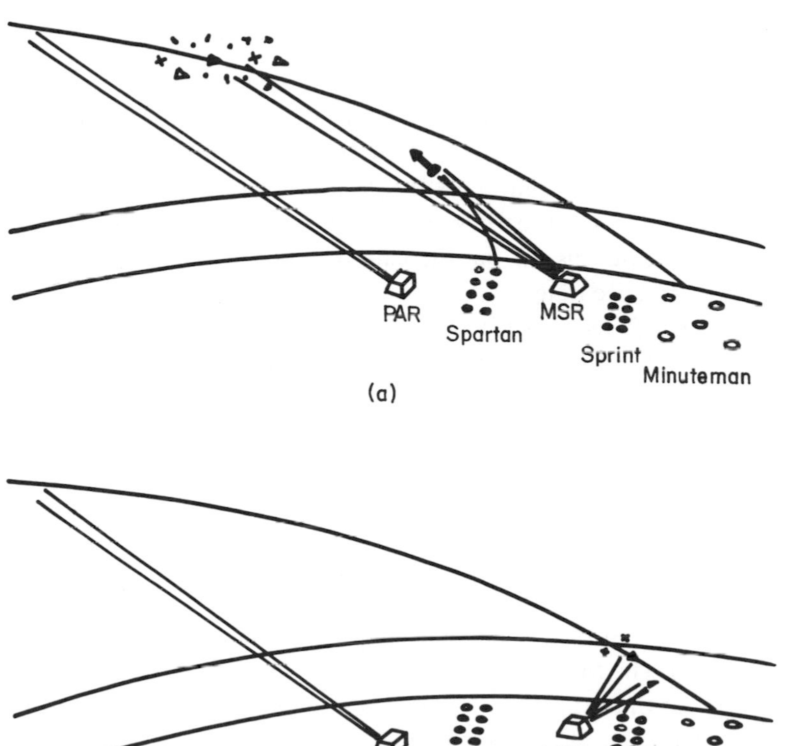

Figure 16. Missile interception by the Safeguard system: (a) exo-atmospheric interception, (b) endo-atmospheric interception

is fired very late, after the objects have already reentered the atmosphere, and intercepts close to the ground.

The American ballistic missile defense system known as *Safeguard* consists of four basic types of components: the two interceptor missiles Spartan and Sprint and two types of radar known as Perimeter Acquisition Radar (PAR), and Missile Site Radar (MSR), netted together by an appropriate system of communications and computers. These two were chosen from several radars developed for BMD under the program known as *Nike X*. Both are phased-array radars, with their beams "electronically steered."

The function of PAR is to detect the approaching objects at long range, to track them, and to provide the information needed to evaluate the threat and make the decisions regarding interception. Information from the early warning systems described earlier should be available and useful, but the data from PAR will be much more detailed and accurate.

The main function of discrimination between warheads and decoys, and the entire function of control of the interceptions, falls to the MSR. The MSR must track the Spartans and Sprints as well as the attacking objects, in order that the interceptors may be sent guidance commands and, eventually, the instruction to detonate the defensive warhead (or to dispose of the interceptor in a safe manner if it has failed to intercept).

The four main components of Safeguard are illustrated on Figure 16. In Figure 16(a) the PAR detects and tracks the cloud of objects and determines that they are threatening to impact on a field of Minuteman silos. The MSR picks them up, and a Spartan is launched under control of the MSR. The warhead of the Spartan will be detonated above the atmosphere. Suppose that it is too far from the real reentry vehicle to destroy it, but that the radiation disposes of the tank fragments, chaff, and light decoys. In Figure 16(b) we see the MSR tracking the remaining objects into the atmosphere and discriminating the decoys by their deceleration. A Sprint is launched under control of the MSR to intercept the attacking warhead at a fairly low altitude.

The Protected Footprint of an Antimissile Battery

Above an antimissile battery is an umbrella-shaped volume in which interceptions can be accomplished. The upper, nearly hemispherical surface is determined by the maximum effective range of

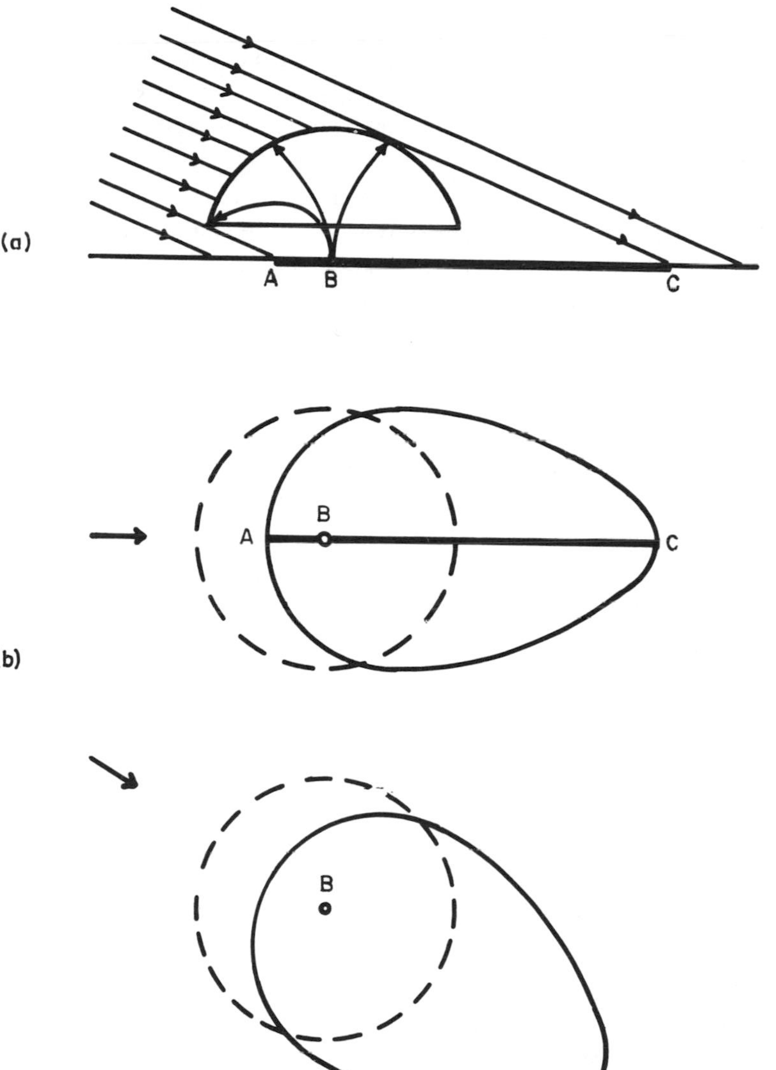

Figure 17. Protected footprint of the ABM battery: (a) vertical section of the umbrella of protection, (b) projection of protected footprint on the ground, (c) rotation of protected footprint on the ground

the interceptor, and the lower, plane-horizontal surface marks the lowest altitude at which the defensive warhead can be exploded to be both effective against the attacking reentry vehicle and safe for the inhabitants and structures on the ground.

The area on the ground which can be protected from impact by attacking warheads is not directly beneath the "umbrella." Because the ICBM trajectories arrive at low angles to the horizontal, they can be likened to rain driven nearly horizontal by a high wind. The area on the ground which the umbrella can keep dry will be displaced downwind from the center (or handle) of the umbrella and will have an ovoid shape.

Figure 17 illustrates this situation. B represents the interceptor battery. In Figure 17(a) a vertical section shows the nearly hemispherical "umbrella" above the battery. The possible ICBM trajectories descending from a particular azimuth and at a vertical angle of 24° will impact on the ground except where they are intercepted by the umbrella. The protected area will extend from A to C.

Figure 17(b) shows the same situation in plan view. The umbrella's projection on the ground is circular, but the protected area is egg-shaped and displaced in the direction of travel of the attacking ICBMs. If the attack should come from a different direction, the protected area would be rotated about B, as illustrated on Figure 17(c).

The protected zone has been labeled as the *footprint* of the ABM battery. The footprint of a Spartan battery is very large. The long dimension depends on the angle of descent of the attacking missiles but is likely to be between 750 and 1200 nm. The scale of protection offered by Sprint is much smaller, the length of the footprint perhaps 45 to 75 nm.

Because of the large size of the Spartan footprint, this interceptor is sometimes said to provide *area defense*.

Deployment Plans for ABM Systems

Of various plans for antimissile defenses of the United States, the most important have been *Sentinel* and *Safeguard*. Sentinel was to

Figure 18. Main options of the Safeguard system

have offered a modest degree of protection to the entire area of the United States, with emphasis on the defense of cities. Safeguard, on the contrary, gives priority to the defense of the retaliatory weapons systems.

Several optional plans for Safeguard were in existence when the first accord was produced from the Strategic Arms Limitation Talks in May 1972. The accord determined the immediate future of Safeguard in a manner different from any of the planned options. However, it is instructive to describe the options, as they are the best example of prospective ballistic missile defenses. It was known for some time that the plans were likely to be altered by the outcome of the SALT.[13]

Two major phases were foreseen, at least as options which might be followed if circumstances dictated.[14] In Phase 1, two ABM complexes would be installed, one near Grand Forks (North Dakota) and the other near Malmstrom Air Force Base in Montana. There is a large group of Minuteman missile silos in each of these locations, marked on Figure 18 and joined by a dotted line. At each ABM complex a PAR, an MSR, a Spartan battery, and a Sprint battery were planned, together with the necessary computers, and the two complexes would have been connected by communication circuits to allow coordination and cooperation.

Three alternative options were planned for Phase 2.[15] The likely developments to which there would be reactions were:

Option 2A: An increased Soviet threat to Minuteman, perhaps due to deployment of more SS-9 missiles and the appearance of operational MIRVs.

Option 2B: An increased threat to bomber airfields, perhaps due to a substantial increase in the number of Soviet missile-launching submarines.

Option 2C: The appearance of a threat to U.S. cities by Chinese ICBMs.

Option 2A would have extended the defense of the retaliatory force by installing MSR, Spartan, and Sprint at two more areas with

[13] See, for example, President Nixon's announcement of March 14, 1969, concerning a modification of the ABM system planned by the previous administration. The text is reproduced in Chayes and Wiesner, eds., *op. cit.*, pp. 254–259.

[14] See *Statement of Secretary Laird, 1971*, pp. 70–74. Also *Hearings on the Strategic and Foreign Policy Implications of ABM Systems*, 1969, pp. 257–296 (Testimony of Deputy Secretary of Defense Packard), and Excerpt from the Defense Posture Report of Secretary Laird, relating to ABM, March 19, 1969, reprinted in Chayes and Wiesner, eds., *op. cit.*, pp. 259–263.

[15] *Hearings on the Strategic and Foreign Policy Implications of ABM Systems*, 1969, pp. 257–296.

Minuteman—Warren (Wyoming) and Whiteman (Missouri)—and at Washington, D.C., because it is the site of the National Command Authority which must make the all-important early decisions regarding reaction to attack. These three locations are joined by a dashed line on Figure 18.

Options 2B and 2C each involved the activation of a total of twelve complexes (including the two of Phase 1). The twelve are shown on Figure 18 by circles. Each had MSR, Spartan, and Sprint. Option 2B, intended to give protection against attack by SLBM, which could come from the directions of the Pacific, the Atlantic, or even the Caribbean, and against FOBS, which could approach from the south, needed to have warning and the capability of interception over 360°. For this purpose a total of seven PARs would be needed, shown on Figure 18 by crosses. Another requirement for Option 2B was that the MSRs, as well as the PARs, should be able to cover all likely directions of attack, so that certain radars of both types needed more than one "face" on their phased arrays. Option 2C, intended to give protection to cities against a small force of ICBMs coming from the direction of China, or against the accidental launching of a missile, would not have needed as extensive radar coverage as 2B.

The footprints of Spartan batteries cover enough area that the twelve sites would have allowed virtually the whole of the United States (including Alaska and Hawaii) to be covered.[16] But the area covered by twelve Sprint batteries would be comparatively small. For these, it would be necessary to give priority to the defense of the crucial elements in the interception system—PAR and MSR. In a full deployment of all options, the four sites located in the Minuteman fields would have had considerably more Sprints than would the other sites.

None of the options, including full deployment of Safeguard, was intended to protect U.S. cities against a full-scale Soviet attack. In

[16] See the diagram in Herbert F. York, "Military Technology and National Security," *Scientific American* 221 (August 1969), 24.

the present state of technology this is not possible, either technically or economically. The objectives were considerably more modest—to wit:

1. protection of the land-based retaliatory forces against a direct attack by the Soviet Union,
2. defense of the American people against the kind of nuclear attack which Communist China was likely to be able to mount within the decade, and
3. protection against the possibility of accidental attacks from any source.

Safeguard is sometimes referred to as "a light defense."

A fact of fundamental importance in judging the practicability of effective defense is that a comparatively small percentage of successful interceptions may be sufficient for the defense of the retaliatory force—if 100 Minutemen survive out of 300, this is probably enough—while anything less than 100 percent defense of a small or medium-sized city means that the city will be destroyed.

At the time that the first SALT accord was reached in Moscow, in May 1972, the Phase I construction of Safeguard was under way, and some preparatory work had commenced on part of Option 2A. Since SALT I limited each country to two ABM complexes, one for retaliatory weapons and one for the national capital, it was necessary to abandon one of the two sites for Phase I. Malmstrom was much less advanced than Grand Forks, so it was stopped, as was all further preparation for deployment except for Grand Forks, with 30 Spartan and 70 Sprint missiles on launchers, one MSR, and one PAR.

Early warning of ICBM, SLBM, or FOBS attack will be provided by BMEWS radar, by early warning satellites, and by coastal radars, including new anti-SLBM phased-array equipment.[17]

Unfortunately, very little information is available concerning the

[17] *Statement of Secretary Schlesinger, 1975*, pp. II–48–49.

Soviet ABM system.[18] It is believed that the U.S.S.R. has a missile early warning system, target acquisition and tracking radar (including one phased array radar larger than PAR[19] and another under construction),[20] together with the necessary command and control. And they have installed around Moscow 64 interceptor missiles known as Galosh, at which number they appear to have halted deployment. Galosh is estimated to have a range of over 200 miles and to carry a nuclear warhead in the megaton range,[21] so that it seems to resemble Spartan more than Sprint. There are reports that an improved interceptor is under development, able to maneuver after a period of coasting.[22] Since the 1972 SALT accord permits six large ABM radars and 100 missiles on launchers around the national capital, it is expected that the Moscow defenses will be increased.[20]

Possible Future Developments of Land-Based ABM Systems

The vigorous research and development programs in the United States and U.S.S.R. are quite likely to offer the possibility of important improvements to BMD. Detection, and especially discrimination, may be able to exploit laser or infrared techniques. It is even conceivable that high-powered laser beams could be used as a means to destroy incoming warheads. The performance of interceptor rockets will probably be improved, particularly in regard to relightable motors to permit effective maneuvering at all stages of the trajectory. And there is every indication that the remarkable progress in computer technology will continue.

[18] A short summary is given in J. Holst and W. Schneider, eds., *Why ABM? Policy Issues in the Missile Defense Controversy* (New York: Pergamon Press, 1969), pp. 149–156.

[19] See the Testimony of Dr. J. S. Foster, Director of Defense Research and Engineering in *Hearings on ABM, MIRV, SALT, and the Nuclear Arms Race*, 1970, p. 427.

[20] No additional launchers appeared between 1972 and 1974.

[21] *The Military Balance, 1975–76,* p. 8.

[22] *Statement of Secretary Laird, 1972,* p. 57, and Holst and Schneider, eds., *op. cit.*, p. 155.

One quite probable undertaking would be the development of a system specifically designed for the defense of hard points, such as missile silos and underground command posts. There are a number of reasons to recommend such a system.[23] If the targets are hard and there is no nearby population, interceptions can be made down to very low altitudes. Therefore, decoys can be filtered out by the atmosphere. If a large footprint is not needed and interception can be at low altitude, the need for a high-performance interceptor missile can be relaxed. If the small number of very expensive components of Safeguard could be replaced by many small cheap hard radars and interceptors, the system would be much less vulnerable to the loss of a crucial component. And, as already mentioned earlier, the objective of saving some of many targets is much more realizable than that of providing 100 percent defense.

Operation of the defenses when electromagnetic blackout is being caused by high-altitude nuclear bursts may be facilitated by the use of several radars (or other tracking sensors) in different locations, all pooling their information in a common data bank.[24]

Other Possible Future Developments in BMD

The interceptions discussed so far have occurred near the end of the intended flight of the attacking missile. In many ways this is the worst place to intercept: guidance is completed, the most delicate mechanisms have already performed their functions, the decoys are already deployed, and if there are multiple warheads they will already be well separated. If the missile could be attacked during its launching phase, it would present a much larger, slower, and more vulnerable

[23] See the Testimony of Dr. W. K. H. Panofsky in *Hearings on Strategic and Foreign Policy Implications of ABM Systems,* 1969, pp. 330–333. See also Hans Bethe, "Hard Point versus City Defense", *op. cit.,* pp. 25–26. Plans for research and development for "site defense" are described in the *Statement of Secretary Schlesinger, 1975,* pp. II–46–47.

[24] *Hearings on ABM, MIRV, SALT, and the Nuclear Arms Race,* 1970, pp. 608–609 and 613.

target. The huge liberation of heat from the burning rockets would provide an ideal target for a heat-seeking interceptor missile. Even a small uncorrected deflection of the trajectory at this stage would produce a large error in point of impact. There is the opportunity to destroy all reentering objects—warheads, decoys, chaff, tank fragments—with one interception.

The difficulties which have so far prevented the implementation of a so-called *boost-phase interception system* are technical, economic, and political. It is clear that such a system would need very rapid warning and a very short reaction time. This would probably demand that the detectors and interceptors be located close to the prospective launching sites and that their reaction be automatic. One project, designed on paper to be based on earth satellites, appeared prohibitively expensive. Moreover, it is easy to see that such a system would be regarded as provocative and dangerous by the opponent, particularly if the interceptors carried nuclear warheads, and that the dangers of mistaken interception (perhaps of a peaceful space launching or of an experimental rocket trial) would be very real.

There have been a number of studies of systems designed to advance the interception away from the terminal phase and into the early part of the ballistic phase if not the launching phase.[25] SABMIS, a Sea-Based Antiballistic Missile Interception System, would place the radars and interceptor missiles on surface ships, able to station themselves in international waters close to the adversaries' coasts. ABMIS, an Airborne Ballistic Missile Interception System, would be carried in a large aircraft. Both would be able to place themselves in good positions to intercept submarine-launched missiles, quite probably in the propulsion phase of their trajectories. And both could be sent to offer protection to a third country should circumstances so dictate.

Up to this point we have given our main attention to the interception of ICBMs. In principle, defense against attack by strategic

[25] Smart, *op. cit.*, p. 21. Also Holst and Schneider, eds., *op. cit.*, pp. 11–13 and 18–19.

ballistic missiles should include defense against SLBM, IRBM, and MRBM, and also against missiles projected from a space vehicle (MOBS). By a slight extension, the ability to destroy space vehicles, whether or not carrying weapons, could be included, especially since the same type of interceptor could probably be employed.

Interception of the shorter-range missiles launched from land or sea presents the defense with shorter warning time and the need for very rapid reaction. This was illustrated on Figure 10. The missile velocities are less and the trajectories lower. The interceptor may be able to make more use of aerodynamic control. Defense of a large area by one interceptor battery does not seem possible, and it is likely that any systems designed specifically for defense against ballistic missiles of less than intercontinental range will depend on short-range interceptors capable of high acceleration.

Early detection of shorter-range missiles poses a difficult problem. Radar on the ground can use a large phased array and gives nearly 100 percent "time on station," but it is more severely limited by the horizon than an airborne radar. The mobility of shipborne and especially airborne radars could prove very valuable, to say nothing of their legal access to international waters and airspace. It is not improbable that the problem of early warning over vast areas (possibly including all of the world's oceans in a few years) will be best solved by satellite-borne detectors, although it is much less likely that the satellites will also carry intercepting weapons.

For defense against SLBM, there is the possibility of using a ship or a large aircraft for detection of the missiles, control of interception, and attack of the launching submarine. A ship can carry a larger radar and more and larger weapons, but an aircraft can observe a larger area and move much faster. On the other hand, there would be little sense in spending a great deal of money to combat the SLBM unless comparable efforts were made against the ICBM. And a defense capable of intercepting ICBMs may have most of the equipment, or at least the infrastructure, needed to provide at the same time defense against SLBMs.

As for the interception of space vehicles, this should not be a technically difficult problem if some delay is acceptable to await the moment at which their orbit brings them into a favorable position. For satellites in low earth orbit, a long-range ABM interceptor of the Spartan type would have sufficient performance. If, however, the objective is to examine the vehicle for information purposes rather than to destroy it, the problem is one of "space rendezvous" rather than simple interception and is more demanding.

CHAPTER IV

The Ballistic-Missile Submarine and Antisubmarine Defense

Twice within the last sixty years Germany came within a hair's breadth of making herself mistress of the Atlantic, isolating Europe from America, and dominating the world from a continent of which she would have controlled both the external and internal communications and, as a result, the political destiny.

What would happen if a great continental power made the attempt again? One scholar, writing twelve years ago, noted that

> turning movement would extend the radius of action beyond the ports of Europe, which would be blocked by mines. . . . There would be a new "Battle of the Atlantic" in parallel with a "Battle of Europe." Unleashed before or at the same time as an atomic war with rocket bombardment, the submarine war would continue after the nuclear exchange. In the end, the submarine and antisubmarine war would determine the outcome of the word conflict.[1]

Today, experts do not agree on the significance of defense of the lines of communication in the nuclear age. Would the outcome of World War III be settled in a few minutes of all-out nuclear destruc-

[1] Jean Savant, *Histoire mondiale de la marine* (Paris: Hachette, 1961), p. 441. Translation by the authors of this book.

tion on land? Or would the conflict be prolonged into a war of attrition lasting for years, on the pattern of its two predecessors? Or is it conceivable that a great maritime contest for control of and access to the seas, as described by Admiral Mahan, could develop without accompanying nuclear warfare? Indeed, is such a contest being waged today, without a shot being fired?

Access to the seas may depend more on geography, political alliances, and land power than on naval strength. As Jean Perré has well said,[2] China is overlooked not so much by Hong Kong as by the large island of Formosa; it is no longer Istanbul which commands the Bosphorus, it is Turkey and Greece; it is not Copenhagen which now bars the Sound, but all of Scandinavia; and Malta and Gibraltar do not close off the western Mediterranean any more, it is northwest Africa, Spain, and Sicily.

One cannot discuss the strategic significance of the submarine without such considerations as these. But today the submarine has a new role, likely to be even more important for the future than control of sea communication. While the surface fleets pay their visits and the flags frequenting naval bases change, the ballistic missile-firing submarines are at sea, always submerged and invisible, alone, avoiding contact, the ideal weapon of deterrence, at once the prisoners and the guardians of the Apocalypse. It is upon this role of the submarine that we will concentrate in this book.

The Strategic Role of the Submarine

Unlike the bomber aircraft, which was used for strategic bombing towards the end of World War I, or the intercontinental ballistic missile, which was conceived specifically for the purpose of long-range attack on cities, the submarine, in the past, was never considered as a weapon to be used against cities or land-based military targets. Up until the commissioning of the first nuclear-powered ballistic-missile firing submarine in 1959, the submarine had been confined to the attack of maritime targets and to other naval functions such as

[2] Jean Perré, *Les mutations de la guerre moderne* (Paris: Payot, 1962), p. 355.

reconnaissance and mine-laying. Starting with the first stealthy attack against the English ship "Eagle" in 1776 by Bushnell's one-man human-powered submarine "Tortue," and including the "wolfpack" attacks by Admiral Doenitz' U-boats against Allied convoys in World War II, the submarine has usually operated like a pirate, attacking the weak and fleeing the strong, sinking cargo ships and tankers, though rarely passenger ships. It had its successes against warships, too, but the big scores, the results of great strategic importance, came against merchant vessels. Between 1914 and 1918 German U-boats sank 13,000,000 tons of Allied shipping; between 1939 and 1945 the total was 14,000,000 tons.[3] American submarines accounted for 2,500,000 tons of Japanese merchant vessels.

The unrestricted submarine warfare of World War I and the Battle of the Atlantic of World War II were contests with truly strategic stakes. In both cases the Atlantic lifeline was held by a narrow margin. But in the Pacific the American campaign against the Japanese merchant fleet, using aircraft, surface ships, and mines as well as submarines, succeeded so brilliantly that the prewar tonnage of 6,000,000 was reduced to 312,000.

Today, the ballistic-missile submarine forms one of the three weapons systems which make up the offensive arm of the strategic nuclear balance. And it is probably the most important of the three for the preservation of stable deterrence. This does not imply that the protection or denial of sea communication has lost all of its former importance. However, the probability of a war of attrition at sea on the scale of either world war appears to be decreasing, while the strategic nuclear balance has assumed dominant significance. Consequently, for the purposes of this book, we shall label as "strategic" the role of the submarine in using SLBM weapons, whether to threaten, to attack, or to retaliate, and also as "strategic" the role of antisubmarine defense when used against ballistic-missile submarines. The other, older, and still important roles of the submarine, such as

[3] In addition to these figures there were sinkings due to aircraft, surface ships, and mines, but submarines accounted for more than all the others combined.

to threaten or to attack surface ships, whether naval or merchant, to lay mines, or to act as a scout or a clandestine replenishment vessel, we shall label as "tactical."

Submarines can carry and launch three types of missile: torpedoes, cruise missiles, and ballistic missiles. Torpedoes are used against ships, including other submarines. Cruise missiles fly as pilotless aircraft, armed with a nuclear or a conventional warhead, and can be used against surface ships or land targets. To launch a cruise missile, the submarine must come to the surface. The SLBM, armed with a nuclear warhead, is intended for strategic targets on land, such as air or naval bases, industry, or population.

Although in a sense outmoded today, there are many hundreds of diesel-engined submarines still in service. Their chief weakness is the need to run the diesel engines for several hours a day, with the snorkel tube[4] above the surface, thus exposing themselves to detection by the noise, the protruding tube, the wake, and the exhaust gases. However, a diesel-powered submarine equipped with either cruise or ballistic missiles, which makes its way close to the enemy coast, can perfectly well attack strategic targets.

The U.S. submarine *Nautilus* in 1955 was the first to be propelled by nuclear power. The revolutionary potential of nuclear power for the propulsion of submarines was dramatically demonstrated in 1958 when the *Nautilus* made its passage under the Polar icecap. Its range seemed quite fantastic to the mariners of the time. Its first uranium "core" sent it 69,000 nm in 26 months, its second 93,000 nm. In its first ten years of service *Nautilus* covered 330,000 nm, of which 255,000 were submerged, and the fuel consumed in the three uranium

[4] A diesel engine consumes a large quantity of air. Before the development of the snorkel tube, it was necessary to bring the submarine to the surface to use the diesel engines. The snorkel tube allows the submarine to remain a few feet below the surface, with only the air intake emerging above the wave tops. The diesel engines are used for two purposes (usually simultaneously) – propulsion and recharging of the electric batteries. The alternate mode of propulsion, using electric motors, is very quiet and can be used at any depth but has limited endurance and speed.

cores totaled only 13 pounds. To cover the same distance, a diesel-powered submarine would burn more than 8,000,000 gallons of oil, the load of a train of tank-cars eight miles long.[5] And this was the first of its kind!

Two years later the nuclear-powered *Triton* completed the first completely submerged voyage around the world. For all practical purposes the duration of the voyage of a nuclear submarine is limited only by the endurance of the crew. It is now normal for the U.S. ballistic-missile submarines to remain at sea, submerged, for two months. On return, a second crew takes the boat out again.

The first submerged launching of an SLBM took place in 1960 from the *George Washington.* This was the first nuclear-powered ballistic-missile submarine, or SSBN.[6] The Soviet, U.S., British, and French navies now have over a hundred SSBNs and nearly 150 other nuclear-powered submarines. However, the same powers still operate about 215 conventionally powered submarines as well. Other countries have another 270, so that only one-third of the world's submarines are propelled by nuclear power, and less than one-seventh are SSBNs.

The great strategic importance of the SSBN results from the fortunate combination (from the point of view of its owners) of three principal factors: its firepower, its mobility, and its difficulty of detection. The present American ballistic-missile submarines carry a total payload of the order of ten megatons, divided among a number of warheads that can be as low as 48 for Polaris A3 but about 200 with the MIRVed Poseidon missile. With the long range of their missiles, the submarines can remain well off the coast and still reach targets far inland.

The mean depth of the world's oceans is about 12,500 feet, with the deepest point nearly 36,000. Military submarines do not go deep enough to use more than about 10 percent of the total volume of the

[5] Jean-Jacques Antier, *Histoire mondiale du sous-marin* (Paris: Robert Laffont, 1968), p. 313.

[6] U.S. Naval nomenclature, commonly used by NATO, is used in this book. SS = conventionally powered attack submarine. SSG = cruise missile submarine. SSB = ballistic missile-firing submarine. SSN = nuclear-powered submarine. Hence SSBN = nuclear-powered ballistic-missile submarine.

oceans, but this gives them over 20,000,000 cubic nautical miles in which to operate. The proportion of this vast volume which is within missile range of their assigned targets is, of course, dependent on the characteristics of the missiles, but for the simple purpose of concealing themselves, the ocean offers a more than adequate element to a vehicle with unlimited range and the ability to remain submerged for months on end.

The maximum speed and depth of the SSBNs are closely kept secrets. However, it is generally believed that they can exceed 30 knots submerged. To remain undetected, lower speeds would be used, since the noise increases with speed, especially beyond the onset of propellor cavitation.[7] Pursued by surface ships, the SSBN would be able to outrun them. According to SIPRI, these submarines can operate safely at depths of 1500 to 2000 feet, but probably collapse at about 3500 feet or lower.[8]

In order to minimize the chance of detection, a submarine should make no radio transmissions. It must, however, be able to receive messages during its long submerged voyages. An antenna protruding from the sea can receive messages on long-wave radio, and it is possible to communicate with a totally submerged submarine (although not at great depth) over great distances by using a very powerful very long-wave transmitter. A transmitting station in Australia, with a power of 81,000 kilowatts and a tower 1400 feet high, is said to be able to contact submarines at a distance of 2400 nm.[9] An even more powerful transmitting station is being planned in the United States, at a cost estimated at $1.5 billion, under the label of Project "Sanguine."[10]

Another purpose for which submarines used to have to come to the surface (or at least expose their periscope) was to make celestial observations for navigation. However, the principle of inertial navigation, which has proven so effective for the accurate guidance

[7] Beyond a certain speed (which increases with depth) the propellor creates bubbles which generate noise when they collapse.

[8] *SIPRI, 1969/70,* p. 124.

[9] Antier, *op. cit.*, p. 346.

[10] *SIPRI, 1969/70,* p. 118. *Statement of Secretary Schlesinger, 1975,* pp. II–53–54.

of ballistic missiles, can also serve submarines. The American equipment is called SINS (Submarine Inertial Navigation System). Although extremely accurate for short periods, there is a tendency for the gyroscopes to "drift." Consequently, to maintain very great accuracy (required for the SLBMs if not for safe navigation of the submarine), it is advisable to check and reset the precise position from time to time. To this end (and for the benefit of surface ships as well), the U.S. Navy has launched navigational satellites known as "Transit," which transmit radio signals receivable in any weather, and whose ephemerides are distributed to the ships.[11] Submarines can also make use of radio navigation beacons and of the grid systems operating for ships and aircraft.

The employment of SSBNs in a nuclear war would depend, of course, on the precise scenario of attack and reprisal. It is quite possible that they would be used as part of a first strike to destroy bomber bases near the coasts and the home ports of submarines. A country planning a first strike and possessing such potent weapons would hardly fail to employ them. Moreover, the opposing defenses could not deny them the use of the open seas prior to hostilities. If the attack were planned some time in advance, more than the average number of submarines could be put in firing position, with a synchronized firing plan prepared in advance. At the same time, the attacking country would alert its own antisubmarine defenses to attack without warning those of the opponent's submarines whose positions were known at the appropriate moment. It is even possible that the attacker would explode a widespread pattern of underwater nuclear depth charges in the areas where submarines were likely to be lurking.

Antisubmarine defense could play an important role in detecting such preparations for a first strike. If the detection system were sufficiently effective and extensive, the arrival of an abnormally

[11] For a description of the methods of navigation see *SIPRI, 1969/70,* p. 119, and *1968/69,* pp. 106–107. A new global positioning system based on satellites and labeled NAVSTAR is under development.

large number of SSBNs to firing stations should be perceived. And if the presence of the defenses cause the submarines to fire from longer range, there would be more time for the ballistic-missile defense to detect and intercept the missiles and to save some of the aircraft.

However, it is for the retaliatory second strike that the characteristics of the SSBN make it especially well suited. Because it is comparatively mobile and invulnerable, and because its missiles have the performance necessary for the destruction of cities, it would seem that the owners of a considerable fleet of SSBNs would rely on them primarily as the main instrument of guaranteed retaliation, the keystone of deterrence.

Functions of Antisubmarine Defense[12]

Although it began during World War I, it was not until the later years of World War II that the search for an effective antisubmarine defense was rewarded by clear success. Major milestones were the practice of collecting merchant vessels into convoys escorted by antisubmarine escorts, the development of sonar, and then radar. But it was only after the creation of a sizable force of long-range antisubmarine aircraft that the hunter became the quarry. His fatal weaknesses were his diesel propulsion, which obliged him to spend long hours at the surface until the invention of the snorkel, and his need to approach his prey to close range while at periscope depth.

The SSBN is freed of these constraints. He can remain at depth, far from his hunters, and deliver his attack from a great distance.

Antisubmarine forces have diverse roles to play, among which are defense of the lines of communication and supply, protection of carrier strike forces, and the hunting of missile-firing submarines.

[12] For background reading see Herbert Scoville, Jr., "Missile Submarines and National Security," *Scientific American* 226 (June 1972), 15–27; Richard Garwin in K. Tsipis, A. Cahn, and B. Feld (eds.), *The Future of the Sea-Based Deterrent* (Cambridge, Mass.: M.I.T. Press, 1973), chap. 6; *SIPRI, 1974,* chap. 10; and Kosta Tsipis, *Tactical and Strategic Antisubmarine Warfare* (Cambridge, Mass.: M.I.T. Press, 1974; and Stockholm: SIPRI, 1974).

And the ships and aircraft capable of antisubmarine defenses are also able to play their part in maritime forces of other types, although it may be necessary for them or companion units to have additional types of armament, perhaps antiaircraft or anti-surface ship. Compared to the other forms of strategic defense (BMD, air defense, and civil defense), the forces for antisubmarine defense are versatile and flexible, able to perform useful service in all types of situations from full nuclear war through limited nuclear war and conventional war to cold war, and against threats other than submarines.

Antisubmarine defense can be divided into five functions: detection, identification, localization, attack, and destruction. The first three can be exercised in peacetime, but, since the open sea is legally accessible to all, attack and destruction are acts of war. And great efforts are made in peacetime to perform the first three functions, partly for training and experience, but also to keep informed of the activities and capabilities of the rival submarine forces.

Conventionally powered submarines offer many opportunities for detection, owing to the noise and exhaust from the diesel engine and the extension of the snorkel tube above the surface, which are completely absent from the nuclear-powered submarine. Antisubmarine forces naturally strive to take full advantage of these opportunities. However, in this chapter, we will discuss in detail the capabilities for defense against nuclear-powered submarines only.

Detection

The electromagnetic waves which carry the signals of radio communication and radar are absorbed by a few feet of sea water. The only reliable means of first detection of a submerged submarine at useful ranges is by the propagation of sound. Sea water is an efficient medium for the transmission of acoustic energy, and if the sea were homogeneous and quiet, the design and operation of sonar would be comparatively straightforward. In fact, the acoustic properties of the sea are remarkably complicated, with layers of different and varying temperatures superimposed on a permanent temperature gradient, variations in salinity, living matter large and small which can reflect or even generate sound, a surface that can be flat and quiet or rough and noisy, and a bottom which can be rough or smooth, rocky or muddy, and possibly strewn with the hulls of wrecked ships and submarines. And, to add to the problems, in the areas near the shipping lanes or fishing grounds there are noises generated by propellors, engines, and hulls of surface ships which compete with the sounds emitted by submarines.

Sonar has two modes of operation: passive and active. Passive sonar depends on the radiation of acoustic energy from the target itself. All ships and submarines emit noise from their propellors, engines, and pumps, and from the motion of the hull through the water. A great deal can be done to minimize this noise, and most countries have taken energetic measures to "quieten" their warships, both surface and (especially) submarine. However, because of the considerable amount of energy required to propel a large hull through the water at high speed, it is probable that any rapidly moving vessel will always generate enough noise to be detected at great distances, perhaps even hundreds of miles, when the conditions of propagation are favorable. An important tactical advantage of using passive sonar is that the target has no indication that it is in operation, or that he has been detected. A disadvantage is that it cannot measure the range to the target, although the direction can be estimated.

Active sonar transmits a powerful pulse of acoustic energy into the water and then listens for the returning echo. The time delay is used to measure the range to the target. The reflecting properties of the hull determine the strength of the echo, and a larger echo will be returned if the signal arrives on the beam than on the bow. To achieve long range, the active sonar must use a pulse of high energy, which will be detectable by the passive sonar of the target submarine at ranges far beyond those at which the active sonar can distinguish the feeble echo of its own pulse. Consequently, a tactical disadvantage of using active sonar is that the quarry will know that the hunter is searching. Another disadvantage is the relatively short ranges that can be achieved, of the order of a few tens of miles at the very best.

Probably the most consistent feature of the results obtained by sonar is their inconsistency. Refraction and reverberation of sound in the sea, and the presence of noise background, are constantly changing. There is a notable contrast with the detection of missiles or aircraft by radar, the reason being the simplicity, emptiness, and quietness of the atmosphere as compared to the sea.

Identification

Once the presence of a "target" has been detected by sonar, it is not always a simple matter to identify it—that is, to determine what it is. A signal received on passive sonar could be coming from a surface ship or a submarine. An echo received on active sonar could come from a whale, a school of fish, a rock, or a wrecked ship on the bottom. Much depends on the ability of the sonar equipment and of the human operators to extract the maximum information from the signal (acoustic qualities of the sound received on passive sonar, physical size of the object returning an echo on active sonar). With active sonar, the motion of the target may be deduced from the Doppler frequency shift.[13]

Localization

Having detected the presence of a target and identified it as a submarine, the defense will probably wish to establish its precise position and then track its progress. This function is known as *localization.* For this purpose active sonar is more useful than passive sonar, because of its ability to measure distance as well as direction.

In addition to using acoustic methods, it is possible to localize

[13] If acoustic (or electromagnetic) waves are reflected from an object which is moving with respect to the source, the frequency of the waves received back at the source will be altered by an amount proportional to the radial speed of the target.

submarines by detecting their effect on the earth's magnetic field. There is enough iron in the steel hull to disturb the natural magnetic lines of force, and this anomaly can be registered on a sensitive magnetometer. The instrument, known as a Magnetic Anomaly Detector (MAD), must be mounted in isolation from magnetic material in the carrying vehicle, and its effective range is limited to less than 3000 feet.

Localization by MAD is quite accurate and can also be useful for identification, since most underwater objects which could be mistaken for submarines are not magnetic. However, in shallow water, MAD can register the presence of a wreck on the bottom, and it is necessary to chart such objects in order to avoid the possibility of false identification.

Destruction

To destroy a submarine it is not necessary to put a weapon into direct contact with the hull. While a submarine's hull must be very strongly built to withstand the hydrostatic pressure at depth, water is a good medium for the transmission of shock waves. The explosion of a mine with a few hundred pounds of conventional charge can gravely damage a ship of any size at a considerable distance, while it is estimated that a nuclear charge of 10 KT could destroy a submarine within 1.2 miles.[14] A direct hit or a near miss with a torpedo, or a conventionally armed depth charge, will be sufficient to sink a submarine, while a lesser shock may serve to damage many of its vital mechanisms.

For defense of the approaches to a port, or the denial of passage through a strait in wartime, it is possible to use moored mines exploded by command. More common are fields of moored or bottom mines automatically detonated by signals that can be acoustic, magnetic, or dependent on hydrodynamic pressure. But mines are unlikely to be useful against submarines in the open sea.

[14] *SIPRI, 1969/70*, p. 117. The calculation is for a submarine with a maximum depth capability of 2000 feet attacked when it is at a depth of 500 feet.

Attack

Of all the antisubmarine weapons the torpedo is probably the most effective. Wire-guided from a ship or submarine, or guided by its own homing head, which may be active or passive, it can be made to detonate on contact, by acoustic signal, or by magnetic influence.

The effectiveness of a torpedo depends on its speed, its range, its maneuverability, and its warhead. It is not possible to optimize all of these at the same time. For example, it is difficult to obtain both long range and high speed from a torpedo of manageable size, and high speed creates so much noise that acoustic homing may not be possible. It is, however, possible to obtain long range by using an aerodynamic or a ballistic vehicle to carry the torpedo through the air close to its destination. The vehicle may be launched from the deck of a ship, and near the end of its flight the torpedo can be parachuted into the water. Alternatively, a torpedo can be carried from a ship to the vicinity of the target by a helicopter.

The first important antisubmarine weapon was the conventionally armed depth charge, dropped off the stern of a ship or from an aircraft and fused to explode at a preset depth. The effectiveness of shipborne depth charges was later improved by projecting them some distance through the air, by mortar or rocket. Today there are nuclear-armed depth charges, propelled by ballistic rockets or droppable from aircraft. The rockets can be launched from surface ships or submarines.

Vehicles for Antisubmarine Defense

Certain antisubmarine defenses are fixed in position. In peacetime, sonars can be installed on the bottom of the ocean, probably along the coasts, in locations determined by the shape of the continental shelf. In wartime, the former mine defenses may be revived, perhaps aided by antisubmarine nets.

However, the main antisubmarine defenses must depend on mobile platforms. There are four main types in service today: fixed-wing

Table 4. Means by which the various antisubmarine functions are carried out from the different platforms

Function	Sea bottom	CVS		DDH	SSK
		Aircraft	Helicopter	Destroyer	submarine
Detection	Passive sonar Active sonar	Sonobuoy	Passive sonar Active sonar Sonobuoy	Active sonar Sonobuoy	Passive sonar
Identification	Passive sonar Active sonar	Sonobuoy MAD	Passive sonar Active sonar Sonobuoy	Active sonar	Passive sonar
Localization	Active sonar	Sonobuoy EER MAD	Active sonar	Active sonar	Passive sonar Active sonar
Attack	Mine	Torpedo Depth charge	Torpedo	Torpedo Rocket Cruise vehicle Mortar	Torpedo Rocket
Destruction	Mine	Torpedo Depth charge	Torpedo	Torpedo Depth charge	Torpedo Nuclear depth charge

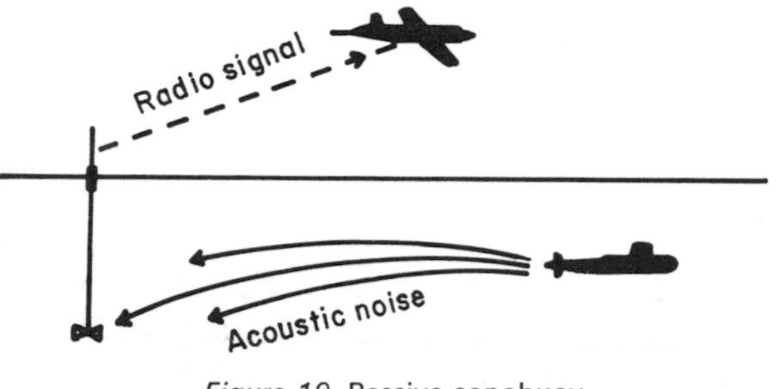

Figure 19. Passive sonobuoy

aircraft, helicopters, antisubmarine surface vessels (destroyers, frigates, A.S. escorts), and antisubmarine submarines (often labeled killer submarines, or SSKs). Table 4 shows the means by which the five functions of antisubmarine defense are executed from the various platforms. A.S. aircraft carriers (labeled *CVS*), helicopter carriers, and helicopter-carrying cruisers may have all of their antisubmarine weapons on their aircraft. But a helicopter-carrying destroyer (labeled *DDH*) is to a certain degree both a destroyer and a helicopter-carrier.[15]

The Antisubmarine Aircraft

Antisubmarine fixed-wing aircraft can be land- or carrier-based. The latter are smaller, with less endurance and payload—but this may be compensated by the presence of their carrier in mid-ocean close to the scene of operations. A complication is that the carrier may need protection against attack not only by torpedo and missile-firing submarines but also by aircraft and surface vessels.

Airborne radar and visual detection, often successful against diesel-powered submarines, are powerless against a discreet nuclear

[15] Most DDHs have room for only one large helicopter. However, the new Canadian 4050-ton DDHs carry two and the Japanese 4700-ton Haruna carries three.

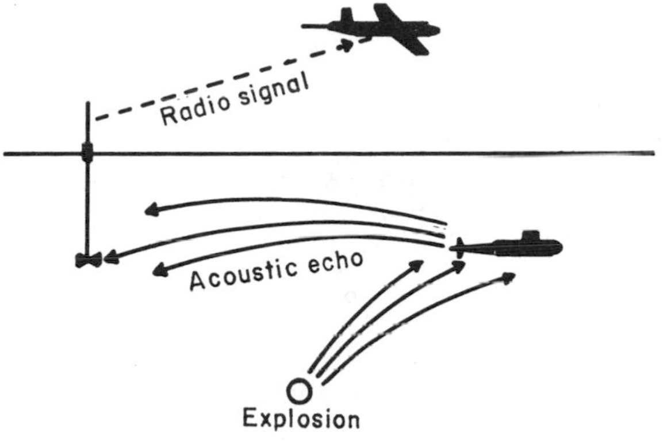

Figure 20. Explosive echo ranging

submarine. The main means of detection is the radio sonobuoy. This expendable device, parachuted into the sea from the aircraft, contains a sonar, a radio transmitter, and batteries. The sonar transducer is automatically lowered on a cable beneath the floating buoy, and a radio antenna is extended above the buoy. The sonar can be active or passive, directional or omnidirectional. Figure 19 illustrates a passive sonobuoy receiving acoustic noise from a submarine and relaying the signals by radio to the aircraft. Some of the advantages of the active mode can be secured with passive sonobuoys if the aircraft drops small explosive charges fused to detonate at depth. The shock pulse acts like a single, very powerful pulse of an active sonar, and energy reflected from a submarine can be detected by the sonobuoy, as sketched in Figure 20. This method is known as Explosive Echo Ranging (EER). The reverberation of the sound from the explosion makes it difficult to employ in shallow water.

A Magnetic Anomaly Detector can be fitted on an A.S. aircraft, usually at the end of a boom to remove it as far as possible from the iron in the engines. Figure 21 shows the lines of force of the earth's

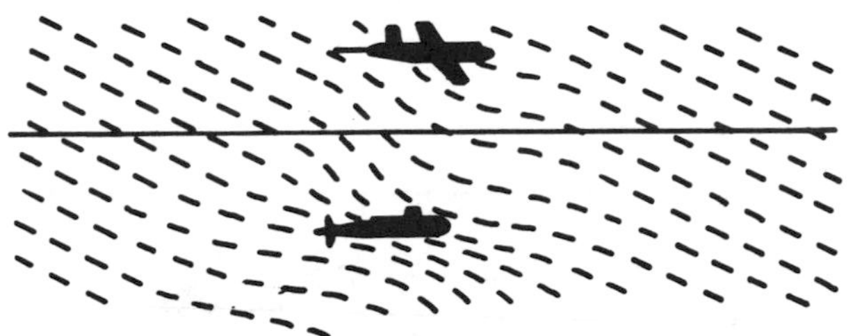

Figure 21. Magnetic anomaly detection

magnetic field, as dashed lines disturbed from their smooth arcs by the presence of the steel hull of the submarine.

Antisubmarine aircraft carry homing torpedoes and depth charges. They are not vulnerable to submarines. Their range, endurance, and speed make them able to search large areas of ocean in a single sortie or to maintain continuous watch on a field of sonobuoys. In addition to antisubmarine defense they are able to carry out many other maritime tasks.

The Antisubmarine Helicopter

The helicopter has less speed, range, endurance, and payload than the fixed-wing aircraft. But it has one significant advantage—its ability to hover in one place for minutes at a time. It can operate a highly effective "dipping" or "dunking" sonar, with the main apparatus inside the fuselage of the helicopter, by lowering the transducer on a cable into the water and then withdrawing it before moving off. It proceeds in jumps, with pauses in between for listening. The submarine may be able to detect the presence of the helicopter by the noise transmitted into the water during the hover but has no way of attacking it. Figure 22 shows an active sonar; it can also be operated in the passive mode.

A helicopter can carry, in addition to sonar, MAD and homing

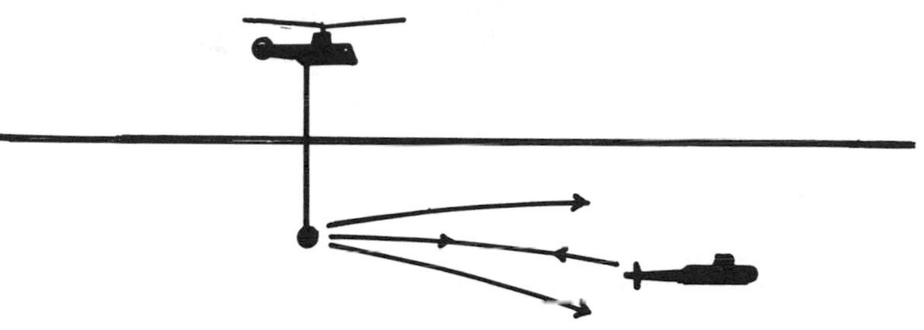

Figure 22. Helicopter-borne active sonar

torpedoes. It is capable, therefore, of conducting all five antisubmarine functions. Alternatively, a lighter helicopter, either piloted or operated by remote control, can be used for carrying the weapon, torpedo or depth charges, with the fire-control information being supplied by a destroyer. This is the principle of the American DASH (Drone Antisubmarine Helicopter).

The Destroyer, the Frigate and the Antisubmarine Escort

A surface ship is no ideal platform for sonar. The noise and vibrations of the engines and other machinery, the sounds of the propellor and hull moving through the water, and the slapping of the waves against the ship's sides all combine to create a noisy background which militates against the detection of weak acoustic signals, especially when the ship is traveling at high speed. Consequently, much more attention has been paid to the development of active than of passive sonar for surface ships.

The second serious difficulty is caused by the considerable irregular and variable refraction of sound in the upper layers of the sea. A common situation is that the topmost water is the warmest, and that sound rays near the surface are curved downwards, but very often the effects of recent weather will produce a layer of cold or of

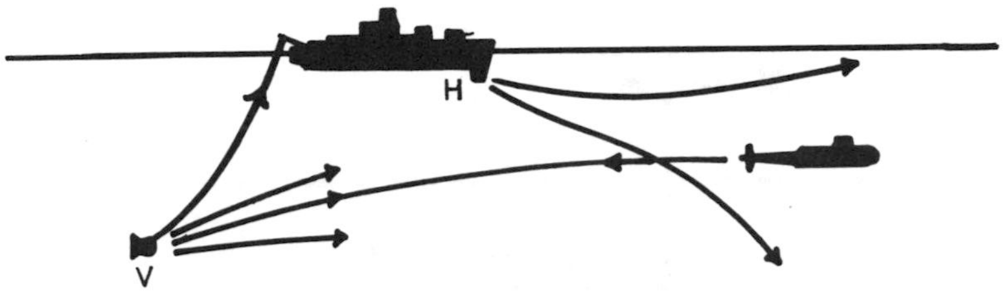

Figure 23. Destroyer-borne active sonar

thoroughly mixed water near the surface. As a result, the sound rays emanating from a sonar on the hull of a ship will often be curved into complicated patterns including "holes" or "shadows" in which sound cannot be received. A submarine can easily measure the temperature distribution in the upper few hundred feet and choose the depth at which detection will be most difficult. Figure 23 shows a destroyer with a hull-mounted sonar (H) in the surface layer; the sound rays from H are refracted in a split pattern, leaving a gap, in which a submarine can remain undetected.

A solution has been found with the Variable Depth Sonar (VDS), which is towed behind the destroyer at a depth below the surface layer. Figure 23 shows the sound rays from V reaching the submarine and returning an echo.

It is possible to mount large, heavy, powerful sonar equipment in destroyers of several thousand tons displacement. The transducer array of the hull-mounted type is commonly protected by a large dome, which shields it from much of the noise. The American SQS-26 sonar, which can achieve ranges in excess of 20 nm, has a dome 65 feet in diameter.[16] A sonar of this size makes considerable demands on the ship, including the provision of large electric power generators. And in the case of the towed VDS the heavy cable and

[16] Antier, *op. cit.*, p. 361.

winch occupy precious space and limit the ship's maneuverability and speed.

The usual antisubmarine weapons of a surface ship are the depth charge and the torpedo. To extend the range, and if possible to outrange the antiship weapon of the submarine, it is highly desirable to be able to project the depth charges or torpedoes to a considerable distance from the ship. Depth charges can be projected by mortar, rocket, or even from a gun. Torpedoes can be launched directly into the water from the ship, but room can be made on the deck for a launcher for a ballistic or winged vehicle which can carry the torpedo some miles through the air, possibly radio-guided in flight from the ship, before it is dropped into the water to search for its target. Three weapons of this family are the American Asroc, the British-Australian Ikara, and the French Malafon.[17] But the best means for projecting the weapon far from the ship is probably the helicopter.

The chief disadvantages of the surface ship are its low speed and its vulnerability to submarines.

The Antisubmarine Submarine

The ideal silent platform for a variable-depth sonar is the submarine. Because of the ideal sonar conditions, and to preserve another major tactical asset in its concealment, the submarine normally uses passive sonar.

An attack submarine designed primarily for the attack of surface vessels, can be used against submarines. However, a submarine specializing in the antisubmarine role is often designated as an SSK (Submarine Killer, or Killer Submarine). A diesel-powered SSK is in danger of being detected while snorkeling by its intended prey, although the hunter will try to lie in wait (perhaps in a strait or near a port) and let his quarry come to him. A nuclear-powered SSK is the most effective of all the antisubmarine platforms. Especially against

[17] Kosta Tsipis, *Tactical and Strategic Antisubmarine Warfare,* estimates the maximum ranges for Asroc, Ikara, and Malafon to be 5½, 12½, and 10 nm, respectively. Asroc can also project a nuclear depth charge.

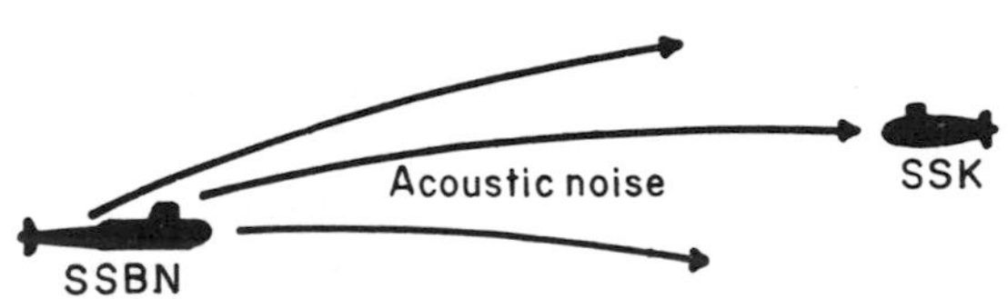

Figure 24. Submarine-borne passive sonar

an SSBN, which has a wide choice of operating areas and which will take great precautions to avoid detection and combat, the nuclear-powered SSK is the only adversary which can hope to engage on roughly equal terms. However, unless the SSKs can intercept the SSBNs near their home port or in a comparatively narrow passage, and there either attack them or follow them to their firing stations,[18] it would appear that the force of SSKs would need to outnumber the SSBNs in order to destroy them quickly.

Figure 24 shows the situation favorable to the SSK, who is lying ahead of the SSBN and listening at the best depth on passive sonar. Just before attacking, the SSK might wish to determine the accurate position of his target by using active sonar, perhaps only for one transmitted pulse.

The normal antisubmarine weapon for a submarine is the torpedo. If it is wire-guided, the firing submarine may use active sonar to follow the maneuvers of the target. However, a much greater attack range can be obtained by propelling a nuclear charge through the air by a ballistic rocket, to sink close to the target and explode at a

[18] Edward Teller has suggested that this can be done if the SSK uses active sonar. See *Hearings on the Strategic and Foreign Policy Implications of ABM Systems,* May 14 and 21, 1969, Part II, p. 597. See also R. L. Garwin in *The Future of the Sea-Based Deterrent,* pp. 98–100. And in Edward Luttwak, *A Dictionary of Modern War* (Allen Lane: Penguin, 1971), p. 23, one reads that Russian submarines are picked up and trailed as they leave port or when they cross narow places such as the Dardanelles. The Russians play the same game on the Polaris vessels.

preset depth. The American Subroc, with a range of 26 to 30 nm, can be launched from the torpedo tubes of the SSK.[19]

Present Strengths of SSBN and Antisubmarine Forces

The upper part of Table 5 lists the numbers of ballistic-missile-firing submarines, both nuclear and conventionally powered. For a valid comparison in terms of strategic strength, one needs to take into account the numbers and ranges of SLBMs, as given in Table 3. The Interim agreement for Strategic Arms Limitation allows the U.S. to have 44 "modern" SSBNs, and the U.S.S.R. 62. For this purpose the 20 conventionally powered SSBs would not count against the Soviet total, so that they could construct another 7 Delta class SSBNs within the limit.

The lower part of Table 5 compares the antisubmarine forces of NATO and the Warsaw Pact Organization. The numbers include units for which the antisubmarine role may be secondary, and also those in refit and reserve, as well as many which are usually deployed out of the normal NATO/WPO areas. French units are included under NATO.

It is very difficult to compare the defensive strength of the two opposing groups. A simple numerical count neglects the facts that most of the ships, aircraft and submarines are also equipped for tasks other than antisubmarine defense and that there are very large differences in the quantity and quality of antisubmarine equipment and training associated with the different units. Another factor which differentiates the effectiveness of the adversaries' A.S. defense but does not appear in the table is geography; this will be discussed in the next section.

Furthermore, the Soviets possess another 66 submarines armed with cruise missiles, likely to divert some of NATO's A.S. effort and to be very effective against surface ships. However, NATO have the most A.S. aircraft, both land and carrier-based. NATO has the advantage in

[19] *SIPRI, 1969/70*, p. 116.

Table 5. Numbers of ballistic-missile submarines and antisubmarine forces

Ballistic-missile submarines	USA	UK	France	USSR[a]
Nuclear propulsion 16 SLBMs each	41	4	3[b]	34
Nuclear propulsion 12 SLBMs each				13[c]
Nuclear propulsion 3 SLBMs each				8
Conventional propulsion 3 SLBMs each				20[d]
Antisubmarine forces			**NATO[a,e]**	**WPO[a]**
Nuclear-propelled attack submarines			72	34
Conventionally propelled torpedo attack submarines of long or medium range			96	163
Multipurpose,[f] AS and helicopter carriers, helicopter and through-deck cruisers			19	2[g]
Large ASW ships			143	42
Destroyers, frigates, and ocean escorts with AS capability			261	181
AS aircraft and helicopters			950	500

[a] *The Military Balance, 1975–76,* pp. 82–88, and *Statement of General Brown, 1975,* pp. 25–28.

[b] Program for five under way.

[c] These are the Delta class with the SS-N-8 missile. At least seven more can be built within the limits of SALT I.

[d] Diesel-powered submarines with SS-N-4 and SS-N-5 missiles may be considered as theater nuclear forces rather than strategic weapon systems. They do not count for the SALT limits.

[e] Including France.

[f] Includes aircraft carriers with a multipurpose role, combining attack, air defense, and antisubmarine operation. The U.S. plans to have eleven such CV or CVN carriers. *Statement of Secretary Schlesinger, 1975,* p. III–79.

[g] Moskva-class helicopter cruisers. Two larger Kiev-class carriers are under construction.

the numbers of destroyers, frigates, and A.S. escorts, but more especially in the quality of weapons and equipment.[20]

The comparative strengths of the submarine forces are not revealed by the simple numbers either. For example, the new American SSN-688 class of nuclear-powered submarines, particularly fast and quiet, should make outstandingly effective antisubmarine vehicles.[21] And it should be remembered that a large part of the Soviet submarine fleet was built some years ago to oppose the American carrier strike fleet, quite a different role than defense against SSBNs.

Geographic Constraints on the SSBN

From Peter the Great to Admiral Gorshkov with his master plan, one objective always in the eye of Russian strategists has been access to the warm waters. In this matter the United States holds an immense advantage. With the Atlantic on the east, the Pacific on the west, the Gulf of Mexico and the Caribbean (the American Mediterranean) to the south, with control of the Panama Canal, and with a friendly ally with immense land territory to the north, geography has been very kind to the United States.

The Soviet Union, on the other hand, possesses a coastline which is extremely short in relation to its enormous area, unless one includes the Arctic coast, along which navigation is blocked by ice for a considerable part of each year. The only northern port usable

[20] For example, in *Soviet Sea Power* (Washington: Center for Strategic and International Studies at Georgetown University, 1969), p. 40, we read: "The Soviet Navy has developed a significant ability to engage in anti-shipping operations, especially in water adjacent to the European landmass. In contrast, its anti-submarine warfare capability still has far to go; among all the branches of naval science, the Soviet Navy lags the United States most in anti-submarine warfare against nuclear submarines." Secretary Laird said: "Today, the U.S. enjoys a substantial, though decreasing, lead in acoustic sensor technology and submarine quietness—two important factors that impact on undersea warfare capabilities." See *Statement of Secretary Laird, 1972*, p. 42.

[21] Construction of twenty-six has been approved. See *Statement of Secretary Schlesinger, 1975*, p. III–90.

the year round is Murmansk, at the western extremity, which benefits from the remnants of the Gulf Stream. But to get out to the Atlantic Ocean from Murmansk, Soviet submarines must negotiate a passage between islands: Great Britain, the Faroes, Iceland, Greenland, or the Islands of the Canadian Archipelago. This gives the Western antisubmarine defense the opportunity to close off passages of limited width instead of trying to cover the broad oceans.

The northern Pacific coast of the Soviet Union is dominated by the great Kamchatka Peninsula, which, prolonged by the Kurile Island chain, encloses the Sea of Okhotsk. The main Soviet eastern naval bases are Petropavlovsk, Sovetskaia Gavan, and Vladivostok. But the first is frozen in for several months in the year, while the other two are on the Sea of Japan, landlocked except for four narrow straits bordered on one or both sides by Japan, and one, the Tartar Strait, only seven miles across, shallow, often blocked by ice, and leading to the Sea of Okhotsk.[22] The strategic importance of Japan and the Kurile chain is very clear.

Although the Soviet Union has good ports and unimpeded access to the Baltic and the Black seas, this does not guarantee her clear passage to the open oceans. A submarine departing the Baltic for the Atlantic must first pass through the Oresund between Denmark and Sweden, or else one of the Danish Belts, and then the Kattegat and the Skagerrak before reaching the North Sea. Even then, unless it passes through the English Channel, it faces the same problem as a boat from Murmansk. Between the Black Sea and the Atlantic lie two famous straits—The Dardanelles and Gibraltar—with ominous histories. The other exit from the Mediterranean, via Suez, leads to the Red Sea, with the Strait of Bab el Mandeb at its southern exit to the Indian Ocean. A main goal of Soviet foreign policy in recent years appears to be to secure friendly neighbors along this route.

Michel Salomon has called the U.S.S.R. a giant with a blocked

[22] Commander Hideo Sekino, "Japan and Her Maritime Defense," *Naval Review 1971* (U.S. Naval Institute, 1971), 120.

nose.[23] Certainly its recent efforts to penetrate into the Mediterranean, the Middle East, and the Indian Ocean are part of a campaign to break out of the shackles which have restrained it in a narrow Continentalism. But it is still short of having the worldwide net of friendly ports and the substantial logistic fleet for support afloat which would permit effective antisubmarine operations in any part of the globe.

In brief, while geography has made the Soviet Union virtually impossible to invade by sea, it has put extreme difficulties in the way of its mounting large-scale offensive naval operations in or across the open oceans.

The Future of the SSBN and Antisubmarine Defense

The U.S. will convert a total of 31 existing Polaris SSBNs to take the Poseidon missile. Later on, the Trident I missile, with a range of 4000 nm, will replace Poseidon in 10 of these submarines. The Trident SSBN will be very much larger than the present Polaris/Poseidon boats (18,700 tons displacement as compared to 8250) and will have 24 missile tubes, initially armed with Trident I SLBM, but later with Trident II, with a range of 6000 nm. The Trident submarine is expected to be both faster and quieter than the Polaris/Poseidon boats.[24] It is expected that the Soviets will continue to build Delta class SSBNs, perhaps elongated to take more than twelve missiles.

The number of new SSBNs built by both powers will be related to the outcome of future strategic arms agreements. It is quite possible that there will be a substantial shift into SSBNs, as the least vulnerable and most stable weapon of deterrence. Plans have been discussed for fixed underwater missile-launching platforms, on the sea bottom or the continental shelf or in caverns excavated beneath the sea bottom. However, the treaty for arms limitation on the sea bed forbids such activity, permitting the installation of weapons of mass destruction only

[23] Michel Salomon, *Méditerranée rouge ou nouvel empire soviétique?* (Paris: Robert Laffont, 1970).

[24] *Statement of Secretary Schlesinger, 1975,* pp. II–30–33, and G. W. Rathjens and J. P. Ruina, in *The Future of the Sea-Based Deterrent,* chap. 4.

within territorial waters (which would include lakes and inland seas),[25] and the parties to the Interim SALT agreement undertake not to use deliberate measures of concealment. It appears that the launching platforms for underwater missiles are likely to continue to be mobile submarines.

Progress is to be expected in the techniques of detection. It is probable that new transducers, perhaps of ceramic, will permit more power to be radiated into the water. Directivity and flexibility of operation may be improved by the use of large transducer arrays conforming to the shape of the hull, and using a technique similar to that of the phased-array radars described in Chapter III for both transmission and reception. Some of the difficulties of refraction may be overcome by reflecting signals off the sea bottom, and others by the extension of VDS to greater depths, where the phenomena of refraction are less variable. This latter technique, however, is bound to exact a heavy penalty in speed and maneuverability, and it may have to be restricted to fixed rather than mobile sytems.

If the silencing of submarines becomes extremely successful, the defense will need to place increasing reliance on active as opposed to passive detection. On antisubmarine submarines, however, this would negate their prime asset of concealment and surprise.

Spectacular improvements are unlikely in the field of antisubmarine aviation. The performance of the airframes and engines is already quite adequate for fixed-wing aircraft, though steady improvement in the speed and endurance of helicopters would be useful and is to be expected. The antisubmarine instruments and weapons, however, are likely to be made considerably better. Airborne computing and data processing will be enhanced, and sonobuoys will be given better range, accuracy, and endurance. It is quite possible that larger moored buoys will replace the small free-floating type for certain types of operations.

Because the large antisubmarine surface vessel suffers from slow-

[25] This subject is discussed in Chapter VIII.

ness and vulnerability, it may be replaced for some of its functions by something much faster and probably much smaller. A prime candidate is the hydrofoil, which can achieve sixty knots when "flying" on its underwater wings. It would probably carry a dipping sonar and operate much like the helicopter, moving rapidly with the sonar retracted and then stopping (floating as a ship) to lower the sonar and listen in silence.

The SSK is likely to be improved in speed, silence, depth capability, and sonar. If it is specialized for the antisubmarine role, it should be able to outdo the SSBN in a duel where each sought to kill the other. The great question is who will succeed in his task if the SSBN wishes to avoid combat. Although submarines have traditionally operated alone, it is quite possible that SSK tactics in the future will call for cooperation with other SSKs, with surface ships, and with aircraft.

All of the antisubmarine vehicles would benefit from improved weapons, especially torpedoes and the means to project torpedoes to considerable ranges. It is possible that antisubmarine mines could achieve a large radius of destruction by projecting homing torpedoes. The mines could be activated and deactivated by remote control and enabled to distinguish the acoustic signature of a submarine as opposed to a merchant ship.[26]

[26] See Richard Garwin in *The Future of the Sea-Based Deterrent,* chap. 6, and *SIPRI, 1974,* p. 319.

CHAPTER V

Strategic Bombers and Air Defense

For many years the aircraft, and particularly the bomber, was the primary strategic weapon in the arsenals of the great powers. The first of the two great technical developments—the nuclear bomb—made the bomber even more dominant, especially with the appearance of jet engines and aerial refueling. But the second—the long-range ballistic missile—displaced the bomber from its proud position. Nearly all of the present long-range bombers cannot exceed the speed of sound, and those that can must restrict their supersonic flight to a comparatively short portion of a long-range mission unless they are prepared to make several refueling rendezvous or to sacrifice their payload. But the ICBM exceeds twenty times the speed of sound for the major portion of its flight. And the bomber is more vulnerable, both on the ground and in the air.

The bomber possesses certain advantages over the missile, among which are the ability to observe, assess, and if necessary change the target, and to report on the success of an attack; the ability to be diverted or recalled in flight; the ability to perform more than one mission; and, under many circumstances, better accuracy. Many countries that do not have missiles do possess bombers (of less than the heaviest category), and there are many missions for which bombers are more appropriate than missiles.

In this chapter we will discuss the main characteristics of bombers and of the defenses against bombers, briefly compare the relative strengths of the two main adversaries, and offer some remarks on possible future developments.

Principal Characteristics of the Strategic Bomber

A heavy bomber can carry a heavy payload and can be allotted several targets considerable distances apart. For example, the American B-52G and B-52H can carry 75,000 lb of weapons.[1] These may be made up of four to six bombs, each of which could have a yield of one to twenty-four megatons, plus two air-to-surface missiles each of four megatons. For comparison, note that the largest ICBM, the Soviet SS-9, carries a 25-MT warhead said to weigh 13,500 lb.[2]

The ability of the bomber to reconnoiter and report depends somewhat on weather conditions and the time over target, although bombing radar should enable most targets to be identified and hit in poor visibility. The flight plan can be modified en route, either by decision of the crew or by instructions from the operations center at home. Or bombers can be sent aloft and armed on "airborne alert" as a precautionary measure, to be ordered to attack or to return at any time. Very long ranges can be attained by aerial refueling, the limit eventually being imposed by crew endurance.

The vulnerability of the bomber on the ground is a serious drawback. It is possible to construct shelters for aircraft which provide some protection against blast and heat, but it is doubtful that the runways of an airbase would be usable after an attack by nuclear weapons.

The bomber's vulnerability in flight can be reduced by flying it at very low altitude over the defended territory, although this imposes a heavy penalty on range for jet engines. The analogy to the ICBM faced by ballistic-missile defense can be seen in this example, corre-

[1] *The Military Balance, 1970–71*, p. 108, and *SIPRI, 1972*, pp. 18–19.

[2] Herbert Scoville, "The Limitation of Offensive Weapons," *Scientific American* 224 (January 1971), 23.

sponding to the use of evasive trajectories, and also in the employment of other penetration aids, with which the attacker attempts to overcome the defender but which are used at the expense of range or payload. ASMs are much harder to shoot down than a bomber, but they are less accurate than gravity-dropped bombs and necessarily smaller in payload. Some ASMs may be used against vulnerable air-defense installations such as radars and interceptor bases. Electronic countermeasures may be used, such as chaff or jamming transmitters to confuse radars, on the ground, in interceptor aircraft, and in homing missiles. The U.S. Air Force is developing a device known as SCAD , Subsonic Cruise Armed Decoy, intended to be mistaken for a bomber. As with ICBMs and BMD, the contest of measure and countermeasure continues, and the existence of a defense believed to be effective by the opposing offense produces "virtual attrition" to the striking power of the offense before a shot is fired, whenever the offense sacrifices payload in favor of penetration aids.

Principal Characteristics of Air Defense

Although it had its successes in World War I against zeppelins and hundred-knot bombers, air defense was never very effective when the only means of detection were by sight or sound. The most important advance came with radar, responsible with the Spitfire for victory in the Battle of Britain, which was fought in daylight in 1940. Before the end of World War II radar had made night fighters an effective weapon (controlled by radar on the ground until the airborne radar made contact), had given antiaircraft (AA) artillery some chance to hit aircraft in the dark, and had enabled AA artillery to defeat the German V1 cruise missile, owing in part to the invention of a radar fuse for the AA shells. The other main improvement in the effectiveness of air defense has been due to the postwar development of guided missiles, both surface-to-air (SAM) and air-to-air (AAM). And behind the control of modern air defenses lie high-speed, high-capacity electronic computers.

The effectiveness of a modern air-defense system depends in large measure on its network of ground-based radars. These should report all movements of aircraft, whether bombers, interceptors, or commercial. In peacetime a radar and communication network is needed for the control of civilian air traffic, and the defense system needs to be able to identify aircraft entering the national airspace to ensure that they are innocent. The normal means of doing this is by comparison of authorized flight plans with movements observed on the radars.

The main weapons of a modern air-defense system are armed interceptor aircraft and SAMs. Interceptor aircraft have an important role to play in the identification of suspicious aircraft, whether in peace or war. If flight-plan correlation, electronic interrogation, and radio conversations fail to satisfy the defense, the last resort is visual inspection by a manned interceptor. The performance of the interceptor should exceed that of the bomber (or of a civilian aircraft which must be visually identified) in speed, maneuverability, and maximum altitude. And the crew (usually only one or two men) must be able to combine instructions from the ground with information from their airborne radar.

There are several types of air-to-air weapons, including cannon and rockets. The more sophisticated rockets are guided either by radar or by infrared energy; their warheads may be nuclear or conventional.

There are various types of surface-to-air missile, some air-breathing and some rocket-propelled, some supported by aerodynamic surfaces. They are guided from the ground but may have automatic homing guidance in the later stage of their interception. They can have nuclear or conventional warheads. In general, a SAM designed for long-range high-altitude interception cannot be made effective against a target at low altitude. If the defense wishes to be difficult to penetrate at low altitude, they will probably need short-range SAMs specialized for low targets, or possibly AA guns with a high rate of fire.

Present Deployment of Bombers and Air Defenses

Bombers

The United States has 432 heavy bombers of the B-52 types, in addition to 615 KC-135 tankers.[3] With aerial refueling, the B-52 can reach any part of the Soviet Union with a heavy payload from bases in America.

The Soviet Union has only about 135 heavy bombers of the Bear and Bison types, together with a tanker fleet of about 50.[4] Hence, in the columns of heavy bombers and aerial tankers, the advantage lies with the Americans.

When we come to medium bombers,[5] the U.S. has 66 FB-IIIAs capable of supersonic flight, and the British 50 subsonic Vulcans. Both types would reach most of the U.S.S.R. But the Soviets possess 755 TU-16 Badgers, subsonic bombers of which about 280 are attached to the naval air force, and 25 supersonic Backfires.[6]

SIPRI[7] lists as "strategic offensive aircraft, including long-range and medium-range bombers of various types," 460 American (not including 50 in reserve), 36 French (not including 20 in reserve) and 840 Soviet (including 700 medium-range bombers which can be expected also to be used in a tactical role, but not including 300 medium-range naval bombers).

As we found for the ballistic missiles, there is no clear line of demarcation between strategic and tactical bombers. Heavy bombers certainly fall within the definition of strategic weapons (although they can be used against tactical targets). It also seems appropriate to class

[3] *The Military Balance, 1975–76,* p. 5. The numbers include 35 B-52s in active storage or reserve.

[4] The U.S. Secretary of Defense estimates the total number of Soviet bombers plus tankers and reconnaissance aircraft to be around 160. *Statement of Secretary Schlesinger, 1975,* p. II–19.

[5] With a maximum range between 3000 and 5000 nm.

[6] *The Military Balance, 1975–76,* pp. 72, 75.

[7] *SIPRI, 1974,* p. 51.

as strategic weapons those bombers of shorter ranges, based in Europe or on board aircraft carriers, carrying nuclear weapons and able to reach the territory of the main adversary. Therefore, the forces of their NATO and WPO allies should be added to those of the two superpowers.

However, a simple addition of all such aircraft would greatly overestimate the force that would be likely to be used in the strategic role. A much more probable role for most of the strike aircraft, light bombers, and fighter bombers would be attack of forward enemy airfields, missions of interdiction,[8] and support of ground troops. The destruction of major military installations in the rear, of industry, and of cities would be the natural task of the ballistic missiles and heavy bombers.

Since aircraft can be loaded with conventional or nuclear bombs, it is conceivable that a "limited war" might be waged for some time, with heavy bombers and tactical aircraft using conventional weapons only. In these circumstances it is probable that ballistic missiles would not be used, since they represent a very expensive way to deliver conventional explosives.

In the face of these difficulties, about all one can do to compare strategic strengths is to list the numbers of aircraft able to reach the main opponent's territory with nuclear weapons. In the category of nuclear strike aircraft,[9] the International Institute for Strategic Studies[10] lists 1500 land-based and 1200 carrier-based[11] American and 2500 land-based Soviet aircraft, but points out that although all are capable of carrying nuclear weapons they may not in fact have a nuclear role. To those they add[12] 112 French and 60 British nuclear

[8] That is, destruction of the enemy's lines of communication.

[9] Aircraft with ranges and payloads less than those of medium bombers, and configured for delivery of nuclear weapons.

[10] *The Military Balance, 1975–76,* pp. 72–73.

[11] Large attack carriers embark 70 to 100 aircraft each, of which a variable proportion would be able to carry nuclear bombs.

[12] *The Military Balance, 1975–76,* p. 75.

strike aircraft, but list other types operated by NATO and WPO countries without estimating how many may have a nuclear role.[13]

Only a portion of the United States aircraft are based in Europe, and some of the U.S.S.R. machines are based in Asia. Record[14] estimates that 684 U.S. nuclear-capable tactical aircraft are deployed in Europe, but that 1854 could be made available for European contingencies thirty days after mobilization. Against this he lists 1610 Soviet nuclear-capable tactical aircraft of the strike category[15] (including some naval machines) and 800 medium-range TU-16 Badgers (of which 300 are naval).

Air Defenses

The air defenses of the Western Powers can be divided into two parts: North America and Europe. For North America, the outer line of detection is the DEW Line (Distant Early Warning Line) across the north of the continent. Further south, covering southern Canada and much of the United States, there is continuous radar cover. Its information is fed into a great communications and computing system known as SAGE (Semi-Automatic Ground Environment), which compares radar plots with aircraft flight plans, keeps track of the readiness of all parts of the air defense system, and performs the computing for the control of interception. Information can also be exchanged with manually operated radars. The operations come under the centralized control of NORAD, the North American Air Defense Command.

NORAD has about 420 interceptor aircraft,[16] but has deactivated all

[13] Mirage IVA, and Jaguar for NATO, and Beagle and Fitter for the WPO, with the nuclear warheads for the Polish and Czech aircraft being held in Soviet custody.

[14] Jeffrey Record, *U.S. Nuclear Weapons in Europe* (Washington: The Brookings Institution, 1974), pp. 24, 41.

[15] Record points out that it is unlikely that many would be used to deliver nuclear weapons, since the U.S.S.R. prefers to use rockets. *Ibid.*, p. 40.

[16] *The Military Balance, 1975–76,* p. 5, gives 374 American interceptors for July 1975, but the *Statement of General Brown, 1975,* p. 44, lists 405 for mid-1975. There are 44 Canadian interceptors.

of its surface-to-air missiles.[17] This represents a great reduction from the 1600 interceptors, 80 Nike Hercules batteries, and 188 Bomarcs present in 1965.[18] However, other tactical aircraft present in North America could be used to augment the air defense force.

The U.S.S.R. also has covered its territory with a solid radar network[19] and has provided itself with over 2600 interceptor aircraft.[20] The Russians' SAMSs are deployed in many thousands for the defense of the homeland,[21] and they also have antiaircraft artillery.

These strategic defensive forces of the Soviet Union are very strong. Moreover, unlike the air defense forces in North America, they can be used against continental as well as intercontinental attackers.

The air defenses of NATO in Europe have about 600 to 700 interceptors,[22] together with SAMs.

Comparison between East and West

As far as air attack at intercontinental range is concerned, the United States has a very substantial advantage in the number of bombers, while the U.S.S.R. has a comparable advantage in the number of air defense weapons.

It is difficult to make a clear comparison between the air forces in Europe with less-than-intercontinental range. The Warsaw Pact countries have a high proportion (34 percent) of interceptors in their force, but the NATO countries have a large number (31 percent) of multipurpose aircraft which can be used for both attack and defense.[23] But it is not very meaningful to simply compare numbers. Many

[17] *Statement of General Brown, 1975,* p. 44.

[18] *The Military Balance, 1965–66,* p. 24.

[19] There are over 4000 radars located at early warning and ground-control intercept radar sites. *Statement of General Brown, 1975,* p. 42.

[20] The number has been dropping at the rate of 100 per year. *Ibid.,* pp. 42–43.

[21] Twelve thousand missiles of four types, representing an increase. *Ibid.,* pp. 42, 44.

[22] *The Military Balance, 1975–76,* estimates 625 (p. 100), while *SIPRI, 1974,* gives 700 exclusively for air defense, plus 50–100 dual-purpose fighter-interceptors. The latter source gave the WPO 2900 air defense and 3050 dual-purpose aircraft (p. 51).

[23] *SIPRI, 1969/70,* pp. 78–80.

writers believe that the Warsaw Pact has superiority in numbers currently available in Europe, but that NATO could provide substantial reinforcement given the incentive and the time, and that the performance of the NATO aircraft is considerably better than that of the WPO taken overall. For example, Enthoven and Smith estimate that NATO aircraft have about 2.4 times as much payload capability per aircraft on typical combat missions.[24] However, an external factor of some importance here is the potent force of 600 IRBMs and MRBMs possessed by the Soviet Union, which would be able to engage the same type of targets as the longer-range strike aircraft. NATO has no comparable force.

Possible Future Developments in Air Offense and Defense

Improvements to Bombers

The future of the manned heavy bomber is uncertain. The three types in the present Order of Battle, the B-52, the Bear, and the Bison, have all been in service since 1956 and are incapable of supersonic flight. Their production ceased years ago. But the more recent large American bombers, while capable of supersonic speeds, have not been very successful. All 60 B-58s have been withdrawn from service, and the construction program for the FB-111 was drastically cut.[25]

The Americans are flight-testing prototypes of the B-1, a new supersonic bomber of intercontinental range.[26] If production is approved it would not enter the inventory in significant numbers until the 1980s.

A new swing-wing supersonic bomber named "Backfire" is entering the Soviet inventory. With aerial refueling it could attack North

[24] Enthoven and Smith, *op. cit.*, p. 154.

[25] In his statement before the Senate Committee on Armed Services, Amendments to the FY 1969 Supplemental and FY 1970 Defense Budget, on March 19, 1969, Secretary Laird said, "The FB-111 will not meet the requirements for a true intercontinental bomber and the cost per unit has reached a point where an Advanced Manned Strategic Aircraft must be considered to fill the void." Quoted in *Naval Review 1970* (May 1970), p. 422.

[26] *Statement of General Brown, 1975*, pp. 30–31; *Statement of Secretary Schlesinger, 1975*, pp. II–34–38.

America, but its high-performance multipurpose capabilities seem better adapted to employment in Europe and over the sea.[27]

Some improvements which would increase the survivability of future bombers would be the capability for sustained high-speed flight at very low level, the use of materials and construction techniques providing greater resistance to blast, coatings to absorb rather than reflect radar energy, a reduction in the infrared energy radiated by jet exhausts, and provision for rapid takeoff with a minimum of preparation.

However, both survivability and effectiveness of future bombers are likely to depend more on penetration aids than on aircraft performance. The most important requirement will be for advanced equipment for electronic warfare, in order to confuse defensive radar and guided missiles. Other weapons intended to attack or to confuse the defenses are the Short Range Attack Missile (SRAM)[28] and Subsonic Cruise Armed Decoy (SCAD).[29] The projected Air-Launched Cruise Missile (ALCM)[30] should decrease the distance through which bombers must go to penetrate the defenses.

Improvements to Air Defense

The future of air defense against the strategic bomber is also full of uncertainties, all the more so because no new generation of intercontinental bombers is on hand to replace the present aging aircraft.

However, as long as there are tactical aircraft, there will be a need for defense against them, so that air defense will be practiced and improved, though possibly on a continental rather than an intercontinental scale.

[27] *Statement of General Brown, 1975*, pp. 31–33.

[28] *Statement of Secretary Richardson, 1973*, p. 59. SRAM carries a nuclear warhead. According to *The Military Balance, 1971–72*, p. 2, the operational range of SRAM is around 60–75 nm, while *SIPRI, 1972* gives 120 nm (p. 19).

[29] SCAD will have a range of several hundred miles. To radar it will look like a bomber. It will be able to carry a warhead. See *Statement of Secretary Richardson, 1973*, p. 59.

[30] *Statement of Secretary Schlesinger, 1975*, pp. II–39–40.

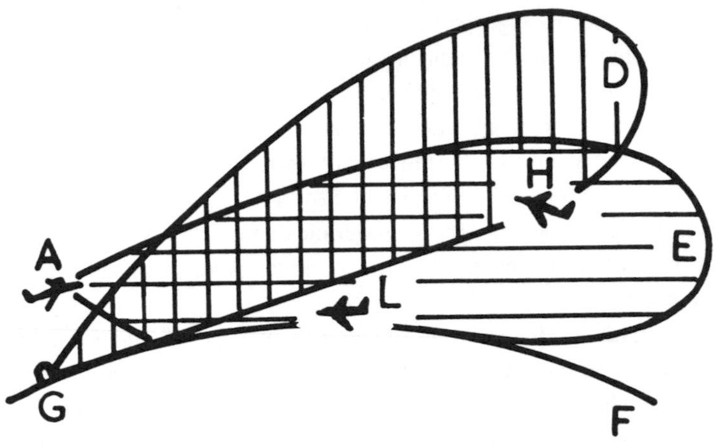

Figure 25. Ground and airborne radar

But there are at least three reasons to believe that air defense will need to be maintained against the strategic bomber, too. For one, if a country were without any air defense, an opponent could completely demolish it unhindered by the restrictions regarding evasive routing, low-level approach, or penetration aids that reduce the hitting power of a bomber force. It would even be possible to use aircraft not originally designed for military use as makeshift bombers. Second, even a superpower may need to consider potential attack by an enemy other than the opposing superpower. The United States built up its air defenses against Cuba, and the Soviet Union can hardly ignore the potential threat from China. Third, for as long as countries wish to defend their sovereignty and lay claim to the airspace above them, it is difficult to see how legal rights can be protected and assured without an air defense system to detect transgressions and prevent their repetition.

Present-day air defense systems suffer three principal weaknesses: (1) the great difficulty in radar detection of aircraft flying at very low altitude; (2) the difficulty in intercepting an air-to-surface missile; (3) the vulnerability of both radars and airfields to attack by either bombers or missiles.

The Americans have hopes of remedying all three of these deficiencies. New types of radar are being developed which should greatly extend the volume of airspace under surveillance, both outwards in distance and downwards to ground level. And the new equipment promises to be less vulnerable than the old.

Figure 25 illustrates the principle of one of the new developments. A normal ground-based radar at G sends out a beam of energy GD (shaded by vertical lines), which just skims above the horizon imposed by local geography and the curved earth GF. Any aircraft which enters the beam GD should be detected by G. An aircraft approaching at high altitude, such as H, will enter the beam at a considerable distance from G and should, therefore, be detected at long range. But if the approaching aircraft is at low altitude, such as L, he will remain below the beam until he is very close to G.

Suppose now that the radar could be lifted a few miles above G, to the point A. Now the beam of energy AE, shaded by horizontal lines, fills most of the area below the ground-based beam. The horizon still exists and cuts off the beam, but at a distance very much further away from the elevated radar A than from the ground-based radar G. This becomes easy to comprehend when one remembers the immense area of ground that can be seen (that is, that is closer than the horizon) from an aircraft no more than a few miles above the earth (30,000 feet is only 5 nm), or even from a moderate-sized mountain, as compared to the field of view from the general ground level. The low-flying L will enter the beam AE at a long range from A.

A serious difficulty is presented by the strong reflections from the ground. The great area of the earth which the eye can see from the air serves as a radar-energy reflector incomparably larger than the target aircraft. This is even a problem for a ground-based radar, which is usually sited in a commanding location, with a good view in the most important direction. But for a fixed radar it is possible to use "Moving Target Indication" (or MTI), which takes advantage of the Doppler effect[31] to distinguish moving reflectors from those which are

[31] See page 106, footnote 13.

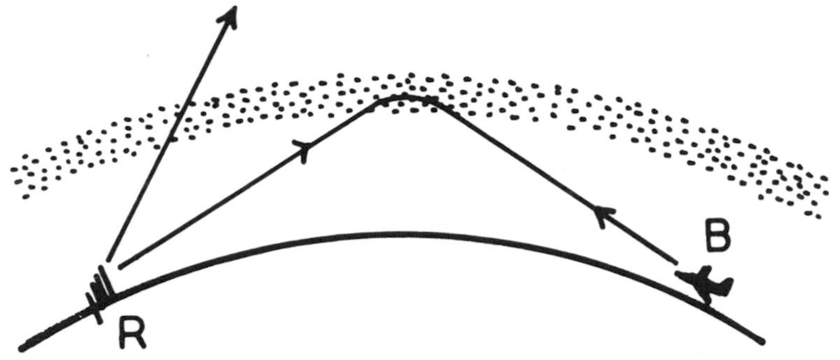

Figure 26. Over-the-horizon radar

stationary. Unfortunately, the airborne radar is moving itself, so that, with respect to it, the enormous body of unwanted reflections are coming from moving hills, rocks, and trees. However, the targets are moving with respect to the earth, and it is possible to design an Airborne MTI (AMTI) which will cancel out reflections whose Doppler frequency shift corresponds to the motion of the radar but will display echoes reflected by objects moving with respect to the earth. The technical problems are difficult but probably surmountable by determined electronic engineers.

The proposed American equipment utilizing this principle is called AWACS, for Airborne Warning and Control System. As its name suggests, it is intended to be not just an airborne detection radar but an airborne control station for collection and dissemination of information and for the control of interceptions. The aircraft would need to carry extensive communications equipment, a computer for the storage, processing, and display of data, and several controllers. And, since a large radar antenna will be required, it is evident that the aircraft must be a big one. It would not be armed, the interceptions being carried out by smaller specialized interceptor fighters operating under control of the AWACS.

AWACS offers several fundamental advantages over ground-based radar, repairing all three of the basic weaknesses of air defense. It should be able to detect bombers at ground level; it extends the area in which interceptors can be controlled outwards from the bombers' targets to a distance beyond the range of air-to-surface missiles; and it makes the key radars much less vulnerable than if they were fixed in a known position on the ground. Also, it allows the defenders to move or strengthen their defenses or to fill gaps quickly.

Although AWACS may be said to move the horizon to a distance (perhaps 200 nm), it still cannot see over the horizon. We saw in Chapter III that it is possible for a low-frequency radar to see over the horizon by scattering its beam off the ionosphere. Figure 26 illustrates a radar on the ground at R and a bomber at B, many hundred of miles from R and well below its horizon. Energy from R directed at a high angle would penetrate the ionosphere, but at a lower angle low-frequency energy is scattered, some of it being deflected downwards towards B. Some of the energy incident on the aircraft is reflected and retraces the path back to R. Even with a powerful transmitter, the amount of energy received back at R is minute, especially since the aircraft does not present nearly so large a reflecting surface as does the ionized gas in the exhaust trail of a large rocket. And, as for AWACS, much stronger reflections from the ground (or the sea) will threaten to obscure the weak signal from the aircraft. However, it is possible to exploit the motion of the wanted target and use the Doppler effect and MTI to distinguish the reflection from the aircraft.

A very small number of these Over-The-Horizon Backscatter (OTHB) radars will enable the periphery of the early warning system to be extended outwards, giving time for AWACS aircraft to take the air and move out to meet the advancing threat.

OTHB radar has its limitations. It will not have the discrimination or accuracy of an interceptor control radar, and it is vulnerable to destruction by ballistic missile or radar-homing ASM. Moreover, its proper functioning depends on good steady reflections from the ionosphere.

In northern regions, the ionosphere is subject to disturbances, caused by radiations from the sun. A visible manifestation of such phenomena is the Aurora Borealis, or Northern Lights, and it is well known that radio communication in the north becomes difficult or impossible during ionospheric storms. Consequently, it is possible that OTHB radar may not be reliable all of the time if used in Canada or the northern U.S.S.R.

So far we have spoken of the difficulties of detecting bombers flying at low altitude. The same difficulties may be encountered in intercepting and in attacking low-flying targets, since the radar in the interceptor aircraft and in radar-guided air-to-air missiles will receive far more reflected energy from the ground than from the bomber. But if electronic techniques can be found to distinguish the echo from the bomber because of its movement relative to the earth, they may be applicable to Airborne Intercept radar and AAMs as well as to AWACS.[32]

To be able to fly alongside an unidentified aircraft and make a visual inspection, perhaps with the aid of illumination at night, the interceptor must be able to match the performance of his quarry in speed and altitude. To be able to attack and destroy an evading bomber, the interceptor will also need to have superior maneuverability, unless armed with a high-performance air-to air missile. But it is possible to build the superior performance into the missile instead of the interceptor aircraft, which would probably be handicapped by a large radar antenna. There is a certain naval analogy with the battleship, which relied on its long-range armament, as compared to the destroyer or the torpedo-boat, which depended on their own speed and maneuverability to close to short range.

Another choice facing the designers of interceptors is between "many and small" or "few and large." The extreme in the latter direction, achieved in conception but not in operational service with the American F-12, is to have an interceptor of extraordinary performance, able to reach the periphery of the defenses from a central location at supersonic speed, and armed with several long-range air-to-air missiles.[33] A modest number of such interceptors

[32] This is often described as "look down/shoot-down capability."

[33] The American Phoenix air-to-air missile is said to have a range between 60 and 90 nm. *Jane's Weapon Systems, 1971–72,* p. 125. Admiral Moorer gives it ranges out to

would provide a substantial capability, but the cost has been considered excessive. The minimum performance necessary to exploit the potential of the AWACS/OTHB combination would include a good radius of action and a "look-down/shoot-down capability." For the United States it appears probable that one of the two new fighter aircraft, the Air Force F-15 or the Navy F-14, or possibly an adaptation of the F-111, the NR-349, or the F-4 can fulfill the requirements of an interceptor for continental defense.

The planners of the air defense systems to which the direct approaches lead across the barren uninhabited lands of the Arctic have a third option: to reduce the requirement for range in the interceptors by siting bases well to the north. This would increase the probability of destroying the bombers before their ASMs could be launched. And, as a measure to reduce the vulnerability of interceptor and AWACS aircraft on the ground, a large number of bases could be given the minimum necessary fixed facilities to allow the operation of these aircraft, and the combat aircraft could be dispersed in a changing pattern. Such a mode of operation would add to the difficulties of maintenance and logistics, but these could be met by a fleet of large support aircraft able to transport technicians, parts, and weapons to the bases in use at any given moment.

Not only radars and aircraft, but also command centers and communications are vulnerable on the ground. The U.S. provides an airborne command post, to be linked to the defense system by satellite communication.[34]

Several components of air defense systems, such as AWACS, the field-force SAM-D, and various tactical fighter aircraft, may be intended for service overseas but also deployable for continental defense.

60 nm and at altitudes up to 80,000 ft. See *United States Military Posture for FY 1974*, Statement before the House Armed Services Committee, April 10, 1973, p. 67. According to the *Statement of General Brown, 1975*, p. 97, it can engage simultaneously multiple supersonic targets in all weather.

[34] *Statement of Secretary Schlesinger, 1975*, pp. II–49–52.

CHAPTER VI

Deterrence

As the experts like to remind us, deterrence is as old as man, as old as the wish to impose one's will on another. It has been practiced by individuals, groups, tribes, and states. The holding of leading citizens of another state as hostages, a recognized custom in the conduct of foreign affairs in Roman times, was a form of deterrence. Deterrence is commonly seen in the animal world—for example, between cat and dog, one hissing, arching its back to seem larger, and showings its claws, the other snarling, barking, and feinting attack. To be effective, the power to hurt or kill must be clearly seen and feared by the adversary. In fact, the effect lies in the belief rather than the reality.

The Definition of Deterrence

It is hard to overemphasize the psychological aspect of deterrence. J. D. Singer[1] and the American behaviorist school define the perception of a threat as the product of the estimated capability of the opponent's forces multiplied by the estimated probability that he will use them. Consequently, there is no threat if there is no apparent intention to use force, even if there is clearly a powerful force available. Britain feels no threat from the United States, although she is well aware of the great American military power. The Soviet Union does feel threatened, because she perceives American hostile inten-

[1] J. D. Singer, "Threat Perception and the Armament-Tension Dilemma," *Journal of Conflict Resolution* 2 (1958), 90–105.

tions, whether correctly or incorrectly. The same idea has been expressed by Claude Delmas,[2] who explains that the policy of deterrence consists in not engaging in warfare, but preventing it, by threatening any attacker with reprisals which would cost him more in damages than he would gain by his resort to force. Delmas then introduces the same two factors already mentioned—the technical strength of the weapons multiplied by the credibility of their employment—and points out that if one of these factors diminishes, the product diminishes, and if one factor goes to zero, the product vanishes.

The Romans used the motto "Si vis pacem, para bellum" to describe the psychological duel between two rivals, at least one of whom hoped to avoid war by remaining armed and alert. Perhaps as common was the situation in which one (or both) would be quite happy to go to war were it not for the fact that he calculated the resulting costs to exceed the gains. A "normal" situation for many states over many centuries was to be at war, recovering from war, preparing for war either for aggressive or deterrent purposes, or abstaining only because the potential adversaries were judged to be able to retaliate too effectively.

The costs of aggression could be exacted in the form of heavy losses to the attacking forces owing to the superior defense of the adversary, or in the form of retaliatory counterattacks against which the original aggressor could not mount an effective defense. Thus the calculation needs to take account of four capabilities: the offensive and the defensive strength of both opponents. The distinction between offense and defense was less important before the modern age, since many wars were decided by pitched battles in the open field between forces similarly armed. But it was significant, for example, to the Venetians, who could retire to their island, unassailable by land forces, or to small states easy to defend because of strong fortresses or mountainous territory. These could embark on

[2] Claude Delmas, *La Stratégie nucléaire* (Paris: Presses Universitaires de France, 1963), p. 56.

a campaign with the assurance that if they lost their offensive force, they would probably still survive.

This century has seen startling changes in the relative strengths of offense and defense. World War I was characterized by the superiority of the defense. Entrenchments, barbed wire, and the machine gun imposed disproportionate losses on the attacker. The main deterrent to a country contemplating an aggression in the 1920s would probably be the heavy casualties to be faced by his own offensive forces. This was the thinking behind the unfortunate Maginot Line.

World War II saw the superiority of the defense overcome, largely by blitzkrieg tactics using armor and close-support aircraft. Carrier strike forces sank enemy fleets right in their own harbors, and amphibious forces successfully assaulted strongly defended coasts. Bombers inflicted heavy punishment on cities.

But it was in the 1960s that the strategic offense really began to outclass the defense. As described earlier, the main causes were the nuclear weapon and the long-range ballistic missile. The same may not be true on the tactical level. It is not certain whether tactical nuclear weapons will be of more assistance to the offense or the defense. But they do assure that the attacker will not escape the battle without very heavy losses to his forces. Thus, for the 1970s, a country contemplating an attack against an opponent armed with modern strategic offensive weapons is likely to be less concerned with the success of his own offense than with that of the adversary's offense. Defense needs to be included in the calculations, but the crux of deterrence lies in the fear of the opponent's retaliation.

Glenn Snyder distinguishes deterrence from defense, relating the former to the power to punish and the latter to the power to deny.[3]

The problem of choice between offensive and defensive forces has not been easy for the countries wishing to practice deterrence. In the United States in the 1950s there was a major dispute between the supporters of strong offensive bomber forces, who hoped to ensure

[3] Glenn H. Snyder, *Deterrence and Defense* (Princeton, N.J.: Princeton University Press, 1961), chap. 1.

deterrence through guaranteed nuclear punishment, and those who hoped to neutralize the opponent's threat by a great air defense network. General Gavin resigned, prophesying a force of uninterceptable rockets with sufficient range to reach the Soviet Union from the United States.[4] Official support for primary dependence on the offense came after the first Soviet Sputnik had demonstrated the feasibility of intercontinental rockets.

If the power of one adversary to resist the will of the other is as great as the power of the other to enforce its will on the first, it would appear that a stalemate has been reached. However, there may still be unequal motivation to undertake initiatives. For example, one will take greater risks to keep what one already has than to obtain what one does not have.[5]

The Logic of Deterrence

There is a fundamental difference between what Thomas Schelling calls strategies of "deterrence" and of "compellance."[6] The first consists of deterring the adversary from imposing his will, the second of imposing one's will on the adversary. Paradoxically, compellance has never been more difficult to enforce than today, when the great powers possess the most powerful arsenals of weapons. It appears that the will to use nuclear weapons decreases to a degree proportional to the number possessed.

One may ask whether war is now impossible, since it would inevitably lead to mutual suicide, and, as a consequence, whether deterrence is not also impossible? In other words, can the threat be convincing if its execution will ensure the destruction of him who utters the threat? Certainly the threat is less convincing if its execution would be contrary to the interests of the one who makes it, but

[4] A penetrating summary of the evolution of United States strategy has been made by General André Beaufre, in *An Introduction to Strategy* (New York: Praeger, 1965), pp. 91–98.

[5] Jean Laloy, *Entre guerres et paix* (Paris: Plon, 1966), p. 188.

[6] Thomas C. Schelling, *Arms and Influence* (New Haven: Yale University Press, 1966), chap. 2.

it can be effective only if it is not safe to ignore the admittedly small probability that it will, in fact, be carried out. A logical consequence is that the threat should not be made lightly, or in circumstances other than ones where truly vital issues are at stake.

From this there follows a second paradox of the nuclear age. If recourse to nuclear arms is unthinkable, except in the ultimate case of deliberate unlimited global aggression by force, then the threat of unlimited reprisal cannot be realistically invoked against a smaller, limited threat. Hence, too much nuclear stability invites aggression at the subnuclear level.

It is, therefore, necessary to deal with conventional aggression by what General Beaufre calls complementary forms of deterrence,[7] where the credibility of the threat is restored by dependence on flexible forces capable of limited war and lesser degrees of force. NATO's doctrine of "flexible response" attempts to meet any threat with no more than the adequate degree of reaction, as measured both physically and psychologically. Up to a certain level of aggression, they would meet offense with an offsetting defense; at any level their objective would be to "make the punishment fit the crime."

One might object that the strategy has failed if the cost of going to war is ever accepted as tolerable, even if only at the nonnuclear level. However, the modern theorists have built up a "ladder of escalation," hierarchically connecting many levels of violence. Clausewitz wrote of resorting to extremes. Each rung of the latter represents a noticeable increase in the severity of the conflict. The deterrence lies in being able to match the opponent at each step, making each escalation more costly for him. The ultimate sanction, that of full-scale nuclear attack on cities, would be considered only in the last resort. But as long as it is there, the opponent will be motivated to stop well short of provoking the ultimate sanction.

Herman Kahn, perhaps the best known expositor of these theories, has defined no less than forty-four levels or thresholds of

[7] General Beaufre, *op. cit.*, pp. 83–86.

violence.[8] To this Thomas Schelling has added the psychological dimension, to take account of the effectiveness of the threats. It is through actions rather than words that the contestants show their will to fight and the price they are willing to pay to secure what they want.[9]

Raymond Aron speaks of "brother enemies," since the opponents would be enemies in combat but are brothers in their desire to avoid annihilation. Their negotiations could well result in the cessation of hostilities, without either's surrendering his wish to destroy the other.[10] Bargaining on the ladder of escalation can be the means by which the balance of deterrence is plotted on the discontinuities of strategic space.[11]

What of this game if there are more than two players? Is the mechanism of deterrence likely to work if it is used for the benefit of allies as well as the owner of the weapons?[12] Here the political and psychological aspects as to how interests, friendships, and responsibilities are perceived may be more significant than the technical. It has been clear since 1941 that the United States is committed to the protection of Britain against armed aggression from the East. And Schelling has observed that the great miscalculation of the U.S.S.R. was to behave in such a way with Cuba as to make the Americans perceive it as a Soviet California.

The ally or country to be protected, then, becomes a two-way mirror or prism through which the two main powers attempt to gauge each other's will. If the stake is a minor one, the protector can always emphasize the elastic nature of the threat and put the crisis in the context of a struggle to the death.[13] But it would seem that after

[8] Herman Kahn, *On Escalation: Metaphors and Scenarios* (New York: Praeger, 1965).

[9] Schelling, *op. cit.*, p. 147.

[10] Raymond Aron, *The Great Debate* (New York: Doubleday, 1965).

[11] André Glucksmann, *Le Discours de la Guerre* (Paris: L'Herne, 1967), p. 210.

[12] Some authors have described these two types of deterrence as active and passive, while others, including Herman Kahn, prefer simply "Type I and Type II."

[13] Glucksmann, *op. cit.*, p. 189.

a certain threshold, which would depend on the case in point, threats of supreme destruction over a minor issue would cease to be credible.

This type of deterrence is thus a question of balance between the stake and the credibility of the threat. The value of the stake is not indefinitely elastic, but it is quite probable that the two adversaries do not estimate it equally or measure accurately the value put upon it by the opponent. It could happen that one country would attach the very greatest importance to a stake which would have no more than minor interest for another. Threats, of course, can extend throughout a very large scale of possible violence, but again their gravity will be differently perceived by different countries, and the assessment by one may be misjudged by his adversary.

Against this type of background one can combine the calculations of nuclear deterrence with the more conventional strategic assets, such as population, area, economic potential, geographic advantages, and social cohesion.

Glucksmann has observed that a priori the issues at stake can be perceived against a discontinuous background of space and time: the only moment at which the two adversaries employ the same space and time is during a crisis.[14] He is speaking of the equality of risk in the context of global nuclear deterrence. But even if there is only one overall strategy, there are several particular strategies appropriate to the stakes and circumstances of the moment.

The strategic situations presenting themselves today exhibit great variety. Contrast, for example, the European theater with the Third World, nuclear war with conventional war, or either of these with guerrilla war. The great powers have been obliged to find means other than direct military conquest to defend their interests and pursue their objectives. The horizons of strategy have widened to the point that they include, in addition to the classic military subjects and questions of international alliances, economics, and logistics, a long additional list including, among others, assessments of political, social, psychological, and scientific developments all over the world,

[14] *Ibid.*, p. 214.

policies regarding economic and military assistance, and the management of military and administrative affairs at home.

The remainder of this chapter, and all of the next, will be confined to a discussion of strategic nuclear deterrence. It is a big enough subject to deserve detailed study. But as soon as one isolates nuclear deterrence from the larger, political, context in which it is embedded, one is seeing only part of the picture.

The Organization of Deterrent Forces

The Search for Stability[15]

We have seen how two technical factors, the nuclear weapon and the ballistic missile, have revolutionized warfare by magnifying destructive power by an enormous factor, and by a large factor the ease of delivering this destructive power. A single one-megaton fusion bomb can kill as many civilians as were killed in all the strategic bombardments of Germany and Japan throughout World War II.[16] This change in offensive power has demanded that strategic concepts be rethought and rewritten.

Another fundamental change brought about by the strategic bomber and the ICBM is the disappearance of distance as a guarantee of immunity from direct attack on the homeland. The Channel and the Navy have served England well for centuries, but they would not have been enough in 1940 if the air battle had been lost, and today the British Isles are pitifully vulnerable to complete destruction by a rather small number of MRBMs, IRBMs, SLBMs, or medium-range bombers. America could plan its strategy in World War II against Germany and Japan without fear of attack on its continental homeland; today nowhere is out of range of the heavy bomber or the ICBM.

Up to a generation ago the strategic strength of a nation was measured by its manpower, wealth, and industrial potential. All

[15] "Stability" will be given a carefully defined technical definition in Chapter VII. In this chapter we use it in its usual more general sense.

[16] The total has been estimated at 800,000 to 900,000.

three of these assets could be transformed into military strength, but only after a period of preparation, which has been lengthening as armaments become more complex to build and the training to use them correspondingly longer. The temptation to attack and overcome a basically stronger but poorly armed nation before it could rearm was ever present, but, when it was attempted, the defender usually managed to trade space and lives for time, convert his great potential into military might, and eventually defeat the aggressor.

The Japanese succumbed to this temptation in 1941, came close to disarming the giant at Pearl Harbor, and drove him out of the part of the world which they coveted. However, he recovered, marshaled his immense strength, and finally overwhelmed them. But Pearl Harbor will never be forgotten as an example of a highly successful disarming surprise attack.[17]

Because of the immensely more destructive weapons now available for a first strike, not offset by any comparable defense, it is questionable that the stricken country would be able to hold out for the months and years required to mobilize, train, and arm large military forces. Rather, it would have to defend itself against the attack, and to strike back, with whatever strategic forces it had already, and which were not destroyed before they could be used. In other words, the only strategic forces that count are those in existence, not potential ones, and the strength of a nation is measured by the number, technical effectiveness, state of alert, and vulnerability of the strategic forces that are active, deployed, and on duty.

During the 1950s, as bombers were armed with fission and then with thermonuclear bombs, countries lived in immediate fear of a nuclear Pearl Harbor, likely to have a different outcome, where he who attacked first would emerge unscathed and victorious. At that

[17] It had a predecessor at Taranto, the most important naval base in Italy, in the same year, although months after war had been declared between Britain and Italy. Both attacks were delivered by carrier-borne aircraft, using torpedoes, and both succeeded in disabling the battleships which were considered at that time to be the key element in offensive naval striking power.

time, it appeared most unlikely that the crime would be followed by suitable punishment.

Since the sword could not now be parried by any known shield, the only means of self-defense lay with another sword. Defense lay in the counteroffensive—but not the old-fashioned counteroffensive against the attacking forces, which would already have executed their functions. The counteroffensive could be against military and industrial targets, but if its main purpose was to be one of terrible retaliation, it would be most effective if directed against population.

To follow such a strategy required strong offensive forces, but it also demanded that they should not be vulnerable to destruction in a surprise attack. In the 1950s the strong offensive forces were nuclear-armed bomber aircraft, and they were extremely vulnerable if attacked on the ground. Consequently, it was necessary to keep the force in a state of constant alert, ready to save itself by taking off on a few minutes' notice. Great efforts were made to increase the length of warning that could be relied upon, and a certain proportion of the bombers were kept in the air, armed, at all times.

These measures provided deterrence. But it was an unstable situation, in which an accident or a misjudgment could easily precipitate an unintended disaster. And the installation of the first ICBMs in the early 1960s made it worse. These were delicate mechanisms, very exposed, and they could be launched only after a long preparatory "countdown." Consequently, if an attack was feared, there would be great temptation to launch these missiles before they were destroyed.[18] This was the period, in Albert Wohlstetter's memorable phrase, of "The Delicate Balance of Terror,"[19] when the operators of the nuclear deterrent forces were strongly motivated to set their retaliation mechanisms on a "hair-trigger response."

Many scholars have been fascinated by the long series of events

[18] There would also be a great temptation for the opponent to destroy the missiles before they were launched.

[19] Albert Wohlstetter, "The Delicate Balance of Terror," *Foreign Affairs* 37 (January 1959), 211–235.

which led up to the initiation of World War I, so well described by Barbara Tuchman.[20] In retrospect it seems as if the defensive alliances, mobilization plans, and detailed timetables for the movement of troop trains, probably all genuinely conceived out of fear of aggression by enemies, constituted an infernal mechanism which, once activated, led inevitably to war. There was a horrible feeling that the same sort of machinery was being created again, with the difference that its irrevocable actions would all take place in minutes instead of days. Fiction writers had no difficulty in composing plausible scenarios.[21]

American and Soviet political and military leaders were well aware of this dangerous situation and took energetic steps to rectify it, behaving exactly like Aron's "brother enemies." They reduced the vulnerability of bombers by dispersing them to more bases and improving early warning. The most elaborate precautions were taken to prevent the release of a nuclear weapon through accident, misunderstanding, loss of communication, or even madness. The newer ballistic missiles were placed in strong concrete underground silos, each well separated from its neighbor. Solid fuels or storable liquids enable the missile to be held indefinitely in a state permitting launching on short notice. The older, highly vulnerable, slow-to-fire missiles were withdrawn from service. But the biggest technical step was to place a substantial fraction of the missiles in submarines and to keep half of these at sea, submerged and invulnerable, with a foolproof communication system. The biggest organizational and doctrinal step was to abandon categorically any concept of automatic instan-

[20] Barbara W. Tuchman, *The Guns of August* (New York: Macmillan, 1962).

[21] A large Soviet air exercise is observed by NATO; as a precaution a number of U.S. bombers take off and, as called for in their prearranged plan, head towards the U.S.S.R. The Soviets detect this, interpret it is a possible attack, and give the order to evacuate their cities. NATO takes this as confirmation of a serious threat and puts its military forces on full alert. The Atlas ICBMs in the United States and the Thor and Jupiter IRBMs in Europe are fueled and begin their countdown. One missile, having reached the final "hold" state, has a short-circuit in the launching control. The reader can no doubt produce his own conclusions as well as other, equally believable preludes.

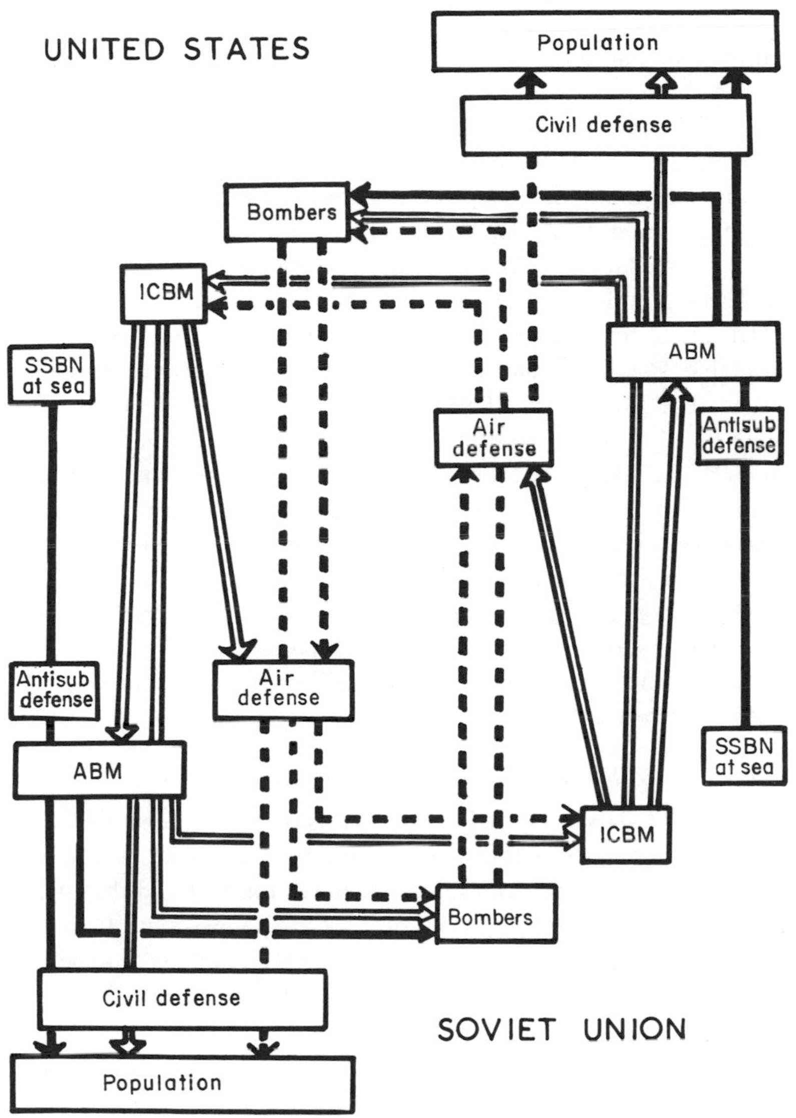

Figure 27. Interactions between strategic offensive and defensive weapons systems

taneous retaliation. Because the retaliatory force was becoming strong and invulnerable, it should be able to endure an attack, with sufficient forces surviving to be able to mete out quite adequate retaliation, in a manner and to a degree appropriate to the occasion. The invulnerability included the provision of secure and alternative communications and command personnel. And a very significant step was the installation of the "hot line" to enable the "brother enemies" to discuss problems and prevent misunderstandings.

Details of Soviet steps to reduce vulnerability of ICBMs are not available. But significant figures about U.S. efforts have been published. The Minuteman ICBMs are located in six large areas. The wing based at Malmstrom has 300 silos spread over 19,000 square miles.[22] The Minutemen are about 250 feet underground and can withstand a blast peak overpressure of 300 pounds per square inch. There have been reports that they have been strengthened to 1000 psi.[23] For comparison, note that an ordinary house will be subjected to heavy damage by 5 psi and a reinforced concrete structure by 25 psi. The most distant silos of this wing are separated by 230 nm.[22]

The relative invulnerability of the ballistic missile submarine has been described in Chapter IV.

Interactions between Offensive and Defensive Systems

Figure 27 shows the main components of the strategic offensive and defensive systems that the two superpowers could have a few years hence. The American forces are in the top half and the Soviet forces in the bottom half. Also shown are the populations of the two nations. The lines indicate attack—dashed for bombers, double for ICBMs, and single solid for SLBMs. Arrowheads indicate the target being attacked.

[22] *Fortune,* August 1963, pp. 125–128. See also the article by Winthrop Griffith in the *New York Times,* reprinted by the *Globe and Mail* (Toronto), May 5, 1969.

[23] The *Statement of Secretary Richardson, 1973,* describes a silo upgrading program, designed to provide improved protection against nuclear blast and radiation effects (p. 58). See also *Offensive Missiles* (Stockholm: SIPRI, 1974), p. 22, which gives 1000 psi for Minuteman 3 silos and 300 psi for the more recent Soviet silos.

To summarize the chief characteristics of bombers, their large weapons and high accuracy permit them to destroy bombers on the ground and missiles in their silos, but their slow speed may have given these targets time to leave before the bombers arrive. They are extremely effective against population, industry, and any other target not able to use warning to escape. They must penetrate air defenses but may be able to "soften up" these defenses by attacking radar stations, interceptor bases, and control centers. On their own bases the bombers are very vulnerable to attack by opposing bombers, ICBMs, and SLBMs. They can expect some warning of attack by bombers, less from ICBMs, and very little from SLBMs.

ICBMs carry less payload and have less accuracy than bombers, but their great speed suits them to "time-sensitive" targets. Their effectiveness against opposing ICBMs will depend very much on the existence of accurate MIRV. ICBMs may have to face ABM defenses but may be able to weaken it by attacking radar stations or using high-altitude precursor bursts to produce electromagnetic blackout. ICBMs should be very effective against cities, even more so with multiple warheads. In their silos they need fear only very accurate weapons.

SLBMs are likely to be particularly effective against bomber bases and cities. They are probably not accurate enough to pose a threat to missile silos. The submarine must cope with antisubmarine forces, and the SLBM with ABM defense (if any). The great, unique advantage of the SSBN is that it is invulnerable to attack by the opposing strategic offensive forces once it is at sea. At its base, though, it could be destroyed by any of the three types of attacking weapons.

The only strategic defensive system not yet discussed here is civil defense. All three attacking systems can be used against population, but civil defense measures would be the same against all three. In fact, one strength of civil defense is that if a new method of delivering nuclear weapons to cities is invented, the civil defense measures designed against existing weapons would probably be equally effective against the new threat. More will be said about civil defense later in this chapter.

As we saw in Chapter III, the scale of ABM defense actually deployed up to 1975 is very small, with warning systems in both countries and a small number of interceptor missiles around Moscow and at Grand Forks. The provisions of the ABM treaty signed in 1972 limit the total strength of BMD to an equal and very restricted level on both sides. However, for the purposes of analysis of the potential effects of strategic offense and defense we will suppose that each superpower has ABM systems with a significant capability to intercept both ICBMs and SLBMs.

The targeting of weapons would probably be different for a first or a second strike. In a planned first strike, the attacker would adopt a counterforce strategy, trying to disarm his rival of the offensive weapons enabling retaliation. There would have to be a choice made between taking all possible steps to obtain strategic surprise or making certain other preparations which would strengthen the offensive and defensive forces but could compromise surprise. For example, if the bombers did not take off until the missiles had been fired, this would give the best chance of surprise, but it would mean that the bombers would encounter alert (though probably damaged) defenses and those of their targets that could depart would be gone by the time the bombers arrived. If an abnormally large number of SSBNs were moved on station, the attack would be strengthened, but an alert antisubmarine defense might detect this and give a general warning. If civil defenses were alerted (and certainly if the order were given to evacuate cities), this would probably become known, and surprise would be lost. However, it might be possible to conceal some of these preparations under the pretext of a routine exercise or a precautionary move against a third party.

Aside from these questions of strategic surprise, the likely priorities for targets would be bomber fields and submarine bases for SLBMs, and ABM defenses, air defenses, and ICBM silos for ICBMs. The choice of targets for bombers is less obvious. They might be sent to attack surviving ICBM silos or non-time-sensitive military targets. A proportion of them might be put into the air but not sent to targets, and if not used on the first strike they would serve as the subsequent threat to cities.

As soon as the attack had been launched, all the defensive forces could go into immediate action. The antisubmarine forces would hunt and attack any SSBNs that they could find. Cities could be evacuated if desired, and other measures of civil defense put into effect. Certain air traffic would be grounded to clear the skies for air defense, and navigation aids, radio transmitters, and lights likely to assist bombers would be turned off.

The aggressor would then have to await the retaliatory second strike by the injured opponent. The great question would be whether the weakened forces making the second strike would be able to penetrate the alerted full-strength defenses and deliver unbearable retaliation against the cities of the aggressor.

The main problem for the delivery of the retaliatory strike would be to assign the depleted forces in the most efficient manner, using a command and control system likely to be damaged, confused, and obliged to use secondary and tertiary communication circuits and alternate commanders. But if the targets were cities, and some were hit several times and some were not attacked at all, the total damage done would probably still be more than the original aggressor could bear to contemplate. If his predictions of the result of his first strike were that he could not bear the subsequent punishment, then he would not make the first strike. In other words, he would be deterred.

Former U.S. Secretary of Defense Clark Clifford explained the American strategy in 1969:

> Many knowledgeable Americans, both within and without the Government, have wrestled with this problem over the years. There is now a very broad consensus that until a truly safeguarded nuclear disarmament agreement is achieved in the context of viable worldwide security arrangements, the only realistic policy we can pursue at this particular juncture is one of deterrence. In other words, we must be prepared to main-

> tain at all times strategic forces of such size and character, and exhibit so unquestionable a will to use them in retaliation if needed, that no nation could ever conceivably deem it to its advantage to launch a deliberate nuclear attack on the United States or its allies.[24]

Later in the same statement, he added the following paragraphs:

> While numbers of Soviet and U.S. warheads, delivery systems, megatons and many other factors are taken into account in the analysis of our strategic force requirements, the soundest measure of the effectiveness of these forces is the "Assured Destruction" role in their ability, even after absorbing a well co-ordinated surprise strike, to inflict unacceptable damage on the attacker. . . .
>
> Our calculations indicate that the U.S. strategic forces programmed over the next few years, even against the highest Soviet threat projected in the NIE (National Intelligence Estimate), would be able to destroy in a second strike more than two-fifths of the Soviet population and about three-quarters of their industrial capacity.[25]

Thus it was concluded in 1969 that even without any American ABM defense the Soviet Union did not possess a "first-strike capability."

There is no doubt that the same situation applies in 1975. It also seems clear that the reciprocal situation prevails in 1975; that is, the United States does not possess a first-strike capability but the U.S.S.R. does have a second-strike capability. This means that we have a state of mutual deterrence.

All of the debates about Safeguard, "overkill," and strategic sufficiency are (or should be) about the situation some years further on, at a time when decisions taken now could have achieved realization

[24] *Statement of Secretary of Defense Clark M. Clifford on the Fiscal Year 1970/74 Defense Program and 1970 Defense Budget* (Washington: USGPO, 1969), p. 47.

[25] *Ibid.*, p. 49.

as operational weapons. It is conceivable, for example, that if Figure 27 were drawn for a date in the future, assuming the SALT agreement to have expired or been abrogated, would show the Soviet ICBM and SSBN forces much larger and equipped with accurate MIRV, and their ABM force built up and able to intercept SLBMs. It could also show the American ABM and air defense forces weak or nonexistent. One should then replay the Soviet first strike and see what the result would be. Certainly, as compared to 1975, less American retaliatory weapons would survive, and of those that did a smaller proportion would be able to penetrate the Soviet defenses.[26] Considerably less than two-fifths of the Soviet population and three-quarters of their industrial capacity would be destroyed. But how much less? And would it still be enough to provide deterrence? Every box in Figure 27 would need to be taken into account, and every interaction.

It might seem prudent to put a major effort not only into establishing strong offensive forces for "assured destruction" but also into reducing the damage that would be inflicted in the event that deterrence should fail. Secretary Clifford defined "damage limiting" as the ability to reduce the potential damage of a nuclear attack upon the United States through the use of both offensive and defensive weapons.[24] Short of making a preemptive first strike, offensive weapons are severely limited in the counterforce role because the missiles or bombers are likely to have gone. Hence the main weapons for damage limiting are likely to be defensive.

If the two policies were mutually supporting, there would seem no theoretical objection to the attempt to pursue both simultaneously: one to prevent the outbreak of war (by deterrence), the other to mitigate the consequences in case the first should fail. However, as has been pointed out by G. W. Rathjens,[27] a successful program of

[26] Assuming the composition of the American offensive forces to have remained unchanged.

[27] George W. Rathjens, *The Future of the Strategic Arms Race* (New York: The Carnegie Endowment for International Peace, 1969).

damage limiting by one country would mean that it was no longer deterred by its opponent. The opponent would probably see this situation developing and would strengthen his offense to preserve (or restore) the threat or would institute damage limiting himself, with the resulting loss of deterrence in the other direction—or, more likely, a countervailing strengthening of the opposing offense. In summary, an attempt to protect population from the nuclear threat would probably result in the maintenance of the present state of assured destruction at increased cost, but it could result in the loss of mutual deterrence. Neither of these results seems particularly desirable.

In the present state of technology, the discussions of damage limiting are rather theoretical, since very few[28] believe that it is technically or economically possible for any country to prevent fatal damage from an all-out missile attack delivered by one of the superpowers.

The recently expressed fears that the existing state of mutual deterrence will be upset illustrate two of the points just made. The Americans feared that the Soviet building program of large SS-9 rockets was intended to give them enough MIRV missiles to destroy virtually all the Minutemen—in other words, to take one, perhaps the biggest, step towards a first-strike capability. And the opponents of the American ABM program feared that it could lead to a full-scale damage-limiting capability which would destroy mutual deterrence, or stimulate the Soviets to an even more aggressive building program.

With all the interacting complexities between offense and defense, the different interpretations that can be put on national programs, and the possibility that great expense may be incurred with no better result than to preserve the present situation, it is encouraging that the two superpowers (or brother enemies!) have decided to hold private meetings to compare points of view and agree on limitations.

[28] Donald G. Brennan is a proponent of full-scale BMD. See "The Case for Missile Defense" in *Hearings on the Strategic and Foreign Policy Implications of ABM Systems*, 1969, pp. 465–476. He labels the present strategy as "assured vulnerability."

Civil Defense

The fourth strategic defensive system, civil defense, needs to be judged in the perspective of the strategic considerations outlined in this chapter. A host of theoretical arguments can be made for and against civil defense, often related to unanswerable questions. Would the evacuation of cities be ordered in time? Would the ordering of evacuation in time of crisis exacerbate the situation? Even if the citizens who remained in their shelters until the radioactivity diminished were able to emerge alive, would the living envy the dead?[29] Would not the credibility of the threat to attack, and hence deterrence, be enhanced if it were known that there were adequate shelters for all citizens? Is there a basic difference in strategic significance between heavy blast shelters and light fallout shelters, the first representing preparation for a first strike (and its resulting counter-city retaliation), and the second being simply a prudent precaution against an enemy counterforce first strike?

It seems strange that, in the West, so many warn of the horrors of nuclear war and predict its imminent descent, but make no effort to prepare for the onslaught they believe so near. At the beginning of this chapter we quoted the formula that the perception of a threat is the product of the estimated capability of the opponent's forces multiplied by the estimated probability that he will use them. Presumably the magnitude of the threat from nuclear attack is the product of the damage if attack occurs multiplied by the probability that there will be a nuclear attack. But in the minds of many this seems to be infinity times zero. The results are too horrible to contemplate, and the probability is too small to be worth considering at all. So we do not "think about the unthinkable."[30] Yet those who have thought about it and studied it objectively believe that although a nuclear war would be a truly dreadful calamity, it would not be the end of the human race or of life on earth, as prophesied by some Cassandras. In fact, if certain preparations were made in advance,

[29] Another compelling expression due to Herman Kahn. [30] Another.

those who survived could well rebuild in a few years a civilization with a standard of living comparable to the 1930s.[31] Most would not consider this with equanimity, but it should hardly be grounds for total despair.

What would be required to save lives, preserve cohesion, and expedite reconstruction would be a soundly organized group of well-trained and disciplined citizens, the buildup of stocks of certain foodstuffs and medical supplies, and a store of tools and machinery suitable for the tasks of decontamination, clearance, and reconstruction. Cost-effectiveness studies have demonstrated that the way to save the most lives per dollar spent is by the provision of fallout shelters, up to the point that there is a space in a shelter for everyone in the country. But by some queer quirk of mass human psychology, we in the West continue to warn one another of the impending Apocalypse but do not choose to take the rather elementary precautions which would greatly reduce its consequences. For mathematicians, $\infty \times 0$ is indeterminate. For the human imagination, it seems to be 0.

It could be that if ABM defenses were installed in the United States, perhaps only around retaliatory weapon bases far from large cities, a program to construct shelters for urban population could be revived. The nation's resolution and the credibility of retaliation might well appear greater if the preparations clearly demonstrated their determination to go on living after the conflict.

The Soviet Union has devoted more attention to civil defense than has the United States, and in particular to the evacuation of urban population but with provision for essential work to continue in the cities.[32]

[31] *Report on A Study of Non-Military Defense* (Santa Monica, Calif.: Rand Corporation Report R-322-RC, July 1958), chap. 4.

[32] "The simultaneous dispersal of workers and evacuation of the plants and institutions will greatly decrease the number of people in the cities; this in turn will sharply reduce population losses in case of a nuclear attack by the enemy. It has been stated in the foreign press that a nuclear attack of an unprotected large city may result in the loss of life of as much as 90 percent of the population. An early dispersal and evacuation could reduce the losses considerably, to a level between 5 and 8 percent." See J. Gailer and C. H. Kearny, eds. and trans., *Civil*

The Psychology of Deterrence

The Plausibility of Deterrence According to Theoretical Models

Assuming that deterrence can be calculated by the multiplication of resources available by the will to use them, one is faced with one calculation in the world of physics and engineering and another in the dimensions of psychology. Given the vagaries of personality and the imponderables of individual and group perception, the second is undoubtedly the more difficult calculation.

Since a comparatively small and weak country will have difficulty in producing overwhelming weapon power, it will probably try to increase the psychological factor in its favor. History gives many examples where weakness of means has been compensated by strength of purpose. Hitler's occupation of the Rhineland in 1936 and the Anschluss in 1938 were carried out in spite of military inferiority with respect to his opponents. He appeared to be determined to use what force he possessed, while his adversaries were irresolute. In more recent years the conflicts over decolonization have usually resulted in victory for the weaker but more determined party.

Any theory dealing with the nuclear arms race must treat the question of deterrence between unequal powers. General Gallois has described "proportional deterrence," which allows a small nuclear power to deter a stronger nuclear power by threatening reprisals whose damage would exceed the limited value of the stake represented by the small power. As an example, he asks whether the seizure of France would be sufficient to compensate the U.S.S.R. for the loss of Moscow. This is the principle behind the independent nuclear deterrent, the French "force de frappe," strongly disapproved by both superpowers.[33] It could be the cause of further nuclear proliferation.

Defense (Oak Ridge, Tenn.: Oak Ridge National Laboratory, April 1971), p. 68, from *Grazhdanskaya Oborona*, edited in Moscow in 1969 by N. I. Akimov. The emphasis is on protection for extended stays in rural areas.

[33] U.S. Secretary of Defense McNamara described a small independent nuclear force as at once "ineffective, useless, and dangerous." See General André Beaufre, *Deterrence and Strategy* (London: Faber & Faber, 1965), p. 86.

Another aspect of deterrence beyond the "two-person game" is the question of third or additional parties, with alliances. This has been treated by General Beaufre.[34] He concludes that the entry of a third power into what had been a bipolar equilibrium restricts the freedom of action of both principals and increases the uncertainties in the calculation of risks. More uncertainty implies more deterrence and consequently more stability. This may well be the case in Europe today, with Britain and France possessing small nuclear forces allied with the West.

Whatever theoretical model may be postulated, the effective exercise of deterrence requires a series of psychological maneuvers intended to convince the rival of one's will to fight rather than cede to threats. There are a host of means to demonstrate determination without resorting to armed force, and it is to be hoped that they will be described and categorized by scholars of international relations.[35] They form a sort of ladder of escalation below the level of violence, giving further evidence of the broad extent over which the strategy of international relations should be studied. In fact, the emphasis on strategic studies in the United States is shifting from nuclear war to a much lower level of conflict, with more attention being given to political, economic, psychological, and social aspects than military.

From Massive Retaliation to Realistic Deterrence

The evolution of American strategic doctrine has depended on many factors, some of which have been technical and others psychological or political. A good strategy is one perfectly adapted to the needs of the moment, but to practice it, the means must be at hand. In 1954 the United States, and NATO, did not have strong enough conventional forces to stop a Soviet thrust in Europe. Hence it was necessary to emphasize nuclear deterrence, exploiting strategic weapons—the only strong asset possessed at the time.

Twenty years later the situation is different. The United States (and

[34] *Ibid.*, chap. 3.

[35] A remarkable study of this nature has been published by Jean-Baptiste Duroselle, on the *Conflit de Trieste, 1943–1954* (Bruxelles: Editions de l'Institut de Sociologie de l'Université Libre de Bruxelles, 1966).

consequently NATO) has plenty of small tactical nuclear weapons and stronger conventional forces in Europe, so that it is possible to talk of warfare limited to the battlefield, perhaps with conventional weapons only. Thus there exists the means to fight at any one of many levels of violence—to offer a graduated response according to the situation.

After it was generally accepted that the Soviets had armed themselves with a large arsenal of strategic nuclear weapons, the United States became increasingly concerned over the possibility that an incident in Europe might require them to make good their threat of massive retaliation, the probable consequence being an all-out nuclear attack on America. This was a principal reason for the replacement of the doctrine of massive retaliation by flexible response. But for psychological reasons, France and Germany interpreted this American initiative as a renunciation of the firm policy of John Foster Dulles and a thinly disguised attempt to withdraw their pledge of military assistance in case of war in Europe.

Although somewhat less biting than heretofore, debates and polemics over the various strategic doctrines continue. But one needs to remember that a doctrine is no more than a doctrine until the moment of truth comes, and in the crisis psychology may have more influence than theory. There is likely to be a tendency to reach towards the supreme weapon, to "silhouette the crisis against the horizon of death." This is what President Kennedy did in the Cuban crisis, in spite of a contrary existing doctrine.[36]

The coordination of nuclear targeting cannot be left until the hectic moment of need. NATO's nuclear planning committee chooses the targets and allots the missions among its various nuclear-armed forces. It is only proper that France should wish to be assured of nuclear support, or that Germany should expect to have a veto on the selection of targets. However, the withdrawal of France from the

[36] The doctrine of flexible response had displaced that of massive retaliation before the crisis of October 1962. But the terms of President Kennedy's declaration that any attack coming from Cuba would be considered as a Soviet attack requiring massive retaliation by the United States were strikingly reminiscent of Secretary Dulles' celebrated discourse of January 1954.

Organization poses new problems. Bilateral negotiations between Paris and Washington may solve them, but it is possible that the fear of an independent French action could not be ruled out of all consideration by a potential attacker, and could deter him from aggression. It is in this sense that General Beaufre postulated that the contribution of a third partner could be stabilizing, always assuming that the purpose was deterrence, and not to act as a detonator for a nuclear explosion which might consume the two great partners rather than the minor one. But it is difficult to conceive of any European country wishing to precipitate a nuclear war.

NATO's doctrine for a conflict in Europe is still for graduated response. As General Beaufre has explained, this does not mean that NATO will always simply mirror the actions of the adversary. For example, a heavy attack with conventional weapons might be met with a tactical nuclear defense, or even with a limited strategic nuclear riposte. It does mean that each case would be dealt with according to the circumstances, with the massive nuclear retaliation being reserved for the final extremity. The purpose is to produce the effective response while limiting the scope of the conflict.[37] Thermonuclear retaliation belongs at the upper end of a continuous spectrum of graduated responses.

In 1971 the American secretary of defense expounded a "Strategy of Realistic Deterrence."[38] It is realistic because the United States does not intend to be the policeman of the world but expects its allies to play their parts in their own and in the collective defense. It is in fact no more than the formulation in terms of the Defense Department of the "Nixon Doctrine," articulated upon the three bases of partnership, strength, and negotiation. Regarding the plans for the U.S. strategic deterrent, Mr. Laird says: "I would point out that whatever the outcome of SALT, our strategic forces will remain the cornerstone of the

[37] *Le Monde*, December 6, 1963, p. 3.

[38] *Statement of Secretary Laird, 1971.* This report, which we have cited many times in earlier chapters, bore the title "'Towards a National Security Strategy of Realistic Deterrence."

Free World's deterrence against nuclear attack and must always be sufficient for this crucial role.''[39]

In fact, there appears to be nothing fundamentally new in the Strategy of Realistic Deterrence. It demonstrates a continuation of the retreat from the more aggressive stands of fifteen years earlier and a readiness to try negotiation whenever there appears to be a real chance of mutually advantageous agreement. That this intention is genuine has already been proven by two presidents' visits to Peking and Moscow, the admission of China into the United Nations and the progress of the Strategic Arms Limitation Talks.

The formulation of these objectives under the title of a new strategy may have been intended more for internal political purposes than as a significant change in strategic doctrine. During the next few years United States foreign policy and military power may have more diplomatic campaigns to win and more lost territory to regain at home than abroad.

Selective Targeting Options[40]

In 1974, Secretary James Schlesinger announced a modification to the doctrine for use of American strategic weapons. The technical capabilities of the weapons should permit the President a far wider choice of options than ''all or nothing.'' A new doctrine now allows the option of limited attacks on a few carefully selected targets, probably of a purely military nature and not in locations risking large numbers of civilian casualties. Although there are programs to improve the accuracy of ICBMs and SLBMs, the Secretary has taken pains to deny any intention to acquire a disarming first-strike capability. The announced purpose is to provide a capability for flexible strategic response.[41]

[39] *Ibid.*, p. 18.

[40] *Statement of Secretary Schlesinger, 1974,* pp. 32–43. *Strategic Survey, 1974,* pp. 66–68. *SIPRI, 1974,* pp. 55–66. W. R. Van Cleave and R. W. Barnett, ''Strategic Adaptability,'' *Orbis* 18 (Fall 1974), 655–676. Barry Carter, ''Nuclear Strategy and Nuclear Weapons,'' *Scientific American* 230 (May 1974), 20–31, also reprinted in *Survival* 17 (January/February 1975), 25–31.

[41] *Statement of Secretary Schlesinger, 1975,* pp. II–1–11.

CHAPTER VII

A Theoretical Model of Deterrence

Much less has been written about the equilibrium of the strategic balance. This chapter will not attempt to repeat or summarize existing works but to put in succinct numerical and graphical (if perhaps oversimplified) form the principal factors which determine the presence or absence of deterrence. In addition, an attempt will be made to define, explain, and examine the real meaning of *stability*, a word used in many different ways.

Several presentations of the strategic balance have been offered in graphical form.[1] We have chosen to follow the approach first published by G. D. Kaye.[2]

[1] A pioneer analysis was by Colonel Glenn A. Kent, "On the Interaction of Opposing Forces under Possible Arms Agreements," *Occasional Papers in International Affairs, No. 5* (Cambridge: Center for International Affairs, Harvard University), March 1963. Other graphical formulations have been made by General André Beaufre, *Deterrence and Strategy* (London: Faber & Faber, 1965), chap. 2. See also Thomas Saaty, *Mathematical Models of Arms Control and Disarmament* (New York: Wiley, 1968), chap. 2.

[2] G. D. Kaye, "A Guide to Deterrence and Arms Control," *Air Force College Journal* (Toronto), 1961, pp. 81–89. Also, by the same author, "An Operational Research Approach to some Defence Problems of Small Powers," *Canadian Operational Research Society Journal* 1 (1963), 39–45. An extensive analysis of the same nature is that by H. Afheldt and P. Sonntag, *Stability and Strategic Nuclear Arms* (New York: World Law Fund, 1971). This is part of a longer study on the consequences and prevention of war entitled *Kriegsfolgen und Kriegsverhutung* (Munich: Carl Hanser Verlag, 1970). See also R. H. Kupperman and H. A. Smith, "Strategies of Mutual Deterrence," *Science* 176 (April 1972), 18–23.

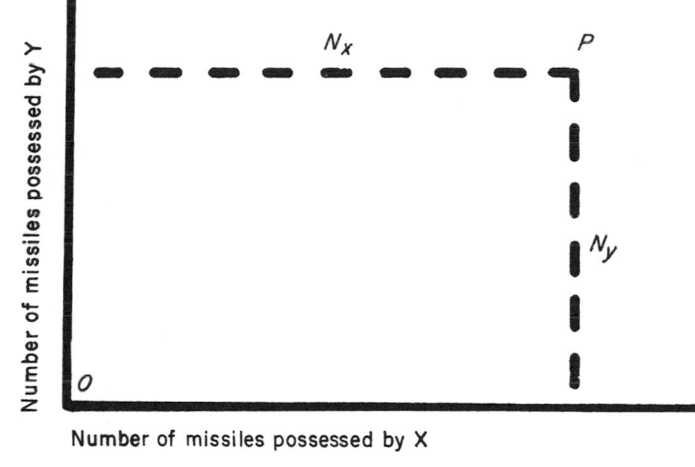

Figure 28. Coordinates indicating the number of missiles possessed by X and Y

Graphical Representation of the Thresholds of Deterrence

Let us represent the opponents in a two-party duel by X and Y. If X possesses N_x weapons of a particular type, and Y has N_y of the same general type, it is convenient to represent this situation by a point P on a graph, such as Figure 28, with cartesian coordinates (N_x, N_y). The graph has two axes at right angles, the distance to the right from the vertical axis, measured parallel to the horizontal axis, being N_x, while the vertical distance upwards from the horizontal axis is equal to N_y. From here on the weapons are assumed to be missiles.

One use of such a graphical representation is to trace the history

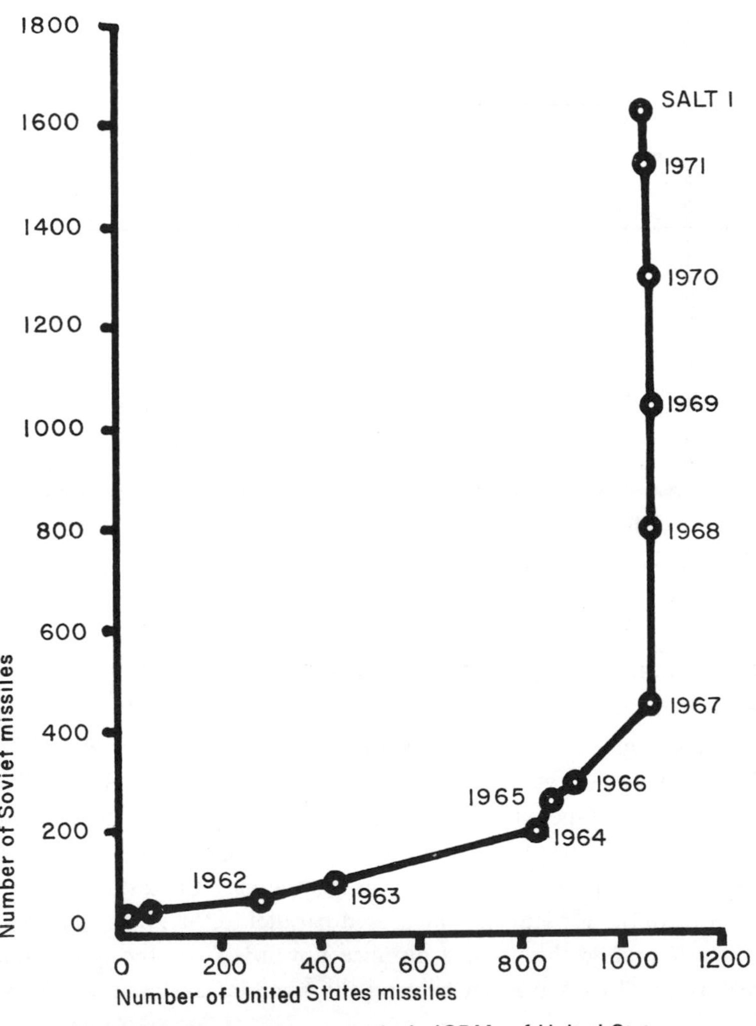

Figure 29. Comparative strengths in ICBMs of United States and Soviet Union

of an armament program.[3] Figure 29 shows the buildup in ICBMs from 1960 to 1971, each point representing N_x and N_y at the middle of the indicated year.[4] It is evident that the Soviets started first,[5] but the United States left them far behind in a large building program during 1961 to 1964. By 1967 the Americans had completed their deployment, and after 1966 the U.S.S.R. began to overtake them. Since 1970 the Soviets have held numerical superiority.

On Figure 29 the point labeled "SALT I" represents the number of ICBMs existing or under construction at the time of the Interim Agreement of May 27, 1972, believed to be 1618 for the U.S.S.R. and 1054 for the United States.

We have noted earlier that deterrence depends on a nation's ability to deliver unbearable or unacceptable damage, even after absorbing a counterforce first strike. A numerical analysis requires us to put numbers in place of adjectives.

How much damage is "unbearable" or "unacceptable"? General Beaufre describes a study at the Institut Français d'Etudes Stratégiques[6] in which it was estimated that a loss of 2 to 10 or 15 percent of a country's resources would bracket the damage that could be risked for most stakes, and for no stake would loss of more than 50 percent be acceptable. U.S. Secretary of Defense McNamara stated that

> it is the clear and present ability to destroy the attacker as a viable 20th Century nation and an unwavering will to use these forces in retaliation to a nuclear attack upon ourselves or our allies that provides the deterrent, and not the ability partially to limit damage to ourselves.
>
> ...the first quantitative question which presents itself is: What kind and amount of destruction must we be able to

[3] "Arms Race" is a fashionable term. But it implies that whoever reaches some finishing line first, whether by a large or small margin, "wins." One objective of this chapter is to demonstrate that such an outcome is unlikely.

[4] *The Military Balance, 1971–72*, p. 56.

[5] The famous "missile gap." In fact, it was very small and soon reversed.

[6] General Beaufre, *Deterrence and Strategy*, p. 35.

> inflict upon the attacker in retaliation to ensure that he would, indeed, be deterred from initiating such an attack?
>
> As I have explained to the Committee in previous years, this question cannot be answered precisely. . . . In the case of the Soviet Union, I would judge that a capability on our part to destroy, say, one-fifth to one-fourth of her population and one-half of her industrial capacity would serve as an effective deterrent. Such a level of destruction would certainly represent intolerable punishment to any 20th Century industrial nation.[7,8]

Afheldt and Sonntag[9] calculate that 100 optimally directed 1-MT warheads would produce about 15 percent casualties in either the United States or the Soviet Union, while 100 10-MT warheads would raise the figure to 38 percent. They therefore use as their "threshold of deterrence" 100 warheads in the megaton range successfully delivered onto as many countervalue city targets.

For the moment, let us retreat from the concrete to the abstract, and from arithmetic to algebra, and accept that there is a threshold, representing the damage that U_y of Y's missiles could inflict on X's cities, which is intolerable for X, and beyond which X would be deterred from any adventure judged likely to provoke such injury. Similarly, suppose that the threshold of deterrence for Y—the level of damage which he cannot bear—corresponds to the destructive power of U_x or X's missiles used in a counter-city strike.

[7] *Statement of Secretary of Defense Robert S. McNamara before the Senate Armed Services Committee on the Fiscal Year 1969–73 Defense Program and 1969 Defense Budget*, January 22, 1968 (Washington: USGPO, 1968), pp. 47–50.

[8] A year later Secretary Clifford estimated that a United States retaliatory second strike could destroy more than two-fifths of the Soviet population and about three-quarters of their industrial capacity, slightly above the thresholds mentioned by McNamara. *Statement of Secretary Clifford, 1969*, p. 49. At higher levels of attack, Secretary McNamara stated that 400 thermonuclear warheads would kill 30 percent of the population and destroy 76 percent of the industry, while 800 warheads would increase these figures to 39 and 77 percent. U.S. Senate, Committee on Armed Services, *Authorization for Military Procurement, Research, and Development, Fiscal Year 1969, and Reserve Strength*, February and March 1968, p. 118.

[9] Afheldt and Sonntag, *op. cit.*, pp. 11–12.

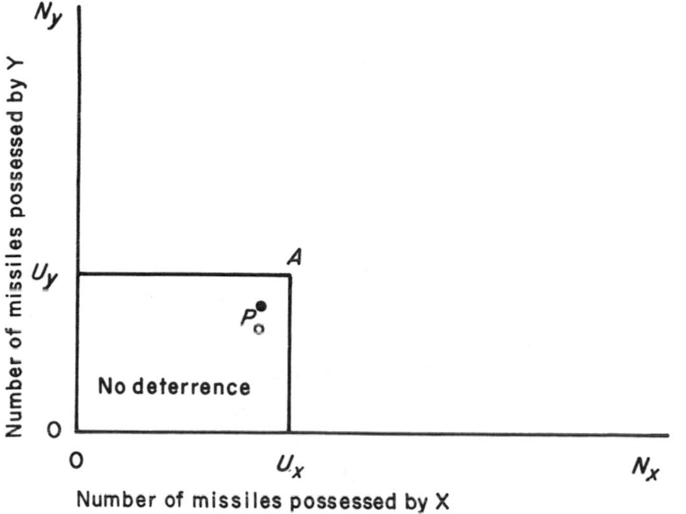

Figure 30. Thresholds of deterrence

The two thresholds U_x and U_y need not be identical. Populations may be differently distributed and differently vulnerable. One nation may be prepared to face greater sacrifices than the other. Moreover, X and Y may not make the same estimatees of U_x and U_y. A point to remember is that it is X's estimate of U_y which does or not result in X's being deterred, although N_y is chosen according to Y's estimate of U_y.

Figure 30 shows a rectangle OU_xAU_y with sides $N_x = 0$, $N_y = 0$, $N_x = U_x$, and $N_y = U_y$. Any point such as P_0 which is inside this rectangle represents a situation in which there is no deterrence in either direction, since $N_x < U_x$ and $N_y < U_y$. Of course it could be argued (quite correctly) that there must be degrees of deterrence, so that if X expected to have his cities hit by $(U_y - 1)$ missiles he would be "nearly deterred." For this elementary model we neglect such partial deterrence and make the simplifying assumptions that X is not deterred by $(U_y - 1)$ missiles or less, but is deterred by U_y missiles or more.

When the point $P(N_x, N_y)$ is outside the corner marking "no deterrence," the situation is more complex. Suppose that X has a number N_x missiles greater than U_x (that is, $N_x > U_x$). X can keep U_x of his missiles in reserve, to threaten Y's cities, and use the remaining $(N_x - U_x)$ to attack Y's missiles. If he did this, a certain number of Y's missiles would be destroyed. Deterrence hinges now on one question: is Y left with more or less than U_y missiles? If more than U_y, Y can retaliate against X's cities with an unbearable reprisal. Calculating all this in advance, X would decide not to make the attack. X does not possess a first-strike capability, but Y possesses a second-strike capability. X would be deterred.

If, on the contrary, less than U_y of Y's missiles would survive X's counterforce first strike, then Y could not retaliate in sufficient strength to deter X from making the attack. X would possess a first-strike capability.

The same reasoning can be repeated with Y contemplating a counterforce attack on X's missiles but being deterred if the number surviving the attack would exceed U_x.

To progress further, we need to introduce additional parameters. Naturally, the number of missiles that would be destroyed in a counterforce strike depends on a number of factors, among which are the accuracy and warhead yield of the attacking missiles and the vulnerability (hardness) of the missiles under attack. Taking these into account, suppose that C_x designates the probability that, if one of X's missiles is fired at one of Y's missiles (in its silo), the target will be destroyed.[10] Conversely, the probability that one of Y's missiles can destroy one of X's missiles is C_y. We can call C_x and C_y the "coefficients of counterforce effectiveness" of X and Y, respectively.

[10] Or, to use a definition which will also cover the case of multiple warheads, C_x can be defined as the expected number of Y's missiles destroyed by one of X's missiles (supposing that none of Y's missiles are targeted by more than one of X's).

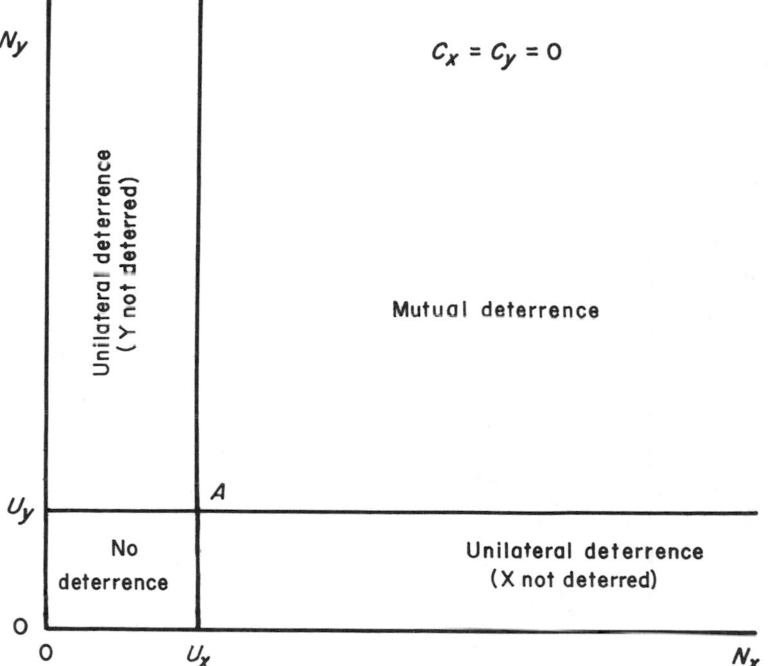

Figure 31. Possible deterrent situations for zero counterforce capability

The Case of Invulnerable Missiles

SLBMs in submarines at sea are invulnerable to opposing ICBMs.[11] There have been exploratory plans for rail-mobile Minutemen, or ICBMs kept in deeply excavated caverns. There may well be missiles whose positions are not yet known to potential attackers. For these and other cases, the counterforce effectiveness of missiles is so low that we could put $C_x = C_y = 0$.

[11] Excluding the case of a "barrage" of underwater nuclear explosions intended to destroy all submarines in a considerable area. This could be delivered by missiles or aircraft.

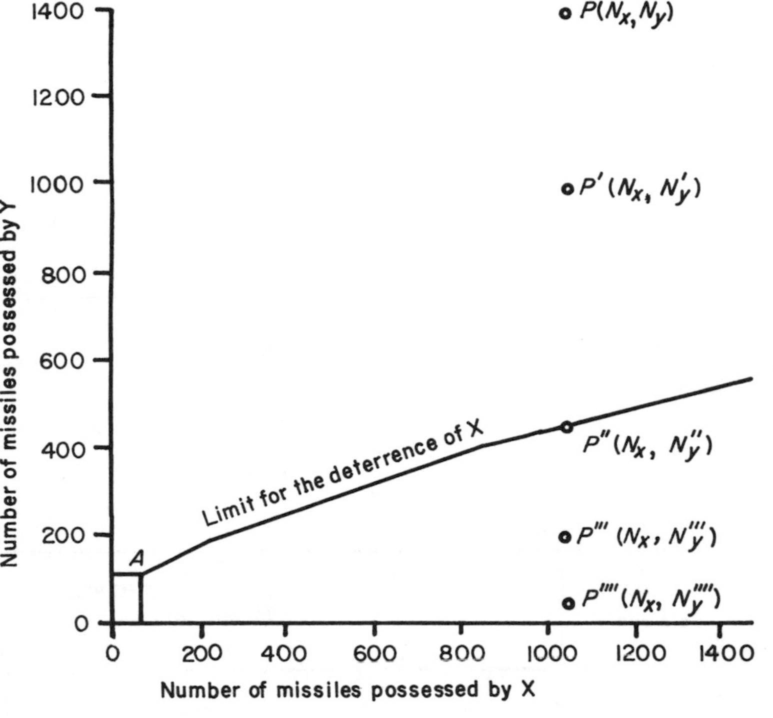

Figure 32. Deterrence of X by Y

In these circumstances there is no counterforce capability. If there is no effective defense for the cities, then the conditions for mutual deterrence are simply $N_x > U_x$, $N_y > U_y$. On Figure 31 all points $P(N_x, N_y)$ in the large area above and to the right of point A represent a state of mutual deterrence. And, as before, if P is in the small rectangle to the lower left, there is no deterrence. But two other zones remain. In the upper left zone, above $U_y A$ on Figure 31, $N_x < U_x$ so Y is not deterred by X, but $N_y > U_y$ so X is deterred by Y. This is called unilateral deterrence. The zone to the lower right is also one of unilateral deterrence, Y being deterred but not X.

The Case of Vulnerable Missiles

Now consider the case where C_x and C_y, the coefficients of counterforce effectiveness, are both greater than zero (but less than one). And consider the calculations of X, with N_x missiles, contemplating a counterforce strike using $(N_x - U_x)$ missiles against the N_y silos of Y. As we saw earlier, everything depends on the number of Y's missiles which will survive: will the number be more or less than the threshold of deterrence, U_y?

As a concrete illustration, suppose that the thresholds of deterrence are $U_x - 50$, $U_y = 100$, so that X is deterred by 100 missiles on his cities but Y by 50 missiles on his. These thresholds are indicated on Figure 32, which also shows a number of points P, all representing $N_x = 1050$ missiles for X, but various numbers N_y for Y. Suppose, furthermore, that the coefficient of counterforce effectiveness C_x is 1/2, so that a missile of X aimed at a silo of Y has a 50 percent probability of destroying it.

Consider first the point $P(N_x, N_y)$, for which $N_x = 1050$, $N_y = 1400$. X could launch $(N_x - U_x) = 1000$ missiles against 1000 of Y's 1400 silos. But with $C_x = 0.5$, he could expect to destroy only 500. $1400 - 500 = 900$ would remain, amply sufficient to destroy X many times over. Clearly P is well within the zone where X is deterred from attempting a disarming first strike. But what if N_y is less than 1400, as illustrated by the series of points P', P'', P''', and P'''', all of which have $N_x = 1050$? Unilateral disarmament by Y could lead to just such a series of points.

At P', Y has $N_y' = 1000$ missiles. The 1000 missiles of X attacking 1000 silos of Y would leave 500 surviving, still five times the tolerable threshold $U_y = 100$. P' is inside the zone where X is deterred.

Now take the case with $N_y'' = 450$, marked by P''. With 1000 missiles to aim at 450 silos, X can afford to aim two of his missiles at each of 350 silos, and three at each of the remaining 100 silos.[12] According to the calculus of probability, the number of silos expected

[12] $(350 \times 2) + (100 \times 3) = 700 + 300 = 1000.$

to survive the attack will be $350 \times \frac{1}{2} \times \frac{1}{2} = 87\frac{1}{2}$ of those attacked by two missiles apiece, plus $100 \times \frac{1}{2} \times \frac{1}{2} \times \frac{1}{2} = 12\frac{1}{2}$ of those attacked by three missiles apiece, for a total of $87\frac{1}{2} + 12\frac{1}{2} = 100$ surviving out of the 450. This is precisely at the threshold of deterrence $U_y = 100$. For $N_y \geqslant 450$, X is deterred from attacking, but for $N_y < 450$ he is not deterred. P'' marks the limit between a state of mutual deterrence and a state of unilateral deterrence. Evidently, P''' and P'''' are well into the zones where X is not deterred.

So far we have assumed the counterforce effectiveness of X's missiles to be $C_x = 1/2$. If it were higher, the critical value N''_y providing deterrence would have to be larger; that is, Y would need to have more silos in order to have at least $U_y = 100$ survive the attack by $(N_x - U_y) = 1000$ missiles. Suppose that the situation already described pertained at a particular time, and that Y had $N''_y = 450$ silos, just enough to deter X. But, remembering that the accuracy of missiles has been improving by a factor of two every five years, suppose that X reduced the CEP of his missiles and raised their counterforce effectiveness to $C_x = 9/10$. In this case, if 100 missiles were to survive, Y would need to have 1000 silos.[13] And, for 100 percent counterforce effectiveness, with $C_x = 1$, Y would need 1100. Clearly, if Y has barely enough silos to provide deterrence, and then X improves his counterforce effectiveness even without increasing the number of missiles N_x, Y must react or lose his power to deter X.

Up to this point we have fixed the number of X's missiles at $N_x = 1050$. Now, leaving U_x, U_y, and C_x fixed, we can vary N_x and determine the geometric locus of P'' for all values of N_x. In other words, join by a continuous curve all the points $P''(N_x, N''_y)$ such that an attack by $(N_x - U_x)$ missiles against N''_y silos would leave precisely U_y silos undamaged. The curve AP'' on Figure 32 shows this locus, and we can call it the limit for the deterrence of X. Every point $P'(N_x, N'_y)$ situated above this curve represents a state in which X is

[13] One thousand fired at 1000 on a one-to-one targeting could expect to destroy $1000 \times 9/10 = 900$.

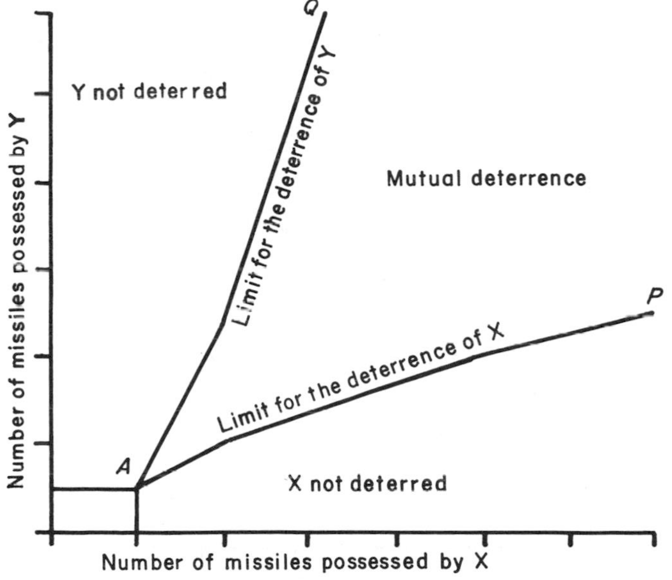

Figure 33. Limits for the deterrence of X and Y

deterred, every point $P'''(N_x, N'''_y)$ below the curve represents a state in which X is not deterred and has a first-strike capability.

So far we have spoken only of the deterrence of X by Y. The entire chain of reasoning can be repeated for the deterrence of Y by X. To every number of missiles N_y possessed by Y there corresponds a number of silos N''_x belonging to X, such that an attack by $(N_y - U_y)$ missiles againt the N''_x silos will leave exactly U_x surviving, just the number needed to deter Y. A curve can be drawn, representing the limit for the deterrence of Y.

Figure 33 shows both curves, labeled *AP* and *AQ*.[14] Any point to the right of *AQ* represents a situation in which Y is deterred; to the left Y is not deterred. Any point in the zone between *AQ* and *AP*

[14] U_x is not the same as on Figure 32.

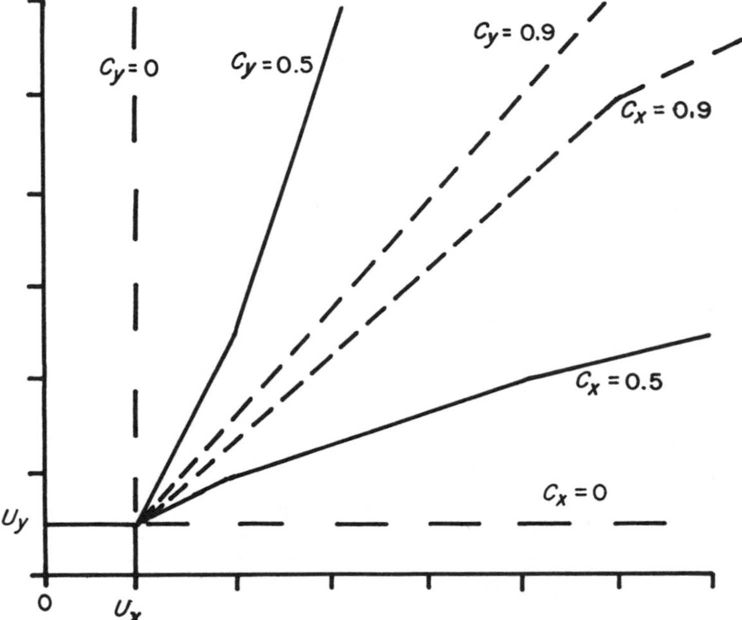

Figure 34. Variation in the limits of the deterrence zones as a function of counterforce efficiency

represents a state where both X and Y are deterred: it can be labeled the zone of mutual deterrence. Thus, N_x and N_y need not be equal (or even nearly equal) to provide mutual deterrence.

The limits AQ and AP shown on Figure 33 were drawn for the case of equal coefficients of counterforce effectiveness $C_x = C_y = 0.5$. Figure 34 repeats these and shows in addition the limits for deterrence for the other examples mentioned, $C_x = C_y = 0$ and $C_x = C_y = 0.9$. Notice that the zone of mutual deterrence becomes much narrower for high counterforce effectiveness.

Readers who wish to work out cases for themselves are referred to Appendix A.

The Case of Very Vulnerable Missiles: The Dangers of MIRV

It has been tacitly assumed up to now that each attacking missile has only one warhead. If the targeted silos of Y are spaced farther apart than the lethal diameter of X's weapon against those silos, then the greatest possible coefficient of counterforce effectiveness of X is $C_x = 1$. However, if each nose cone contains n_x separate warheads, then one missile may be able to destroy several silos. This could be true for unguided MRV, but let us concentrate on the case of individually guided MIRV, where the single missile targets n_x separate silos. Now define C_x as the probability that one of the warheads will destroy the silo at which it has been aimed. C_x will be less than 1, but it is quite possible that $n_x C_x > 1$—that is, that the expected number of silos destroyed by one attacking MIRVed missile will be greater than one. This is the situation illustrated at the bottom of Figure 12.

Mathematically, the expected number of silos destroyed in a counterforce attack by $(N_x - U_x)$ missiles, each with n_x individually targeted warheads, and each warhead with an individual probability of C_x of destroying a silo, is the same as for an attack by $(N_x - U_x)\, n_x$ single missiles, each with a coefficient of C_x. However, there is a difficult question concerning the thresholds of deterrence. In this case the retaliatory missiles are being used for a counter-city attack. As we saw in Chapter II, n_x small warheads will carry less total explosive yield than one large warhead of the same total weight, but they may be able to distribute their destructive power more efficiently over the shape of the city. Or, they can be used against several (perhaps n_x) cities, depending on the possible separation between the individual targets for the warheads from one nose cone. They are, of course, more likely to penetrate active defenses, although these are not being taken into account at this stage. For simplicity, we will assume for the moment that the thresholds U_x and U_y depend on the number of missiles, not the number of warheads, but if another assumption is preferred, one has only to change U_x and U_y.

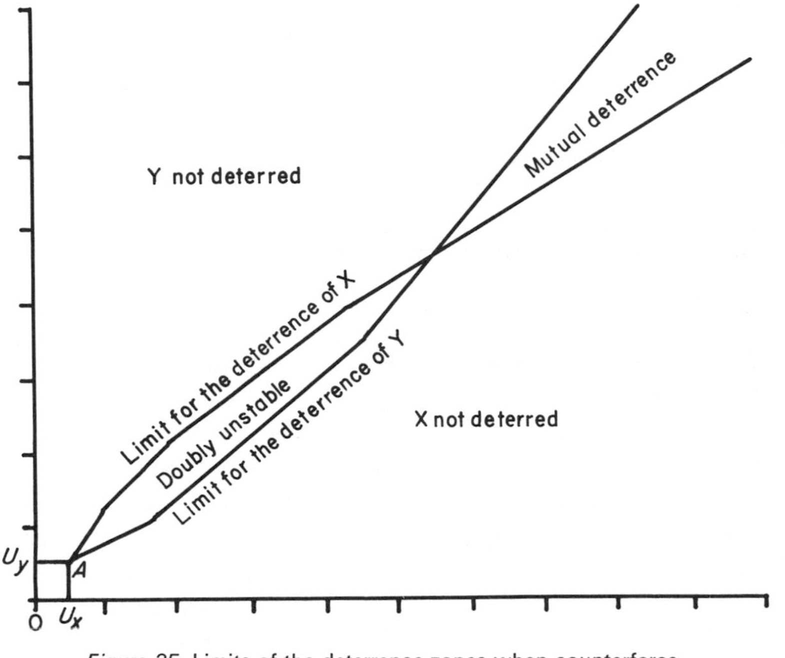

Figure 35. Limits of the deterrence zones when counterforce efficiency exceeds unity

Figure 35 shows the curves for the limits of deterrence of X and Y, assuming that both $n_x C_x$ and $n_y C_y$ are greater than one. As before, the curves start at the point $A(U_x, U_y)$, the upper righthand corner of the "no deterrence" rectangle. But there is one very significant difference. The curve marking the limit for the deterrence of X starts from A with a slope of $n_x C_x$, making an angle of more than 45° to the horizontal axis of N_x. For larger values of N_x (actually when there are more attacking warheads than target silos) the slope is reduced. Similarly, the curve marking the limit for the deterrence of Y starts from A with a slope of less than 45° to the horizontal, although this slope increases for larger values of N_y. The mathematical details of this phenomenon are outlined in Appendix A. The consequence is that near A the two curves enclose a lozenge-shaped zone in which neither X nor Y is deterred. For larger values of N_x and N_y a zone of mutual deterrence does appear, in the upper righthand corner but it is narrow as compared to the cases of missiles with single warheads and C_x considerably less than 1. The enclosed zone adjoining A, labeled "Doubly Unstable," is especially dangerous for the reason that either side can win (disarm the other and still have enough missiles left to destroy his cities) by striking first. It is for fear of such a situation that so much concern is being expressed over the development of MIRV as an effective counterforce weapon.

The introduction of MIRV affects deterrence differently according to the values of the technical parameters. For example, if the extent of the damage inflicted in a counter-city reprisal were directly proportional to the number of warheads, rather than to the number of missiles, then there are circumstances under which the introduction of multiple warheads on a fixed number of missiles could reinforce rather than reduce deterrence.[15] But in other circumstances, and for most values of N_x and N_y, multiple warheads compromise deterrence.[16]

There is a historic precedent for a situation of double instability. It came in the 1950s when both sides depended for deterrence on bombers with nuclear weapons, but the aircraft were deployed to a small number of airfields where many bombers could be destroyed on the ground by a single bomb. Under those circumstances, a surprise first strike could possibly disarm the opponent and leave him at the mercy of the attacker. In the preceding chapter it was explained how urgent steps were taken to reduce this vulnerability and re-establish deterrence.

Stable and Unstable Deterrence

We have identified three basic states for the strategic situation: mutual deterrence, unilateral deterrence, or no deterrence. It is

[15] I. Bellany in *Nature* 226 (1970), 412.

[16] G. D. Kaye and G. R. Lindsey in *Nature* 227 (1970), 696–697.

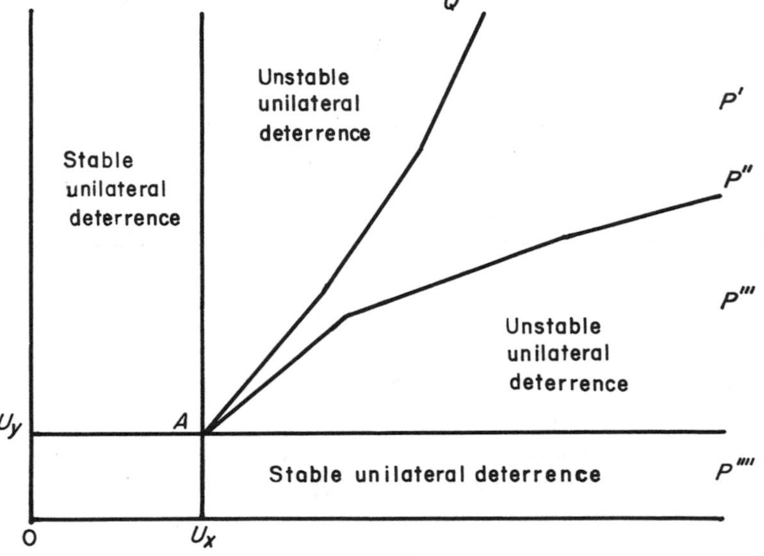

Figure 36. Stable and unstable deterrence

deterrence which prevents attack. But it is time to analyze another fundamental concept: that of *stability*. We could define a state of stability as the absence of rational motive to launch an attack. When there is a rational motive for either (or both) antagonists to launch a first strike, there is instability. But when he who launches a first strike must expect unbearable retaliation, there is deterrence.

Instability is *not* the simple converse of deterrence. We shall show that it is possible to have a state of stable deterrence or of unstable deterrence. Neither is stability necessarily associated with near equality of the forces on the two sides.[17] If, for example, X possessed

[17] The words "stability" and "balance" conjure up the picture of a weighing instrument with equal weights in the two pans. This is unfortunate. We use *balance* more in the sense of a "balance sheet" which describes the state of a commercial enterprise, and *stability* as a measure of the improbability of an attack.

a very large force but Y did not even have enough to seriously injure X by an unopposed counter-city first strike, neither would have any rational motive to attack, and we would have a stable state of unilateral deterrence. But if Y began to arm, X would have a motive to disarm him before his strength reached the threshold of deterrence U_y, and the state of unilateral deterrence would have become unstable.

These points are illustrated on Figure 36. The curve AP'' represents the limit for the deterrence of X. If the situation is represented by a point lying below AP'', then X is not deterred from making a counterforce strike first on Y's missile silos but could hope to disarm Y by such an act. On the contrary, Y is deterred from attacking X. So all the zone below AP'' represents a state of unilateral deterrence. Nevertheless, there is a difference between the state marked by the point P''' (for which $N_y''' > U_y$) and that marked P'''' (for which $N_y'''' < U_y$). If Y has more missiles than the threshold of deterrence, he could inflict intolerable damage on X's cities if he were to launch a counter-city first strike. Such a policy would be irrational, probably suicidal, since X has far more than enough power to obliterate the cities of Y in retaliation. Nevertheless, such an act by Y is possible, and X has the power to prevent it by making a counterforce first strike against the weapons which Y would use. X has the motive and the means to attack. Hence the point P''' lies in a zone which can be labeled Unstable Unilateral Deterrence.

The situation is different for P''''. Here Y does not possess the power to inflict unbearable damage to X's cities under any circumstances whatever. Hence X has no rational motive for attacking Y. P'''' is in a zone of Stable Unilateral Deterrence. It could also be labeled Absolute Superiority for X.

The reciprocal arguments can be employed to show that the zone to the left of the curve AQ marking the limit for the deterrence of Y marks an area of unilateral deterrence, divided into two subareas—one between the axis of N_y and the vertical line $N_x = U_x$, representing stable unilateral deterrence (because Y has absolute superiority and no motive to attack), and the other between $N_x = U_x$ and AQ, representing unstable unilateral deterrence (because Y has the power to prevent an unbearable, though irrational, attack by X).

The other two zones of Figure 36 have been identified on Figure 31. The rectangle OU_xAU_y represents a zone without deterrence or instability. The wedge-shaped zone QAP'' represents a state of mutual deterrence. This can be stable or unstable, for reasons to be discussed shortly.

This graphical method is best adapted to analysis of confrontation between two opponents only. In the past, at the level of superpower strategic capability or of East–West rivalry, there have been only two. But with China growing in strength as a potential third principal center of power, it may soon be necessary to deal with a "three-person game." The International Institute for Strategic Studies believes that current Chinese nuclear weapon systems programs are emphasizing a medium-range capability, with medium bombers and single-stage MRBMs and IRBMs.[18] However, a multistage ICBM with range sufficient to reach the European U.S.S.R. is nearing operational status. Work is proceeding on a very large ICBM able to deliver a multimegaton warhead at least 7000 nm and hence to reach America. This weapon is not expected to be operational for many years.[19] Therefore, during the past years both the United States and the Soviet Union have been in positions of absolute superiority vis-à-vis China. The situation has been stable. But the day when China will have the capability to destroy a dozen American or Soviet cities may not be very far off, and it needs to be foreseen in the long time-scale required for the planning of new weapon systems. The prospect of mutual deterrence is farther off, probably not until the 1980s. So for some years between 1975 and 1985 we can expect a state of unstable deterrence, unilateral as between U.S.–China and U.S.S.R.–China.

The introduction of a third partner into the nuclear strategic game complicates the calculations between the United States and the Soviet

[18] *The Military Balance, 1975–76,* p. 48.

[19] *Statement of Secretary Schlesinger, 1975,* pp. II–16–17.

Union. Either might feel that the number of missiles needed to deter China, or perhaps the number that could be destroyed in a Chinese first strike, should be subtracted from the total available to deter the major adversary. However, a Chinese intermediate-range nuclear capability could pose a direct threat to large parts of the Soviet Union and only an indirect threat to the United States, through vulnerability of her Asian allies or overseas bases. The effect of the third player will not affect the other two in a symmetrical manner.

Concern for a future Chinese threat could offset arms control agreements between the United States and the Soviet Union in terms of types of weapons as well as numbers. Each might be willing to restrict or even renounce its capability for counterforce action or possibly for damage limiting against the other, but would they be prepared to do the same vis-à-vis China? It does not seem possible to have either counterforce or damage-limiting systems effective against one opponent but not another, unless one restricts the discussion to systems of less than intercontinental range. Soviet IRBMs, or even MRBMs, suitably located, and Soviet bombers of less than trans-atlantic range, could be used against Chinese weapon sites. However, they can also be used against the European countries of NATO.

In brief, the growing strength of China will endanger stability before it alters the present state of unilateral deterrence, and if the Chinese buildup continues towards a status of trilateral deterrence, there will be further dangers to be faced.

Now, let us return to the state of bilateral mutual deterrence and discuss the question of its stability. Every point such as P' in the wedge-shaped zone bounded by the lines QA and AP'' of Figure 36 represents a state of mutual deterrence. But motivations to attack or to fear attack can easily arise if P' is very close to either of the boundary lines. Suppose, for example, that P' is near the upper lefthand boundary, AQ, marking the limit for the deterrence of Y. If Y's intelligence service reports (whether correctly or erroneously) that a number of X's missiles have become unserviceable, or that a techni-

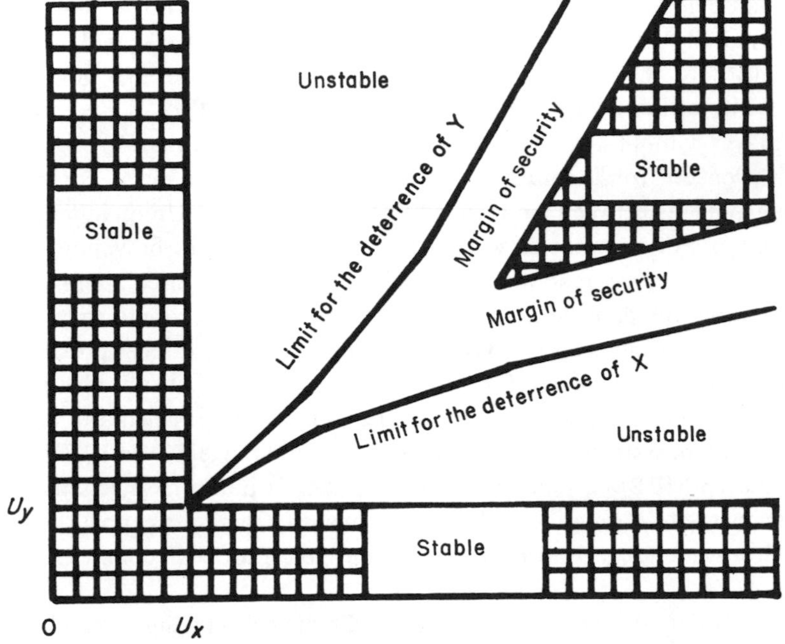

Figure 37. Zone of mutual stable deterrence with marginal zone of security

cal fault has been discovered which calls into question the vulnerability or the counter-city effectiveness of X's missiles, this will have the effect of moving P' across the boundary (or moving the boundary across P') to put it out of the zone of mutual deterrence. Y might believe that he can strike first without having to face unacceptable reprisal. Y might even believe that his opportunity to disarm X is fleeting and should be exploited at once. Another possibility leading to the same result is that Y could actually increase the number N_y of missiles by the small margin necessary to stop him from being deterred by X. If X's intelligence service reports signs of an impend-

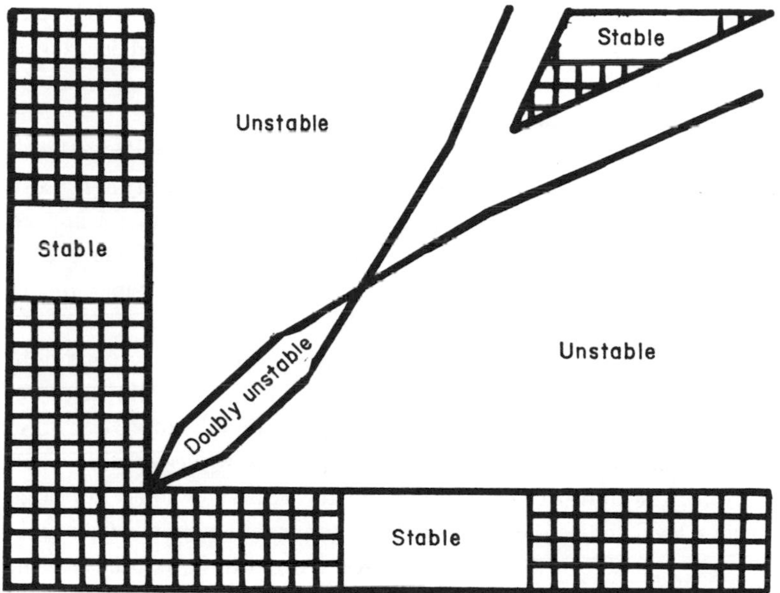

Figure 38. Areas of stability and instability when counterforce effectiveness exceeds unity

ing buildup of N_y, X may be tempted to precipitate action before he loses the power of deterrence, or he may decide to increase his weapon strength in a "crash" program of building or of technical improvement. For all these reasons, the margin of the zone of mutual deterrence close to the limits is unstable. A precarious state in which the deterrence of one opponent can be erased by a small change is subject to a real loss of deterrence if the stronger force is slightly strengthened or the weaker slightly weakened. Perhaps even more important, there are likely to be fears on the one side and ambitions on the other which cannot be considered as likely to facilitate peaceful coexistence.

Figure 37 shows the zone of mutual deterrence divided into a central area of stability and a marginal strip just inside the limits of deterrence. This "Margin of Security" represents a state of unstable mutual deterrence. The zones of stable unilateral deterrence and the zone of no deterrence, which is stable, are shaded and labeled "Stable," as is the central stable part of the zone of mutual deterrence. It is evident on Figure 37 that the two areas of stability are separated by an extensive area of instability.

Figure 37 describes the situation for missiles with single warheads and C_x and $C_y < 1$. With multiple warheads and $n_x C_x > 1$, $n_y C_y > 1$, the additional "Doubly Unstable" zone would appear, as illustrated in Figure 38. The area of stable mutual deterrence is displaced to a greater distance from O and A, and the wider area of instability includes the doubly unstable zone.

In order that a state of stable deterrence apply, three conditions must be fulfilled. First, neither adversary must have both the power to disarm the other by launching a first strike and the motive to do so because he can remove the opponent's ability to destroy his cities. Second, the numbers of weapons on the two sides must not be at such a level that either one or the other has to estimate with great accuracy the size of the opposing force in order to be assured that the opponent is deterred, or that a small increase or decrease to either force can threaten the existence of deterrence. Third, neither adversary must feel obliged to "fire on warning" for fear that his capacity to retaliate will be removed.

To summarize, when both adversaries are strong, there is mutual stable deterrence. Unstable unilateral deterrence occurs when one is considerably stronger than the other, and stable unilateral deterrence when one is strong and the other so weak as to be virtually powerless. Deterrence ceases if both are very weak. Instability can occur in a state of either mutual or unilateral deterrence; it is most probable when the number of weapons is rather limited and their counterforce effectiveness high. The most dangerous situation is that of double instability, when each of the rivals has both the ability and the motive to strike first.

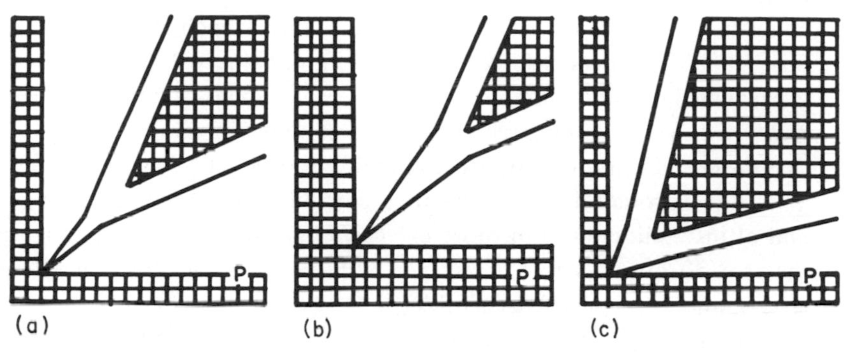

Figure 39. Variations in the zones and thresholds of deterrence as a result of ABM defense: (a) no ABM, (b) ABM defending cities, (c) ABM defending missiles

Effects of Antimissile Defense on Stability

It is important to discuss the effect of ABM defense on deterrence and on stability. We shall so do in terms of a numerical example. Assume the thresholds of deterrence to be equal, $U_x = U_y = 100$, and the coefficients of counterforce capability equal at $C_x = C_y = 0.9$. Figure 39(a) shows the zones; the stable areas are shaded.

Now suppose that X and Y install antimissile defenses. Depending on their nature and location, these may be able to defend population, retaliatory missiles sites, or both. If the radius of action of the defensive missiles is great, or if the silos of the offensive missiles are located close to large cities, it may be impossible to distinguish whether it is population or weapons which are being defended. However, let us suppose that we can designate which type of defense is installed.

Let us examine the case for which the defenses are designed to protect cities. This can be interpreted to mean that the thresholds of deterrence will be increased. If the effectiveness of X's defenses were such that a counter-city attack by 200 of Y's missiles would result in 100 penetrating to their targets, and 100 was the number whose destruction marked the limit of damage which X could bear, then we could say that U_y was now 200—that is, Y must launch at least 200 missiles at X's cities in order to inflict intolerable damage. Figure 39(b) is calculated on this assumption, with $U_x = U_y = 200$—that is, symmetrical capabilities on each side, and assuming as in Figure 39(a) that the coefficients of counterforce capability are still $C_x = C_y = 0.9$. With BMD around the cities, the areas of stable unilateral deterrence and of instability are both more extensive than without BMD, and the area of mutual stable deterrence is displaced in the direction of large numbers of offensive missiles.

In Chapter III it was noted that one possible variant of the American Safeguard ABM system was to install a "light" defense of cities to counter a buildup of ICBMs by China. It is interesting to examine the effect of such a development on the stability of deterrence. If the horizontal axis on Figures 39 represents the number of American missiles N_x, and the vertical axis the number of Chinese missiles N_y, the present situation would be indicated by a point well out on the horizontal axis, at $N_x = 1054$, $N_y = 0$, below the point marked P.[20] But if the Chinese began to install intercontinental missiles and reached the point P, with $N_y = 100$, the situation would be ready to change from stable unilateral deterrence to unstable unilateral deterrence. The United States would be motivated to disarm China before she attained the strength that would enable her to inflict unbearable damage (however irrational and suicidal such an action might be). But if the United States installed BMD around her cities, in a strength capable of intercepting 50 percent of 200 counter-city missiles, she would have doubled the width of the area of stable unilateral deterrence and P would no longer be at the boundary of instability. Ballistic-missile defense of missile sites or installations of

[20] The upper part of the diagram would not be as in Figure 39(b), unless we assume Chinese BMD. But the points describing the situations under discussion are all in the lower righthand area.

more offensive missiles would not achieve this useful accomplishment. Of course, if it were assumed that China would inevitably continue to increase N_y until the zone of mutual stable deterrence were reached, and the desired policy was to reach this state with a minimum period of instability en route, the objective of widening the area of stable unilateral deterrence might be subordinated to that of narrowing the area of instability. In this case, BMD of United States missile sites would be the better policy.

A conclusion might be that the installation of ballistic missile defense around cities will increase the number of offensive missiles which the adversary would need to launch in a retaliatory second strike in order to provide deterrence. Consequently, he needs a larger number of offensive missiles if he is to have "assured destruction." The result is to increase the size of the area of instability which separates the two stable areas. The installation of BMD around cities could easily convert a situation of mutual stable deterrence into unstable mutual deterrence, or even unstable unilateral deterrence. On the other hand, if a state of stable unilateral deterrence applies because of the overwhelming superiority of one of the two adversaries, but strengthening of the weaker side threatens to make the situation unstable, it is possible that the stronger power can keep it stable by deploying BMD around his cities.

Now consider the effect of BMD deployed to defend retaliatory missile sites. The coefficient of counterforce efficiency indicates the probability that a missile fired at an opposing silo will succeed in destroying it. Effective defense reduces this probability, so that if X defends his missile sites, C_y will be reduced. And we have already seen (for example, in Figure 34) that lower values of C_x and C_y enlarge the zone of mutual deterrence. Consequently, as is evident on Figure 39(c), the area of stable mutual deterrence is extended and includes considerably smaller numbers of missiles N_x, N_y. The zones on Figure 39(c) are calculated for $U_x = U_y = 100$, as in Figure 39(a), and for $C_x = C_y = 0.5$, as compared to 0.9 for the first two cases. Even though the areas of stable unilateral deterrence are narrower

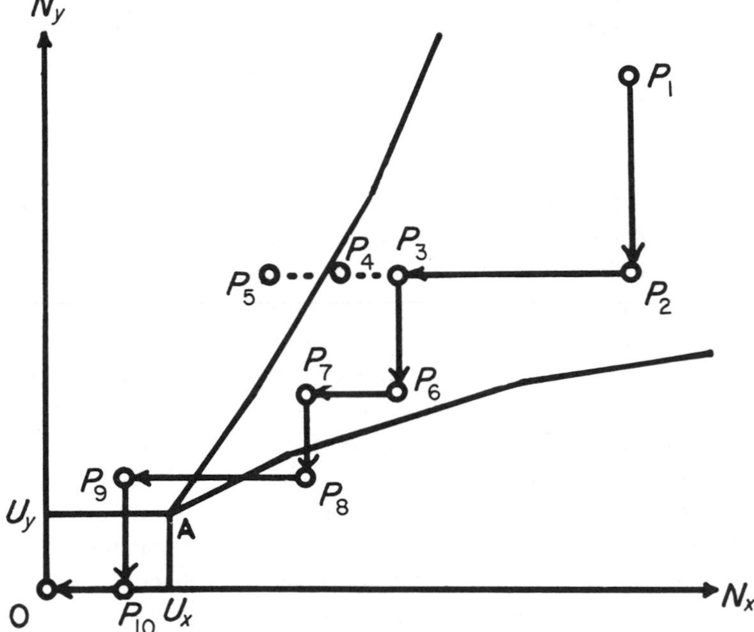

Figure 40. Paths towards disarmament

than for the case of BMD for cities, the area of instability is much narrower with BMD of missiles.

The conclusion is that defense of retaliatory missile sites improves stability.

Disarmament and Stability

Deterrence and stability are usually discussed in respect to present strengths or of planned or potential increases in armaments. But those who advocate disarmament, or substantial reductions in strategic armament, have a responsibility to study the effects of such a course of action on deterrence and stability and to plan the moves that might be undertaken by the two (or several) participants in such a sequence that the dangers would be minimized.

Figure 40 illustrates a step-by-step disarmament program. P_1 could represent the present state of strategic armaments of the United States and the Soviet Union. The situation represented by P_1 is one of stable mutual deterrence, since the point is between the lines representing the limits for the deterrence of X and Y, and not close to either limit.

Y could commence a unilateral program of arms reduction and continue as far as the point P_2 without endangering stability. But if he continued much beyond P_2, X could calculate by only a small misjudgment that he could disarm Y in a counterforce first strike. Now if X reduced his forces, he could take the situation to P_3 and still preserve mutual stable deterrence. But if he continued further, mutual deterrence would be lost near P_4, and at P_5 Y would have a first strike-capability. By agreement, the two rivals could continue to reduce through P_6 to P_7, but below P_7 stable mutual deterrence would cease to exist.

Below the level represented by P_7, X and Y could decide, either in concert or independently, to reduce further, but they would immediately renounce the advantages of stability, quite soon of mutual deterrence, and eventually of all deterrence. A genuine concerted effort to go from P_7 to O would, presumably, try to get directly from P_7 to A and then to O, in a brief interval, with satisfactory verification for both parties. But in the absence of genuine good faith and trust on both sides, the path from P_7 to O is dangerous and narrow, threading its way towards safety[21] with precipices on both sides. How can the dismantling of the weapons be truly simultaneous? How

[21] "Safety" in this case signifies stability, in the sense that neither party would have the power or the motive to make a nuclear attack. Whether the world would actually be a safer place without nuclear deterrence is another question. The great powers, and other powers not so great, will continue to have disagreements and the will to exert pressures on one another. Without nuclear weapons there would be a strong temptation to resort to conventional weapons. Arguments could be settled by the Big Battalions. And one must not ignore the possibility that smaller powers, perhaps less responsible than the larger ones, could acquire nuclear weapons.

can each be assured of the compliance of the other? Can either take the risk of placing himself at the mercy of his recent enemy, even for a matter of hours?

Suppose, for example, that the path from P_7 towards O led via the points P_8, P_9, P_{10}. At P_8, X could disarm Y and retain the strength to obliterate Y's cities. At P_9, Y would possess the power to obliterate X's cities, while X would be unable to retaliate. By P_{10} the worst dangers would have been passed, although X could threaten a certain amount of destruction which Y could not reciprocate.

It is easy to see why a country not completely convinced of the good intentions of another will feel much safer when both have many weapons than when both have only a few. In the second case, there is far more opportunity to gain a decisive advantage by the clandestine retention or acquisition of a small number of weapons, and much more dependence on accurate intelligence and forecasting to ensure security.

If multiple warheads are deployed, and a situation similar to Figure 38 pertains, with large numbers of missiles on both sides making the situation one of mutual stable deterrence, the road to complete disarmament is evidently much more dangerous than for the case of Figure 40. On Figure 40, a path leading from P_1 through A to O kept the inevitable danger of instability to a minimum. But on Figure 38, the path from the area of mutual stable deterrence to O, or even into the area of stability where $N_x < U_x$ or $N_y < U_y$, has to cross a wide area of instability, and the direct path leads through the most dangerous doubly unstable zone in which he who fires first wins.

It should be clear that much more is involved in nuclear disarmament than the simple abolition of an unmitigated evil.

The Situation as Regards Ballistic Missiles in 1972

We shall now use the methods just described to analyze the situation in 1972 as regards ICBMs between the United States and the U.S.S.R. If the thresholds of deterrence and the coefficients of

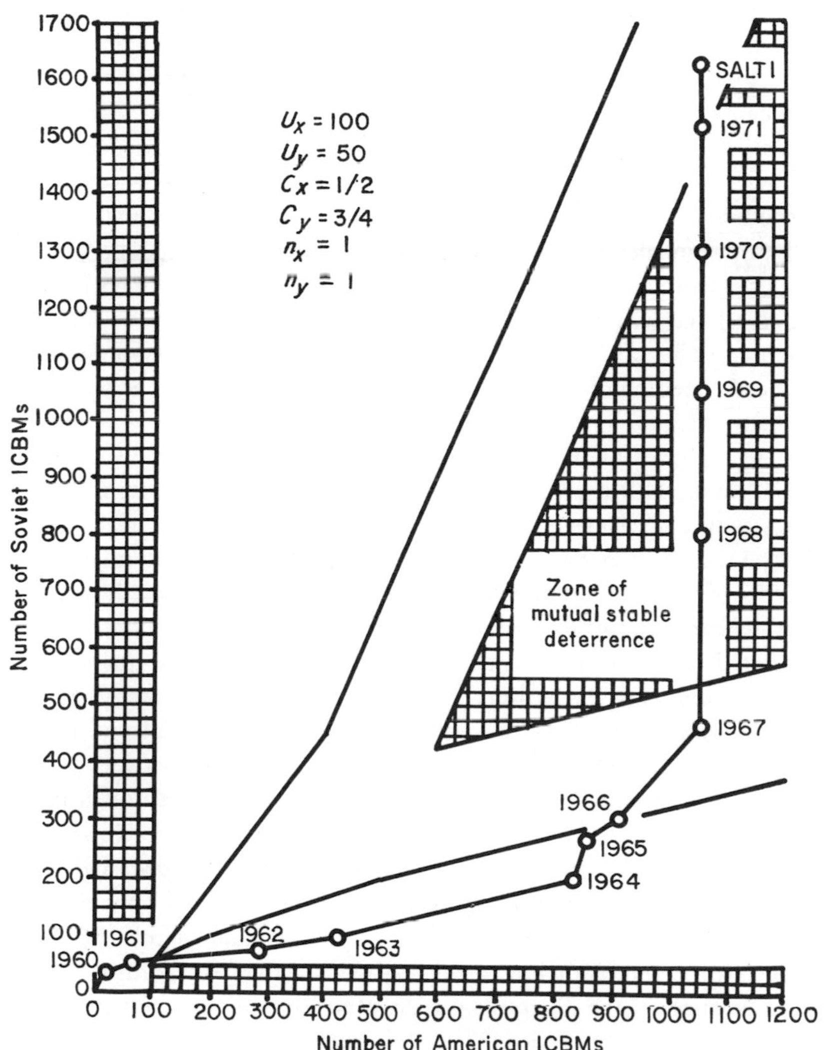

Figure 41. History of the strategic balance since 1960 through different areas of deterrence and stability

counterforce effectiveness were known to the countries themselves, the figures were secret, but we can make rough estimates for illustrative purposes. Suppose that the United States, X, could not tolerate the damage done by $U_y = 50$ Soviet counter-city missiles, but that $U_x = 100$, because the Soviet population is more dispersed and because they have experience in enduring heavy losses in wartime. Until MIRV is widely deployed we can put $n_x = n_y = 1$. Because the Soviet SS-9 missiles have such a large payload, we will take the coefficient of counterforce effectiveness to be $C_y = 3/4$. Minuteman, with the smaller payload, appears less efficient against missile silos, so we assume that $C_x = \frac{1}{2}$. For the "margin of security" to cushion against inaccurate intelligence or the sudden appreciation of technical faults, let us take a figure of 200 missiles. With these assumptions, and the method of calculation explained in Appendix A, one obtains Figure 41.

Also shown on Figure 41 is the year-by-year total of American and Soviet ICBMs. Of course the counterforce effectiveness C_x and C_y certainly changed between 1960 and 1972. But it seems that the U.S.S.R. may have reached a position of stable unilateral deterrence for a few months late in 1961,[22] soon to be changed by the rapid American buildup to unstable unilateral deterrence in favor of the United States which lasted until 1966. Thus for five years the Americans had the power and a rational motive to carry out a counterforce first strike, at least insofar as ICBMs were concerned. Their critics should remember that they did not do this. Between 1966 and 1968 the rapid Soviet buildup took the situation through unstable mutual deterrence into stable mutual deterrence. However, with the number of American missiles fixed at $N_x = 1054$, and the Soviet total N_y rising year by year, with 1530 estimated operational by mid-1972 and another 88 under construction, stable mutual deterrence could soon have given way to instability, as regards ICBMs in isolation. If the diagrams for the other strategic weapon systems showed the same tendency, prudent American planners would be

[22] Offset, of course, by the existence of the large American bomber force.

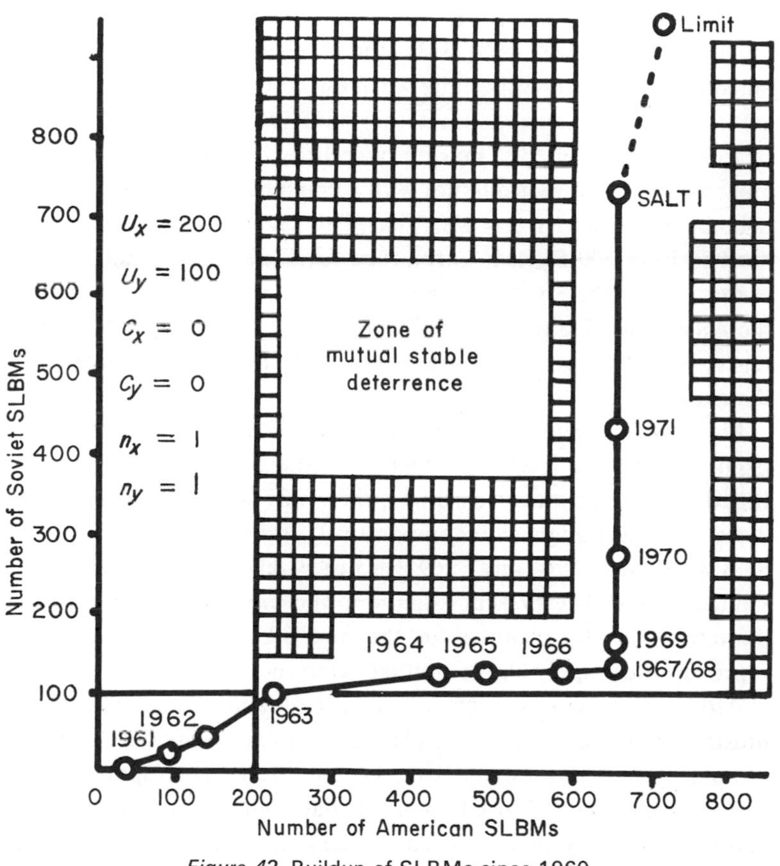

Figure 42. Buildup of SLBMs since 1960

quite justified in fearing an approaching Soviet capability for a first strike. Figure 41 explains why, in the SALT, the Americans wished to halt the increase in N_y and to provide BMD for some missile silos.

The same type of diagram can be drawn up for submarine-launched ballistic missiles, using modified parameters. Against opposing SLBMs in their submarines at sea, the counterforce effectiveness is $C_x = C_y = 0$. However, the submarines are vulnerable in port, to other weapons as well as SLBMs, and to a certain extent at sea from antisubmarine forces, especially when the latter can initiate a surprise attack against submarines in international waters. To allow for these factors and also for the "margin of security," which need not be as great as for the case of missiles with a counterforce capability, let us take $U_x = 200$ and $U_y = 100$; that is to say, the Americans would need to have 200 SLBMs earmarked for counter-city retaliation in order to deter the Soviets, while the Soviets would need 100 to deter the Americans. Figure 42 shows a large area of mutual stable deterrence, bounded by two narrow bands of unilateral deterrence along the axes.

Figure 42 also shows the buildup of American and Soviet SLBMs, from 1960 to the levels agreed in the first SALT accord in 1972. Based on the parameters assumed, there was no period of unilateral deterrence, although the comparatively small number of Soviet SLBMs between 1963 and 1969 was just barely sufficient to deter the United States. The present situation, and any increases within the limitations of the protocol to the first SALT accord, appear to represent thoroughly stable mutual deterrence.

Although diagrams such as Figures 41 and 42 are helpful for illustrating trends and principles, each treats only one offensive weapon system and the defensive system directly corresponding.

We have explained in Chapter VI that there are important interactions between systems. Moreover, the significant measure of deterrence is the cumulative sum of the contributions from each type of counter-city weapon.

It is, of course, possible to assume any combination of weapons on each side, with attendant parameters, and to calculate whether a counterforce first strike would succeed to the extent that the total counter-city retaliation by the surviving weapons, after they had suffered further attrition by the alerted defenses of the original attacker, would still be more than he could bear. However, it does not seem possible to plot the large number of combinations on a simple two-dimensional diagram.

Subsequent Changes due to Technology

During the three years following the SALT I agreement of 1972 the only important change in numbers of strategic missile launchers actually deployed has been the increase in Soviet SLBMs, but this was foreseen and allowed under the agreement. However, the total number of American warheads has more than doubled, because of the increased number of Polaris A3 with 3 MRV, of Poseidon with 10 MIRV, and of Minuteman 3 with 3 MIRV. Thus $n_x > 1$ for U.S. ICBMs and SLBMs. C_x will also be different, since warhead accuracy, warhead yield, and the hardness of Soviet silos have all changed.

In a calculation attempting to combine all of these factors,[23] SIPRI consider the counterforce capability of the U.S. missiles to have doubled between 1972 and 1975, with the largest contribution coming from Minuteman 3, due primarily to its high accuracy. For the Soviet Union, $n_y \approx 1$ in 1975, but both n_y and C_y will soon be increased when the MIRVed SS-18 replaces SS-9, and the MIRVed SS-17 and SS-19 replace SS-11.[24] However, the SIPRI calculations show both improved forces still far short of the power to destroy nearly all of their opponent's land-based missiles.[25] And they still have little capability to destroy SLBMs in submerged submarines.

[23] *Offensive Missiles* (Stockholm: SIPRI, 1974); and Kosta Tsipis, "The Accuracy of Strategic Missiles," *Scientific American* 233 (July 1975), 14–23.

[24] *Statement of General Brown, 1975,* pp. 9–20.

[25] See also D. R. Westervelt, "The Essence of Armed Futility," *Orbis* 28 (Fall 1974), 689–705.

CHAPTER VIII

From Disarmament to Arms Control

Considered as a compelling necessity by some, and as an idealistic utopia by others, disarmament has polarized the attention of the international community since 1945.

At the first sitting of the United Nations Atomic Energy Commission, the American delegate Bernard Baruch declared:

> Colleagues of the United Nations Atomic Energy Commission,
> Citizens of the World,
> We are here to decide between Life and Death.
> That is our task . . .
> We must choose between World Peace or Universal Destruction.

Some fifteen years later, at the sixteenth session of the United Nations General Assembly, President J. F. Kennedy declared no less solemnly:

> Humanity must put an end to War, or else War will put an end to Humanity. We must abolish weapons of mass destruction before they destroy us.

The supporters of disarmament have always believed that armaments generate tension, and that the arms acquired by a state will be used, sooner or later. Humanity has a propensity for war, and the only way to save it from the nuclear scourge will be to get rid of all nuclear weapons forever.

But war, as stated in the preamble to the Charter of UNESCO, has its roots in the minds of men. Are armaments the cause or only a symptom of international tension? Which should come first, safety and security to make détente possible, or détente to lead to safety and security? France has proposed an intermediate formula: "détente-entente-cooperation." But one can offer another tryptique: security-cooperation-détente. Or suggest that thesis combine with antithesis with détente and security arriving together.

What the states have actually accomplished on the road to general and complete disarmament hardly deserves to be described as even a step toward the ultimate goals. Moscow, Washington and many other capitals are unprepared to renounce the security, prestige, and power which they feel their armaments bring them, unless there are comparable and assured advantages to be gained. With no real prospect of actual disarmament in the near future, efforts have turned towards more modest goals, such as agreements not to begin armament programs in areas where there are none today, or agreements to control rather than abolish certain types of weapons or military activities. From small beginnings more could follow, and laboriously obtained agreements over rather small items, occupying ponderous debates for months at a time, appear to be all that can be accomplished at present. However, even if the substance at these first treaties is not of primary significance, the process of discussion, comprehension of the various points of view, and discovery of the mechanics by which agreements can be reached may well create the background against which important steps can be taken in future years.

In this chapter we shall discuss the fruitless efforts towards general and complete disarmament and then outline the very limited agreements on arms control that have been negotiated.[1]

[1] According to Hans Morgenthau, "while disarmament is the reduction or elimination of armaments, arms control is concerned with regulating the armaments race for the purpose of creating a measure of military stability." *Politics among Nations* (4th ed.; New York: Knopf, 1967), p. 375.

The Undiscovered Route to General and Complete Disarmament

We will now mention some of the obstacles that have blocked attempts to achieve general and complete disarmament. Instead of repeating this rather cumbrous phrase, we will use only the one word "disarmament."

One of the principal impediments to disarmament has been the problem of inspection and verification, in order to assure the parties to an agreement that its terms are being rigorously observed by the others. The Soviets have always maintained that inspection is no more than a form of espionage. But the Americans insist that disarmament is impossible without verification, since, without verification, mistrust will persist, and without trust one cannot expect meaningful disarmament. The first plans for nuclear disarmament collapsed in 1946 over this difference.

This problem seems insoluble as long as sovereign states continue to govern their policy in accordance with their national interests.[2] But will it be resolved if the day comes when states are prepared to surrender some of their national sovereignty to a supranational authority? This is by no means certain. Even if inspection were allowed, it is probable that the capacity for concealment and fraud exceeds the power of discovery by foreign inspection. It is true that modern techniques allow remarkable capabilities for inspection of certain types, in many cases without the need for voluntary cooperation by the party being inspected, but it seems likely that a country desiring to thwart discovery could manage successfully to conceal a significant number of the most effective types of armaments, including nuclear weapons.

Another basic difficulty hinges on the organization which would supervise and police disarmament agreements. Ever since 1960 the

[2] To quote Morgenthau, "What, then, are the chances for agreement upon a ratio of armaments to be reached when most or all of the major powers are seeking general disarmament, while at the same time pursuing their contests for power? To put it bluntly, the chances are nil." *Ibid.*, p. 383.

Soviet and American plans have envisaged a supranational body to supervise the execution of promises undertaken. A parallel body, perhaps under the aegis of the United Nations, would be responsible for the maintenance of international peace and security. An explicit accord to transfer the authority to control nuclear weapons to a supranational nonaligned body is not an inconceivable development. But as Raymond Aron has written, unless a common danger makes us wiser, it is very unlikely that in the near future the great powers will come to neutralize the weapons which assure their superiority and at the same time maintain their distress.[3] And, whatever may develop, it is difficult to imagine why the "more equal" of the states would be willing to submit to the will of the large majority of "less equal."

This leads us to the great paradox of the United Nations Charter, which confers on the members of the Security Council the principal responsibility for keeping the peace, although recognizing the right of concurrent interest of the other countries. There is a difficult choice to make: if the egalitarian principles of the League of Nations are applied, then the evident conflict between judicial fiction and political reality leads to inevitable anarchy; if the United Nations are to operate as an organized political hierarchy, as indicated by the Charter, then the superior authorities are not going to submit to control by the inferior. And if the members of the Security Council prefer to retain their armaments, . . .

A further problem is to know just how far disarmament ought to be conducted, in the event that the other obstacles were overcome. The states expressing a desire for general and complete disarmament normally add the proviso that they must retain a certain level of armed force in order to maintain internal order and security, and frequently add to this the power to enforce (perhaps in concert with others) their international obligations. It does not seem necessary to cite historical examples to remind the reader how easily forces necessary for the preservation of law and order at home can be used to

[3] Raymond Aron, *Paix et guerre* (Paris: Calmann-Lévy, 1962), pp. 743–744.

overthrow the law and order of a neighbor. And, when one remembers that the large powers will claim the need of larger and more powerful forces than the others, it is not by any means certain that the security of the small countries would be better assured after disarmament than before.

Yet another difficulty is related to those just described. With no world government or paramount empire, there is no established force stronger than all the others together, or even stronger than the strongest of the others, able to impose its will or enforce adherence to agreements. Thus sanctions cannot be enforced, unless the world community can solve the hitherto insoluble and install a world authority stronger than the strongest nation, yet not under the control of the strongest nation. Domination by the strongest is conceivable, but the existing distribution of nuclear weapons makes extremely improbable a transformation of the present duopoly into a monopoly. And if this should ever come to pass, it is by no means obvious that the prospect of continuing internecine struggle would be much more reassuring than the spectre of war between nations. Or if, instead, the hope is for a supreme authority based on the voluntary surrender of national sovereignty, we must await the development of cosmopolitan citizens of the world, unmoved by nationalism but dedicated to the respect for law, morality, and international justice. Such a wait may require considerable patience.

Three other problems which need to be solved before disarmament can become a reality are more strategic than political. The first is to decide whether the process should begin with the most or the least dangerous weapons. Should nuclear weapons go first, or conventional weapons? And which are really the more dangerous, nuclear or conventional armaments?

This is not a simple question. Conventional weapons were effective enough to cause some 8 million military deaths in the First World War and 15 million in the Second. And the total of civilians killed in these two conventional wars would be comparable. One great air attack on Tokyo in March 1945, using incendiary bombs, killed

83,793, more than the nuclear weapons at Hiroshima or Nagasaki.[4] For that matter, in the thirteenth century Genghis Khan is said to have killed 1,600,000 people in a week after the fall of Herat, a counter-city retaliation for a rebellious act, and a deterrent for other cities whom might be entertaining similar plans. While it seems evident that nuclear attacks on cities would result in far more deaths than any previous human disaster, the prospect of World War III with conventional weapons is certainly no acceptable substitute.

If one accepts the thesis that stability comes from mutual deterrence, depending on substantial nuclear armaments on both sides, then one must examine with care the strategic situation that would face a world without this stabilizing force but with no limitations on conventional armaments. It seems that the older determinants of strategic strength would apply once more, to the advantage of countries with vast demographic potential as well as those endowed with wealth and industry.

On the other hand, if disarmament began in the conventional domain, a quarrel could face states with the absurd alternative of "all or nothing," or of "capitulation or suicide." It seems that the only practical schedule would be to reduce both nuclear and conventional armaments in concert. But past experience offers little hope that the process will get under way without prior progress on the settlement of political difficulties.

The second problem of a strategic nature, which has always caused difficulty in attempts to negotiate agreements on disarmament (or even arms control), is the relative strengths of the forces which are to be disbanded or retained. Not only numbers but types and quality must be taken into account. From the Washington Naval Conference

[4] Air Marshal Sir Robert Saundby, *Air Bombardment* (London: Chatto and Windus, 1961), p. 218. About 70,000 died over a period of ten days in a series of fire raids on Hamburg in the summer of 1943, and when nearly a million refugees were subjected to heavy air attack in Dresden in February 1945 without protection or defense, the number of deaths is believed to have been measured in hundreds of thousands. See Martin Caidin, *The Night Hamburg Died* (New York: Ballantine, 1960), pp. 10 and 156, and *SIPRI 1973*, p. 143.

of 1922 to the most recent negotiations regarding mutual force reductions in Europe, history is full of plans by which states were going to fix the sizes of their forces according to various ratios or formulas. But it is difficult enough to compare forces of approximately the same composition, as we have already seen in previous chapters, and virtually impossible to establish the equivalence of different weapon systems. To how many conventional divisions does a wing of nuclear-armed bombers correspond? How many infantry battalions balance a regiment of artillery with tactical nuclear weapons? Or, to cite a very pertinent problem already mentioned in Chapters II and V, how does one equate Soviet IRBMs to NATO strike aircraft? And if it is necessary to balance human potential with armaments, how many soldiers are worth one missile-firing submarine?

A third strategic factor arises from the advantages and disadvantages of geography, already illustrated in the naval context in Chapter IV. Should a state which is isolated or well protected by nature be entitled to as many defensive armaments as others left more vulnerable by geography? Ought maritime states and continental powers to claim the same composition of forces? The emphasis given to different plans for disarmament by the various powers between the two world wars revealed very clearly where each believed its national interest to lie. The maritime powers sought stabilization of the arms competition at sea, while the continental powers thought in terms of regional accords for European security. There is a certain similarity to the position today, with the two superpowers concentrating on limiting strategic nuclear weapons, while the European states are more interested in a security conference. Now, as before, it seems that the compass course leading to disarmament is read by different nations to lie in different directions, which makes it virtually impossible to find a global accord satisfactory for every national claim.

The final difficulties to be mentioned are of a psychological nature. An approach attempted at the World Disarmament Conference of 1932 was to outlaw aggressive or offensive weapons but to permit defensive weapons. But it proved impossible to obtain agreement on the category befitting each weapon. Each nation claimed (and perhaps even believed) that the weapons it needed were defensive, while those it feared were offensive. In many cases, rivals produced precisely opposite lists. Analogous problems have often arisen in the establishment of aggressive actions under international law.

Another problem verging on the psychological stems from the commonly accepted principle that countries demanding disarmament must not obtain any advantages from it. But nations only make proposals with the object of furthering national interests. It has been said that disarmament negotiations between two powers constitute a double game in which the objective of each is to obtain some advantage at the expense of the other.[5] In fact, though perhaps more with multilateral than bilateral negotiations, there may well occur situations in which all, or at least most, parties can hope to gain. Bargaining over security between two mortal enemies may be a "zero-sum game" where one loses what the other wins. But if a large group of countries came to an agreement which reduced the probability of war and/or saved large expenditures on armaments, without exposing the participants to increased threats or pressures which they might be unable to oppose successfully, then all have gained something.

A danger which could reverse progress towards disarmament after a time is the fact that, while it may be possible to destroy weapons, and to verify that they have been destroyed, it is not possible to destroy the knowledge of how to make them again. And it would be much easier to witness a bomber bonfire or the transfer of fissile material to international custody than to ensure for years afterwards that there was no clandestine fitting of high-performance transport aircraft with the apparatus necessary to allow them to drop bombs, or no diversion of a small fraction of the plutonium output from power reactors.

In terminating this long section on the many obstacles to general and complete disarmament, we should note that, failing a sudden

[5] J. W. Spanier and J. L. Nogee, *The Politics of Disarmament* (New York: Praeger, 1962), p. 15.

widespread and altogether remarkable change in human nature and behavior, any workable future political system must depend on respect for order guaranteed by some military power. Even though the route to general and complete disarmament is blocked, we can be glad of the respite from world war granted by nuclear deterrence, and we can hope that the fear which is necessarily associated with deterrence may stimulate the development of the improved international political relations which form the only real hope for a more stable world.

As Morgenthau says, "Men do not fight because they have arms. They have arms because they deem it necessary to fight. . . . What makes for war are the conditions in the minds of men which make war appear the lesser of two evils."[6] If the presence of arms of frightening potency makes war appear to be a very great evil indeed, and at the same time deters its outbreak, and if fear provides the necessary motivation to reorder the way in which the nations carry on their international affairs, then the experience of living in the shadow of the Apocalypse will have been a salutory one, and the nuclear terror can be quietly retired when it is no longer necessary.

The Gradual Achievement of Limited Arms Control Agreements

Leaving general and complete disarmament with its long list of apparently insuperable difficulties, we take up the various partial, limited, or collateral measures for arms control, which fill a lengthening list of modest successes. We shall select for discussion only those which have already reached bilateral or multilateral agreement. These "collateral" measures are mainly agreements to renounce certain activities which have never been started rather than to relinquish arms already possessed.

It should be noted in passing that important understandings can be reached without being made the object of formal agreements. In fact, some important understandings represent no more than a tacit accord between the participants, or a reciprocal interpretation of

[6] Morgenthau, *op. cit.*, p. 392.

rules to be observed. It has been suggested that mutual example and coordinated parallel actions may be more practical than formal legal agreement.[7] An example is the Soviet and American unilateral decisions simultaneously announced on April 20, 1964, to reduce the production of fissile material for use in weapons.

For convenient presentation, we will concentrate on five principal objectives which the negotiators have attempted to pursue. These are:

(a) to reduce the manufacture of armaments;
(b) to prevent the proliferation of nuclear weapons;
(c) to prevent new areas of the world from becoming the scene of deployment of nuclear weapons;
(d) to prevent the outbreak of a nuclear war;
(e) to limit the effects of a nuclear war if one does break out.

The rest of this chapter will describe some of the measures suggested or agreed upon to further these five objectives.

Checking the Production of Armaments

Most of the plans for arms control have had as one of their objectives a retardation, if not a complete arrest, in the manufacture of new armaments. This is often described as "putting a brake on the arms race," but as we have already remarked, the language is not accurate. A large military force requires considerable production to remain at constant strength, not only for consumable material like aviation fuel and ammunition for training, but to replace major items such as ships, aircraft, and land vehicles which have a limited service lifetime. However, the usual practise is to replace the worn-out vehicles or weapon systems by new ones incorporating the latest technology, costing more, and having increased effectiveness. But the replacement may not be on a one-for-one basis. If ten old piston-engined transport aircraft are replaced by four new larger jet aircraft, costing more in 1975 dollars than the ten old ones did when

[7] Allan Gotlieb, *Disarmament and International Law* (Toronto: Canadian Institute of International Affairs, 1965), pp. 80–83.

they were bought new with 1955 dollars, and with a carrying capacity representing less ton-miles per flight but more ton-miles per month, has the arms race been accelerated or braked? Two other indicators of armament activity often used in addition to manufacture or deployment of weapons and equipment are total military budget and money devoted to military research and development.

Four kinds of control have been suggested on the manufacture and improvement of armaments. The first would be to "freeze" levels at their present figures. The quantity to be "frozen" could be military expenditure, number of conventional weapons, or number of nuclear weapons. All attempts of this nature initiated since 1945 have failed, including the Gomulka plan of March 1964, which hoped to freeze the number of nuclear weapons in Central Europe at their current level.

A second possible type of control is to cut off production. This has been suggested for many weapons systems, including bombers, ICBMs, and fissile material. Although there has never been a formal agreement regarding production of fissile material, as mentioned earlier the United States and the U.S.S.R. informed the international community in April 1964 of their unilateral decision to reduce their production of fissile material for use in weapons.

Third, there can be many types of specific prohibition for the testing, manufacture, or deployment of weapons. This is usually suggested for weapons still in the development stage, although the treaties for nonnuclearization contain clauses prohibiting the manufacture or deployment of weapons of known design. As a rule, such treaties do not forbid programs for which procurement is already under way, but obligate the signatories to refrain from certain activities in which they have never engaged. In particular, they attempt to prevent the acquisition of nuclear weapons by countries not now possessing them.

The only formal accords for the prohibition of the testing of arms are the nuclear test-ban treaty, to be discussed in the next section, and the ABM treaty, which contains an agreement not to test multiple antimissile launchers or missiles, or to test radars, launchers, or missiles not originally designed for the ABM role, in such a manner as to convert them to an ABM role.

The fourth approach is rather general and covers attempts to reduce or limit armaments of particular types. New suggestions appear about as frequently as new types of weapons. Only two agreements have resulted in actual elimination of existing weapons. One was the Washington Treaty of 1922, after which seventy large warships were scrapped by the United States, Britain, and Japan. Two other naval treaties made between the world wars, the London Treaty of 1930 and the Anglo-German Agreement of 1935, established limits to warship strength that were higher than the countries wished to reach at the time. However, the Convention on the Prohibition of the Development, Production, and Stockpiling of Bacteriological and Toxin Weapons and on Their Destruction, opened for signature in April 1972, and signed by 107 states by the end of that year, is being accompanied by actual destruction of biological warfare agents.

SIPRI have recorded world military expenditures between 1951 and 1971, corrected them for inflation, and calculated an average real increase of 2.9 percent per annum.[8] It hardly seems that many of the propositions to reduce the production of armaments have had much effect, although the influences for increase and for decrease may be coming closer to equilibrium. The 1975 Conference on European Security and Cooperation may have contributed to an atmosphere of detente, and could have cleared the way for some progress in the talks on mutual force reductions on the Central European front.

Discouraging the Proliferation of Nuclear Weapons

Before the United States acquired the nuclear bomb in 1945 she was concerned over the possibility that Germany would have it first. And as the "nuclear club" grew from a membership of one to five, both the members and the nonmembers have been apprehensive

[8] *SIPRI, 1973*, p. 207. The rate of rise was faster than this between 1965 and 1968, but after 1968 expenditure has leveled off.

about who the next member might be and what he would do with his terrible new power. A country suspected of having pretensions to the ownership of nuclear weapons is often called the "*N*th country"—the potential next member of the nuclear club.[9] If an applicant to this club could be prevented from joining by a black ball, its membership would remain at five forever.

The two superpowers have been led by circumstances to guarantee the security of many smaller countries by vast military alliances, including integrated military forces and a widespread deployment of nuclear weapons outside their borders. The American and Soviet owners may permit an ally the right of veto over the use of nuclear weapons on his territory, but they carefully retain not only the organizational veto but the actual custody and control of the nuclear weapons in the persons of their own nationals. Britain has her own nuclear weapons, but it is very difficult to conceive of circumstances under which she would even threaten to use them except as part of NATO. But France has had much to say about the independence of her nuclear deterrent, and China's independence is absolute.

The twelve members of NATO who do not possess nuclear weapons are probably all extremely satisfied to be able to shelter under the American nuclear umbrella without having the expense and responsibility of designing, testing, manufacturing, and controlling their own weapons.[10] However, they feel entitled to a voice in the nuclear strategy of the alliance for the very good reason that their fate depends on its success. To outsiders it may appear that these twelve allies have, in fact, for all practical purposes "acquired nuclear weapons" by a process of *dissemination*. Some of the proposals for

[9] If the club already has N members, the apprehensions are with the potential $(N + 1)$th country. Albert Wohlstetter entitled his perceptive essay on the subject "Nuclear Sharing: NATO and the $N + 1$ Country." See *Foreign Affairs* 39 (April 1961), 355–387. Somehow it has become more usual to speak of the *N*th country.

[10] In adhering to the Treaty of Brussels in October 1954, the Federal Republic of Germany undertook "not to manufacture on its territory atomic, biological and chemical weapons."

"denuclearization," such as the Rapacki plan,[11] were intended to prevent dissemination. Much more serious is the possibility that a state with modern scientific and industrial facilities and not a member of a strongly integrated nuclear-armed alliance will decide to embark on its own independent nuclear weapons program. This contingency as well as dissemination from another country are sometimes described as *horizontal proliferation*, in contrast to the *vertical proliferation* of nuclear weapons in greater numbers or of new types by continued manufacture and development in countries that are nuclear powers already.

There has never been any agreement properly described as "denuclearization." Undertakings by states not possessing nuclear arms to renounce their acquisition have been called "treaties of denuclearization," but a better term would be "nonnuclearization." Even if the end result is the same—that is, the creation of a geographical zone in which nuclear weapons are forbidden—there is still a difference between the action of a state which, having no such weapons, renounces the right to make them, and one which has them but agrees to their complete and permanent removal. The prevention of the spread of nuclear weapons into new geographical areas is a special part of the wider problem of nonproliferation, which will be treated later in this chapter.

To this date, the acquisition of nuclear weapons by additional countries is restricted only by two multilateral treaties. The first, which prohibits the testing of nuclear weapons in the atmosphere, in outer space, and under water, was first signed in 1963 and has now been ratified by 106 states. The second, first signed in 1968 and now binding 96 parties, concerned the nonproliferation of nuclear weapons. Appendix B gives their main characteristics.

[11] A plan named after the foreign minister of Poland, who suggested in 1957 that no nuclear weapons be produced or stockpiled within the territories of Poland, East Germany, or West Germany.

The Partial Test Ban Treaty

Because the first treaty permits nuclear weapons to be tested underground, it is also known under the title "partial test ban." There is, however, a partial control even on underground testing, in that release of radioactive material beyond the territory of the testing state is forbidden. This escape of radioactive debris from a subterranean explosion, known as *venting*, has occurred in a number of instances.[12]

There are at least four reasons for the exclusion of underground tests from the ban. One is that the most serious immediate concern regarding testing in the atmosphere was the increasing level of worldwide radioactive fallout. Underwater explosions could add to this, but it was hoped that underground explosions would not. Second, nations were not prepared to agree to restrictions unless they were assured that violations by other signatories would be detected. It appeared that the means of detection of nuclear explosions were adequate to report tests anywhere in the atmosphere, in outer space, or under water, but the seismic methods of detecting and locating underground explosions were not sufficiently effective in 1963 to ensure that a small nuclear explosion could be identified or distinguished from a natural earth tremor.[13] Third, there was an expectation in some quarters that nuclear explosions could have useful peaceful

[12] See *SIPRI, 1968/69*, pp. 249–255, *SIPRI, 1969/70*, p. 387, *SIPRI, 1972*, p. 463 and *Summary Information on Accidental Releases of Radioactivity to the Atmosphere from Underground Nuclear Detonations designed for Containment* (Washington: U.S. Atomic Energy Commission, June 1971).

[13] Techniques for the detection of underground explosions have progressed considerably since 1963. See, for example, the article by Dominique Verguèse in *Le Monde*, May 11, 1967, and by F. M. Anglin in *Nature* 233 (September 3, 1971), 51–52, as well as Henry Myers, "Extending the Nuclear Test Ban," *Scientific American* 226 (January 1972), 13–32, *SIPRI, 1972*, pp. 410–417, *Seismic Methods for Monitoring Underground Explosions* (Stockholm: Almqvist and Wiksell, 1969), and P. Olgaard, "Verifying a Comprehensive Test Ban," *Survival* 14 (July/August 1972), 162–168. The former director of the U.S. Arms Control and Disarmament Agency has stated: "With our present means of instrumentation and other sources of information it is not conceivable that the Soviets could carry out clandestine testing on a scale which could affect the strategic balance." *SIPRI, 1972*, p. 527.

applications for excavation, essentially an underground operation. And, perhaps most important, the nuclear powers who wished to continue with testing believed that they could conduct their experiments successfully underground.

The principal results of the Partial Test Ban Treaty have been to reduce worldwide radioactivity and to make it slightly harder for a nonnuclear signatory of the treaty to acquire nuclear weapons. It is most unlikely that a country would design, manufacture, and deploy nuclear weapons without confirming their performance by tests. The simplest, cheapest, and probably the most informative tests in the early stages of design of a complete weapon system and the measurements of its effects would be low-altitude trials in the atmosphere. However, a state attempting a clandestine test would almost certainly explode their device underground in any case.

There have been suggestions that the ban be extended to subterranean tests, perhaps only for energy yields above the level now reliably detectable by the improved methods. In the Moscow Soviet-American Summit of 1974 a bilateral agreement was made [14] to limit the size of underground nuclear weapon tests performed after March 1976 to 150 kilotons.

In fact, if the success of the Nuclear Test Ban Treaty is measured by the change in the worldwide rate of nuclear testing, it must be judged a signal failure. Between 1951 and the signature of the treaty in 1963 there were an average of 40 tests per year.[15] After the Test Ban the rate rose to 45.[16] However, only about 11 percent of the post-test-ban explosions have been above ground,[17] so there has been less worldwide fallout.

[14] For the text, see *Survival* (September/October 1974), 237–238. Critical comments are given by A. Chayes, F. A. Long, and G. W. Rathjens in "Threshold Treaty: A Step Backward," *Bulletin of the Atomic Scientists* 31 (January 1975), 16.

[15] In 1958 the Soviet Union, the United States, and the United Kingdom each unilaterally suspended the testing of nuclear weapons. They did not resume until 1961.

[16] Averaged to the end of 1974, *SIPRI, 1975*, p. 510.

[17] Forty-one French and fifteen Chinese tests between August 5, 1963, and the end of 1974, out of a total of 512. *SIPRI, 1975*, p. 510. The French and Chinese atmo-

The Nonproliferation Treaty

The formulation of the Nonproliferation Treaty is complete rather than partial, but it distinguishes between nuclear weapon states and nonnuclear weapon states and places different obligations upon them. It defines a nuclear weapon state as one which has manufactured and exploded a nuclear weapon or other nuclear explosive device before January 1, 1967.

A nuclear weapon state signing the treaty undertakes not to transfer nuclear weapons or other nuclear explosive devices to any other country, whether directly or through an alliance. Neither can the control of nuclear weapons be transferred. In addition, nuclear weapon states must not assist, encourage, or induce nonnuclear weapon states to acquire nuclear weapons or devices.

A nonnuclear weapon state must not manufacture or otherwise acquire nuclear weapons or devices, including devices for peaceful purposes. A controversial obligation requires nonnuclear weapon states to accept the inspection, control, and safeguards applied by the International Atomic Energy Agency. The purpose is to prevent diversion of nuclear material from peaceful uses to nuclear weapons or other nuclear explosive devices. The necessity of this obligation rests on the fact that over fifty countries are now engaged in research, development, or production of power with nuclear reactors, and we saw in Chapter I that an inescapable result of using nuclear fission for power is to create material which can be used to make fission bombs.[18] However, many of the nonnuclear weapon states resent the fact that the nuclear weapon states are not obligated to accept the same inspection, and some feel that international inspection may become an unfair infringement on commercial security.

The limitations of the Nonproliferation Treaty bear unequally on

---

spheric tests have continued since then, against increasing international disapprobation. See *SIPRI, 1975,* pp. 487–489.

[18] *SIPRI* estimates that by 1980 the generation of nuclear power in nonnuclear weapon countries will be producing plutonium at a rate sufficient to make 100 weapons of nominal size per week. *SIPRI, 1972,* p. 288. See also *SIPRI, 1975,* pp. 22–29.

the two classes of nations. The nuclear weapon states merely promise not to do things which they had no intention of doing anyway, while the nonnuclear weapon states undertake not to do some things which it might be in their interests to do. However, as a measure of compensation, the treaty confirms that nonnuclear weapon states have every right to pursue research, production, and use of nuclear energy for peaceful purposes; it affirms an obligation of those states with a highly developed nuclear technology to help the others (for peaceful applications); and it urges the nuclear weapon states to make available to the others the beneficial applications of nuclear explosions for peaceful purposes.

Perhaps the most useful result of the Nonproliferation Treaty may be an improvement in the psychological climate among states contemplating the manufacture of nuclear weapons. If a nonsignatory were concerned at the prospect of his main rival's acquiring nuclear arms his fears could be allayed if the rival signed the treaty.

Unlike the Partial Test Ban Treaty, which has unlimited duration, the Nonproliferation Treaty calls for a conference to determine its future after twenty-five years. In both cases, a party can withdraw from the treaty if it decides that extraordinary events related to the subject-matter of the treaty have jeopardized the supreme interests of its country. No country has signed the Nonproliferation Treaty without having signed the Test Ban Treaty too. Those who have signed the Test Ban but not the Nonproliferation Treaty are probably concerned over possible disadvantages for the development of their commercial nuclear programs. Of the five nuclear powers, the United States, the Soviet Union, and the United Kingdom have signed and ratified both treaties, but France and China neither.

The nuclear powers had done their best to encourage the nonaligned countries of the Third World to sign the Nonproliferation Treaty. They have also stated in a resolution adopted by the U.N. Security Council on June 19, 1968:

> Aggression with nuclear weapons, or the threat of such aggression, against a non-nuclear weapon state would create

> a qualitatively new situation in which the nuclear weapon states which are permanent members of the United Nations Security Council would have to act immediately through the Security Council to take measures necessary to counter such aggression or to remove the threat of aggression in accordance with the United Nations Charter.

This was their attempt to reply to the objections raised by Third World states who felt that they were being asked to renounce nuclear weapons without any assurance that they could expect to be protected under all circumstances against the threat of nuclear blackmail.

By May 1975, 96 states had signed and ratified the Nonproliferation Treaty, and another 15 had signed without ratifying. Japan had not ratified, and India,[19] Israel, Brazil, Argentina, South Africa, and Spain had not even signed. A review conference, held in Geneva in 1975, achieved little beyond technical discussions.

Opposing Regional Proliferation

Although the repeated attempts to denuclearize regions of Central Europe have all failed, schemes intended to define zones into which the deployment of nuclear weapons is forbidden have been much more fruitful in other areas. The four zones which have already been made the subjects of formal agreements are Latin America, Antarctica, outer space, and the sea bed. Other attempts have been made, in particular for the nonnuclearization of Africa and of the Indian Ocean,[20] but have not yet succeeded. The four treaties will now be discussed; Appendix B gives their main characteristics.

The Antarctic Treaty

The first of the series of postwar multilateral agreements for the

[19] India tested a nuclear device in 1974. Although detonated underground, described as a peaceful nuclear explosion, and not putting India into the category of a nuclear weapon state by the terms of the NPT, this development is generally considered to be a case of horizontal proliferation. See *SIPRI, 1975*, pp. 16–22.

[20] See *SIPRI, 1972*, chap. 20, *SIPRI, 1974*, pp. 388–394, *SIPRI, 1975*, chap. 5, and William Epstein, "Nuclear-Free Zones," *Scientific American* 233 (November 1975), 25–35. The U.N. declaration wished the Indian Ocean to be completely demilitarized.

limitations of armaments was the Antarctic Treaty, signed in December 1959, following up the peaceful character of the International Geophysical Year of 1958. Everywhere south of the 60th parallel of south latitude is covered by the treaty, which includes all of the Antarctic Continent and a few small islands. The duration of the treaty is thirty years, but it is subject to modification at any time by unanimous agreement.

Only peaceful activities are authorized. There can be no nuclear explosions or release of radioactive wastes in the Antarctic. Military personnel may participate in scientific research or other nonmilitary activites, but the establishment of military bases or fortifications and the conducting of military exercises or weapons tests are prohibited.

The main purpose of the treaty is to prevent military activity, whether nuclear or conventional, and to emphasize the desire of all humanity that the Antarctic shall never become the theater or the cause of international conflict. However, another clause which prepared the way for later similar accords was that no action taken during the life of the treaty would constitute a basis for sovereign territorial claims in the Antarctic. Eighteen countries have ratified or acceded to this treaty.

The Outer Space Treaty

The Outer Space Treaty, signed in January 1967, and now ratified (or acceded to) by 71 countries, concerns itself with space beyond the earth's atmosphere, including the moon and other celestial bodies. No claims of territorial sovereignty will be entertained, even if based on use or occupation. The signatories bind themselves not to place in orbit around the earth any object containing nuclear armament or weapons of mass destruction, not to place such arms on a celestial body, nor to introduce them into outer space in any other way.

It is specified that all stations and installations, material, and space vehicles on the moon or other celestial body are to be accessible on a reciprocal basis to representatives of other states party to the treaty. But objects launched into space, including objects delivered to or constructed on a celestial body, remain the property of the original owners. Astronauts making emergency landings are to be assisted and returned to their country of origin.

No form of control is specifically provided, and the treaty has no time limit. There is no prohibition against the use of military personnel, or indeed against military activity, in outer space—only against nuclear weapons.

In spite of many statements to the contrary, it does not seem that the moon or planets are likely to have great military significance. A rocket placed on such a body for the bombardment of a target on the earth would be unusable for long periods because of the rotation and orbital motion both of the moon or planet and of the earth. The "launching window" which limits the times available for the launching from the earth of space vehicles intended to reach the moon or planets operates in the reverse direction as well. The vehicle attacking the earth would take many hours to arrive from the moon, and weeks from a planet. Moreover, such a complex installation would probably require periodic visits for inspection and maintenance. It would be fantastically expensive. In fact, from every rational point of view, a space-based missile is so much less efficient than an earth-based ICBM that it offers no attraction unless it is a psychological one.

Possession of all or parts of a celestial body, or denial to a rival, are unlikely to become rational subjects of conflict. If they should ever become so, it will probably be for reasons of prestige or as a result of competition over the operation of some device such as a station for relay of communications from and back to the earth. Battles between manned space ships are very appealing to the producers of television serials for juvenile viewers, but it is likely that they will be left in sole command of this activity. The responsible nations appear to be taking commendably unbellicose attitudes towards the exploitation of outer space, although a cynic might suggest that the explanation is that, whatever the rewards may be in terms of knowledge and satisfaction, in financial terms the costs are (literally) astronomical, and the cash profits nil.

As regards the prohibition of nuclear weapons in orbit, the treaty follows the recommendation of a previous U.N. General Assembly resolution. Of the two systems FOBS and MOBS described in Chapter II, the Fractional Orbital Bombardment System would not be banned,[21] but the Multiple Orbital Bombardment System, which makes more than one complete orbit of the earth, would be disallowed. However, as already explained, MOBS would be severely restricted in the times at which it could attack, and it does not appear to be a very efficient weapon.

The military activities for which orbiting vehicles do offer very important advantages are observation and communication. The area of the earth's surface visible from a satellite, and the new area swept per hour, are superior by orders of magnitude to the best accomplishments of aircraft. Surveillance, reconnaissance, and warning are all legitimate functions, as are the reception and relay of information. Manned orbiting laboratories are permitted to carry out military as well as scientific or commercial activities, provided only that they do not carry nuclear weapons or weapons of mass destruction. Infringement on territorial sovereignty occurs only if the vehicle enters the air space, within the atmosphere, above another country. So far, there has been a clear gap between the regimes of aircraft, which are supported by aerodynamic surfaces, need air for their propulsion system, and therefore remain well within the dense portion of the atmosphere (say below an altitude of 15 nm), and orbiting space vehicles, which are hindered by air and therefore remain beyond the dense atmosphere (say above an altitude of 100 nm) until they make their reentry. However, it is quite possible that rocket-propelled "aerospace" vehicles will be built, moving at suborbital velocities and using wings for aerodynamic lift, either for level flight or gliding descent. If such vehicles are used for military purposes over other countries, it may not be clear whether they are cruising in international space or violating national territory.

21 Although ICBMs and SLBMs could be said to carry nuclear warheads into space beyond the atmosphere, they are not prohibited because they do not go into orbit.

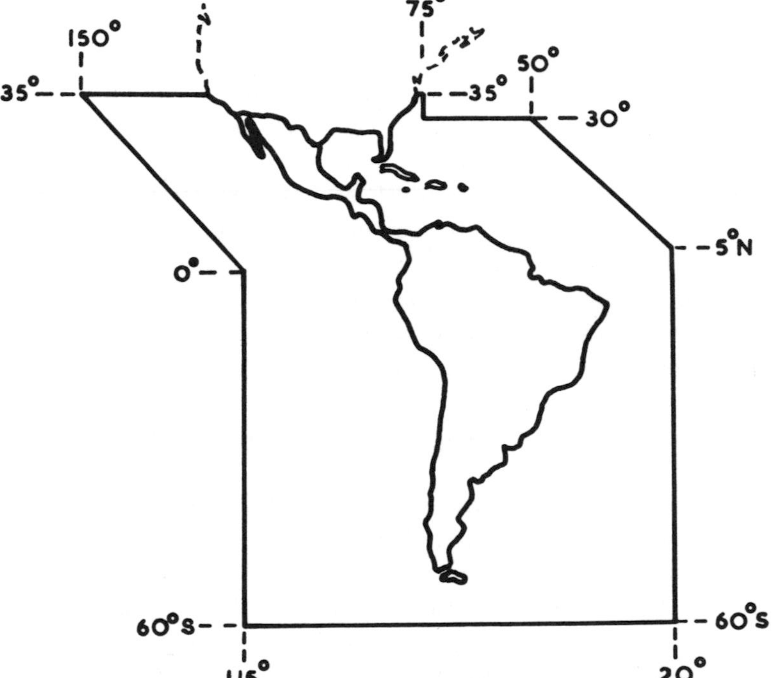

Figure 43. Geographical limits of the zone of application of the treaty for the prohibition of nuclear weapons in Latin America

The Treaty for the Prohibition of Nuclear Weapons in Latin America

Signed in Mexico City in February 1967, the "Treaty of Tlatelolco" is open to Latin American countries as parties, but can involve other countries through two additional protocols. So far, twenty-six nations have ratified the treaty, but it is in force for only twenty, not including the two largest—Argentina and Brazil.

The contracting parties undertake to "use exclusively for peaceful purposes the nuclear material and facilities which are under their jurisdiction and to prohibit and prevent in their respective territories" both "the testing, use, manufacture, production or acquisition by any means whatsoever of any nuclear weapons" and "the receipt, storage, installation, deployment and any form of possession of any nuclear weapons" by the parties themselves, directly or indirectly, on behalf of anyone else, by anyone on their behalf, or in any other way.[22] The transit of nuclear arms is not expressly forbidden, perhaps because of the Panama Canal.

The zone of application of the treaty includes the territorial sea, air space, and any other space over which each signing state exercises sovereignty in accordance with its own legislation, as well as a considerable area of the oceans of the Western Hemisphere, bounded by parallels of latitude, meridians of longitude, loxodromic lines, and the territorial waters of the United States (which cannot be a party to the main treaty while retaining nuclear weapons). The zone of application is illustrated on Figure 43.

The treaty provides for an elaborate system of verification and control. Each state undertakes to negotiate bilateral or multilateral accords with the International Atomic Energy Agency for the application of its safeguards to its nuclear activities. In addition, a new international organism known as OPANAL[23] is established, to prevent the clandestine introduction of nuclear weapons and to ensure compliance with the obligations of the treaty.

If a violation is suspected, IAEA or OPANAL may conduct a special inspection. Reports of violations go to the U.N. Security Council, the U.N. General Assembly, and the Council of the Organisation of American States.

The treaty remains in force indefinitely, but any party may

[22] *SIPRI, 1969/70*, p. 222. A special article on this treaty was prepared by Dr. A. G. Robles. See also *SIPRI, 1972*, chap. 19.

[23] The Spanish acronym for "Agency for the Prohibition of Nuclear Weapons in Latin America." It began its work in 1969.

denounce it with three months notice[24] in circumstances where supreme interests or peace and security are in jeopardy.

Additional Protocol I is open to states exerting a de jure or de facto jurisdiction over territories situated in the zone of application. These comprise the United Kingdom, the Netherlands,[25] the United States, and France. States signing the protocol agree to respect the statute of nonnuclearization for military purposes of the treaty in the territories for which they are responsible.

Additional Protocol II is for the five states now possessing nuclear weapons. All but the Soviet Union have signed, but the latter objects to permission of transit for nuclear weapons. Adherents to the protocol undertake to respect the statutes of the treaty and not to threaten the use of nuclear weapons against the contracting parties of the treaty.

The Treaty of Tlatelolco is the most far-reaching act of nonnuclearization, potentially covering nearly six million square nautical miles. It gives reason to hope that the nuclear rivalries of the great powers will not extend to Latin America. And it is the first treaty of nonnuclearization due entirely to the efforts of nonnuclear weapon powers.

The Sea Bed Treaty[26]

The full title of this accord, signed in February 1971, and engaging 55 parties by the end of 1974, is "The Treaty on the Prohibition of the Emplacement of Nuclear Weapons and Other Weapons of Mass Destruction on the Sea Bed and the Ocean Floor and in the Subsoil Thereof." Structures, launching installations, or any other facilities specifically designed for storing, testing, or using such weapons also

[24] Controversy arose over whether the treaty should enter into force when a majority, or when all of the eligible countries, had signed. The resulting compromise allowed immediate denunciation of the treaty by states submitting to it before all had signed. See *SIPRI, 1969/70*, p. 225.

[25] Only these two had signed by December 1974.

[26] A good discussion of the sea bed treaty and the militarization of the deep ocean is given in *SIPRI, 1969/70*, chap. 3. See also *SIPRI, 1972*, chap. 18.

are forbidden, but mobile submarines are permitted, even if temporarily resting on the bottom and loaded with nuclear missiles. The signatories are not limited in their actions on the bottom of their own territorial sea or the contiguous zone, fixed at twelve miles from the coast.

Nothing in the treaty interferes with any rights or claims that nations may have regarding waters or the sea bed. The duration is unlimited, but a conference for possible revisions will be held five years after its entry into force. A state can withdraw from the treaty with three months' notice, but should explain to the other countries and to the U.N. Security Council what extraordinary events it considers to have jeopardized its supreme interests. Any state has the right to inspect an installation suspected of contravening the treaty, using its own means or with the full or partial assistance of any other state. This last provision is important, since very few countries possess the advanced technology necessary for inspection of objects at considerable depths.

Although this arms control treaty does not differentiate between the continental shelf and the ocean floor, other international agreements dealing with sovereign rights and commercial exploitation distinguish the two zones in a manner likely to be very significant as the techniques of prospecting, drilling, and mining the sea bottom develop. A coastal state has the exclusive right to commercial activity on the floor of the continental shelf, where the depth is usually less than 600 feet, so that in a few years there could be many mechanical installations on the bottom, perhaps manned, perhaps serviced by nonmilitary submarines or other submersible vehicles. But the water above the bottom is international, except for the narrow territorial and contiguous strip, and the air above that also is international, although certain zones are treated as sovereign for the purposes of air defense. If increasing reliance for deterrence is placed on missile-firing submarines, and it becomes possible to service them and change crews from an underwater base in order to avoid observation and possible targeting by ballistic missiles, one can imagine a mixture of military and commercial installations on the continental shelf, all perfectly legal in the eyes of the proprietor state, but the objects of intense curiosity by commercial competitors and suspicion by other military forces. Repeated demands for widespread inspections to verify absence of weapons contravening the treaty could well lead to uncooperative behavior and real friction.

Antisubmarine detection systems fixed to the bottom are not prohibited by this treaty, nor are antishipping mines, whether moored or lying on the bottom.[27] Missile-firing submarines are such effective offensive weapons that it seems difficult to believe that a country would prefer some underwater missile launcher resting on the bottom. It is conceivable that a very large nuclear mine could be placed on the sea bottom near an enemy coastal city, with a remotely controlled firing circuit.

No nonnuclear weapon state which has signed the Nonproliferation Treaty is further limited by the Sea Bed Treaty. It is doubtful that the United Kingdom, France, or China have either the technology or the inclination to place nuclear devices on the sea bed. So the only two countries who might be prevented from deploying a new weapon system by the treaty are the United States and the U.S.S.R. But both show every indication of depending on submarines as the platforms for their ocean-launched missiles. Thus, it does not seem that the signing of the Sea Bed Treaty will cause anybody to do, or not to do, anything different from what he would have done without it. It may, however, serve to allay certain suspicions and to direct attention towards additional arms control measures or clarifications of international law in the marine environment.

For all four of these treaties, designed to impede the extension of nuclear weapons into regions where they have not yet appeared, it can be said that progress has been made in solving many of the difficult questions such as definitions, procedures, organization, and arrangements for verification, which can be put to good use in future treaties. And the signing of such agreements, limited in scope as they

[27] Unless they contained nuclear explosive. This hardly seems a likely weapon.

may be, improves the psychological climate necessary for the negotiation of more significant measures.

Preventing the Outbreak of Nuclear War

Of the anxieties felt by those responsible for the defense and security of their countries since the appearance of nuclear weapons, perhaps the sharpest has been the possibility of the sudden outbreak of nuclear war, by surprise, technical accident, or misunderstanding. The fear of a nuclear Pearl Harbor produced the suggestion that countries should permit overflights for aerial photography and possibly other types of inspection. President Eisenhower presented his "Open Skies" proposal in Geneva in 1955, and a Conference of Experts on Prevention of Surprise Attack met in 1958, without result. It has been observed that the Western delegates proposed technical solutions while the Eastern delegates discussed organization and procedure, a dichotomy not unknown when nations encounter large-scale internal difficulties involving technical, social, and political aspects. In this case, technology and a fortuitous quirk of international law allowed the aerial photography, which was illegal from aircraft without permission for overflight, to be replaced a decade later by photography from orbiting satellites, not considered to be an act of trespass.

An important step taken unilaterally rather than by mutual agreement has been to improve the security and precautions with which nuclear weapons are designed, handled, and managed inside each of the national military systems (and throughout NATO). Physical devices minimize the chances of an accidental nuclear explosion. Several dozen accidents in which nuclear weapons were involved in fires, aircraft crashes, or fall from great heights have never resulted in an unintended nuclear explosion.[28] Both physical and procedural precautions, including the "electronic lock," have been developed to a high degree in order to ensure that nuclear weapons cannot be

[28] *SIPRI, 1968/69*, pp. 259–270, lists 33 American accidents and believes that there must have been many others in the five nuclear-weapon states.

exploded without the proper authority or through misunderstandings or failure to receive orders. Stringent precautions are taken to scrutinize the psychological stability of all personnel closely concerned with the handling and control of nuclear weapons. The delegation to tactical units of the power (both physical and institutional) to release nuclear weapons is very carefully controlled.

These measures have several beneficial consequences in addition to the virtual removal of the possibility of outbreak of nuclear war by accident. They minimize the dangers of "horizontal proliferation" and of the use of nuclear weapons to a greater extent than authorized after their use has begun. The "double key" system, requiring representatives of two countries to collaborate in the firing procedure after receiving independent authorization through their national channels, provides an effective veto for each partner. And it is easy to imagine the dangers of escalation if the commander of an army division, cut off by an overwhelming enemy force using conventional weapons, and finding his troops facing annihilation on the battlefield, had the capability to release tactical nuclear weapons.

Another procedural precaution which has received the attention of novelists is the system known as "fail-safe," which ensures that a breakdown in communications must cause an attack to be abandoned rather than delivered.

Concern has been expressed lest the host of safety precautions might prevent the use of nuclear weapons at a time when their owners really wish to employ them.

A significant action to facilitate consultation between adversaries in a crisis, and possibly correct misunderstandings before irrevocable acts have been taken, was the establishment of a direct communication link between Washington and Moscow. In the aftermath of the Cuban missile crisis, the so-called "hot line" was instituted in 1963. This permitted cyphered teleprinter communication but proved technically unreliable.

Two far-reaching agreements were made in 1971: "The Agreement on Measures to Reduce the Risk of Outbreak of Nuclear War between the United States of America and the Union of Soviet Socialist Republics" and "The Agreement between the USA and the USSR on Measures to Improve the USA–USSR Direct Communications Link." The first, commonly described as the "Nuclear Accidents Agreement," dealt with notification of missile tests, nuclear accidents, or other events that could be misinterpreted with consequent risk of war; the second, often called the "Hot Line Modernization Agreement," improved the direct communications by using satellite relays. In a U.S.–U.S.S.R. agreement, signed in 1973, both parties agree to refrain from the threat or use of force against the other, and, should a risk of nuclear conflict arise, to enter into urgent consultation.[29]

It is fashionable to blame technological progress for making the world more dangerous; we have just seen, however, that technical methods are also being used to reduce the probability of accidental outbreak of war.

The proposals for the exclusion of tactical nuclear weapons from Central Europe in the 1950s, like the Rapacki plan of 1958, were largely motivated by the fear of an accidental outbreak of nuclear war. With the present safety precautions this apprehension is much less acute today, and most of the recent suggestions for denuclearization of certain areas[30] have political purposes or else are attempts to impede horizontal proliferation.

The period of the greatest danger of nuclear war by accident came in the unstable era when the retaliatory weapons were vulnerable and when each nation was tempted to poise its strategic forces "with fingers on the triggers." It has been explained earlier how the two superpowers took urgent steps to correct that situation by decreasing the vulnerability of their weapons through increasing numbers, hardness, dispersion, and mobility.

Although the two nuclear superpowers have made no progress

[29] *SIPRI, 1972*, pp. 36–37, and *SIPRI, 1974*, pp. 366–370.

[30] The Gomulka plan for Central Europe, the Kekkonen plan for Scandinavia, the Soviet plan for the Mediterranean, the plan of Sri Lanka (Ceylon) for the Indian Ocean, and several plans for Africa.

towards denuclearization, they have behaved with considerable prudence and restraint. In the crucial area of nuclear deterrence, they have been determined to establish and to preserve stability, and they have exhibited great concern as regards safety precautions and fool-proof control of nuclear weapons.

Limiting the Effects of a Nuclear War

The unilateral physical measures that might be taken to limit the effects of a nuclear war have been discussed in earlier chapters. They were called *damage limiting* and distinguished from *assured destruction*, which had as its objective the prevention of war. They depended on ballistic missile defense, air defense, antisubmarine defense, civil defense, and possibly on offensive counterforce weapons.

Another means to limit the effects of a nuclear war could be to negotiate a bilateral reduction in the strength of the strategic offensive weapons which would inflict the damage. To do this, it might be necessary to limit at the same time the strengths of defensive systems. This subject of strategic arms limitations will be discussed in the next chapter.

What steps other than altering the strength of the strategic forces can be taken to reduce the effects of a nuclear war? Possibly something can be done in the field of strategic doctrine. Even though Secretary of Defense McNamara was a supporter of Assured Destruction, he expressed in a speech at Ann Arbor, Michigan, in June 1962 the hope that civilian population would not, in fact, have to be attacked even if a nuclear war did break out. He said.:

> Principal military objectives, in the event of a nuclear war stemming from a major attack on the Alliance, should be the destruction of the enemy's military forces, not of his civilian population.
>
> The very strength and nature of the Alliance forces make it possible for us to retain, even in the face of a massive surprise attack, sufficient reserve striking power to destroy an enemy

> society if driven to it. In other words, we are giving a possible opponent the strongest imaginable incentive to refrain from striking our own cities.[31]

There have been many objections to this doctrine. Is it possible to make rules that would be kept in a nuclear war? Can military targets be destroyed without damaging cities as well, especially in densely populated areas such as Europe? And, even if the United States adopted this doctrine, would the Soviets follow it too?

In spite of the reservations regarding the "no cities" doctrine, expressed by Secretary McNamara himself as well as by his successors, it has received considerable support. In fact, it seems quite evident that both sides would have a series of targeting combinations worked out in advance, so that options are available for various contingencies. If the dreaded moment of choice has ever to be made, previously declared policy and assessments made in the peace long before the crisis will no doubt influence the decision, and both sides will probably reserve the ultimate vengeance for the last extremity. What is unpredictable is when they may judge the last extremity to have been reached.

Even if doctrines cannot be considered binding and infallible guides to actual conduct, they do serve to establish an atmosphere and indicate a most probable course of action. The same can be said for the declaration accompanying the announcements of military budgets or of new arms projects. They are analogous to unilateral declarations of intentions regarding arms control. It is probable that the American declarations to the effect that the objectives of the full Safeguard ABM system were to protect their command and control system and a fraction of their retaliatory force against a Soviet attack, and their cities against a Chinese attack, were quite genuine statements of policy and were interpreted as such by other countries. But we also know that they were disbelieved by many Americans and were believed by others to be only a temporary stage en route to a system

[31] *Survival* 4 (September–October 1962), 195.

with more ambitious objectives. In the present climate of suspicion, it is only to be expected that adversaries will consider statements or declared doctrines of their opponent as an item of intelligence to be studied and assigned a credibility dependent on collateral information. Disarmament negotiations would have a better chance in an atmosphere where national announcements could be accepted at face value.

Declarations renouncing the use of force or the first use of nuclear (or biological or chemical) weapons, or signatures of nonaggression pacts, or agreements to avoid warlike propaganda fall into the realm of psychological maneuvering. In view of the dismal record of such activities in the past, it seems doubtful if they sound very convincing even to those who formulate the undertakings. However, the wording of this type of declaration is usually more closely related to prevention than to limitation of war. They are mentioned to illustrate the genuine difficulty in determining which propositions are really fit to be treated as legitimate subjects of negotiation.

CHAPTER IX

The Strategic Arms Limitation Talks

The current literature on strategic subjects has accustomed its readers to abbreviations and acronyms. A recent addition which has stimulated even more than the usual flow of ink is SALT: the Strategic Arms Limitation Talks, bilateral secret discussions held between the United States and the Soviet Union on the possible limitations of strategic armaments. Desired for a long time, but delayed when the Warsaw Pact troops intervened in Czechoslovakia in August 1968, the first meetings opened officially in Helsinki in November 1969. Six subsequent sessions were held alternately in Vienna and Helsinki before the first accords were signed in May 1972 during President Nixon's visit to Moscow. These accords are commonly given the label "SALT I," with subsequent negotiations being assumed to be directed towards further agreements called "SALT II."

Reasons for the Talks

There are a number of reasons to explain the interest in these negotiations, carried on by the two superpowers but closely watched by the rest of the international community. One reason is economic: between them since 1950 the United States and the U.S.S.R. have spent many hundreds of billions of dollars to establish and maintain the nuclear balance.[1] Another reason is to encourage nonnuclear

[1] *Strategic Survey, 1970*, p. 12. The Fiscal Year 1973 program for the United States called for $7.4 million on strategic forces specifically—9.1 percent of the

weapon states to remain in that category. But most important, probably, is apprehension lest developing technology stimulate each of the two to new weapons programs, each fearing that the present state of mutual stable deterrence may be disturbed in favor of the other. The two possible outcomes of such competitive programs are either that stability and even possibly deterrence could be lost, with great consequent danger, or (more probably) that actions would be neutralized by reactions so that mutual stable deterrence would be retained, which amounts to spending a lot of money to maintain the status quo. If the status quo can be retained more safely and cheaply by agreeing not to build expensive new systems which would simply neutralize each other, then it would be in the mutual interest of each competitor to make such an agreement. If the situation, considering all the factors of technology, intelligence, and economics, is such that any action by one side which threatens to give it a first-strike capability will be discerned by the other, who will have the time and the means necessary to offset the action, then the two might do better to confirm to each other the validity of such a situation and to cooperate rather than compete when it would be to their mutual advantage.

Some see in these negotiations additional proof of existing collusion between the two superpowers in a master plan to share the world in agreed zones of influence, and to counter the activities of potential competitors, such as China. Others believe that the SALT constitute the beginning of an institution which will permit a permanent dialogue, through which the two will make each other aware of their reciprocal intentions and achieve a degree of arms control to an

---

total defense budget. Since 1966 the average value of this item has been about $7.5 billion current dollars, 10 percent of the total. The belief that defense expenditures are dominated by the costs of strategic missiles and antimissiles is not correct. However, in addition to the sum budgeted for strategic forces specifically, it should be recognized that a share of other items, such as research and development, central supply and maintenance, training, medical and other general personnel activities, and administration, go for the support of strategic forces. This could increase the gross figure by a factor as large as 2.5.

extent that could not have been foreseen in the early and very uncooperative years just after World War II.

In this chapter we shall not pursue the possible reasons for undertaking the SALT or the possible consequences that may follow from the talks beyond the area indicated by the title—that is, the limitation of strategic arms.[2] Assured preservation of a stable strategic balance, hopefully without excessive cost, is probably the principal reason for the interest in SALT shown by both partners, with their concern properly heightened by the imminent effects of multiple warheads and ABM systems.

Planners uneasy over the possible vulnerability of their retaliatory weapons are disinterring once-abandoned schemes for mobile missiles mounted on railways cars, road vehicles, canal barges, or ships. For improved protection, missiles could be kept in galleries excavated into the sides of mountains, from which they could be rolled out to the entrance for a delayed launching. Other schemes favor concealment underwater, whether in submarines, on the sea bottom, or beneath the surface of lakes. Another group supports the procurement of a new high-performance long-range manned bomber. The relative merits of these various systems are often judged with marked institutional bias, depending on whether their proprietors would be the air force, navy, or army.

Although none of the offensive systems just listed is operational or in an approved program today, they all have their proponents with plans prepared. And, perhaps a generation further along in technological sophistication, other concepts are the subjects of current research.

[2] The significance is likely to extend far beyond the actual changes in deployment of strategic weapons. John Newhouse, *Cold Dawn: The Story of SALT* (New York: Holt, Rinehart & Winston, 1973); W. R. Kintner and R. L. Pfaltzgraff, Jr., eds., *SALT: Implications for Arms Control in the 1970s* (Pittsburgh: University of Pittsburgh Press, 1973); M. Willrich and J. B. Rhinelander, eds., *SALT: The Moscow Agreements and Beyond* (New York: The Free Press, 1974); Morton A. Kaplan, *SALT: Problems and Prospects* (Morristown, N.J.: General Learning Press, 1973).

Trident, the improved SSBN with very long-range SLBMs, a logical extension to the brilliantly successful series of ballistic missile-firing nuclear-powered submarines, is being expedited in the present American program, and will in its day outrange the Soviet Delta class with its SS-N-8 missile.

With ICBMs, the qualitative race shows the U.S. near the end of a program to fit multiple warheads,[3] and now concentrating on improved accuracy, penetration aids, and the new MX. The U.S.S.R. is bringing in a family of much-improved ICBMs, with large throw-weights and MIRV. Both nations are working to reduce silo vulnerability, and may develop mobile ICBMs.

It is possible that strategic cruise missiles, which can be made very accurate, and could be launched by a land vehicle, a surface ship, a submerged submarine, or an aircraft, may be built to supplement the ballistic missile force.[4]

Of nearly comparable importance are the strategic defensive systems, and much has been said already concerning ballistic missile defense. But a significant change in the strength of any one of the three offensive or four defensive systems has its effect on the strategic balance and might or might not jeopardize stability.

Thus, a very large number of considerations enter into the SALT. But some of them may not be open to discussion at all, and more may not be negotiable. A great deal of effort must have been expended during the first meetings simply to identify what topics could profitably be discussed and which were eligible for negotiation.

As the next step in our analysis of SALT, it will be useful to consider what forms of agreement might be possible concerning the

[3] The U.S. now has about 7600 separate reentry vehicles, as against the Soviets' 2600. But Secretary Schlesinger is concerned about the possibility of 7000–8000 large-yield Soviet reentry vehicles, as a counterforce threat. See D. R. Westervelt, *op. cit.*, pp. 689–705.

[4] Kosta Tsipis, "The Long-Range Cruise Missile," *Bulletin of the Atomic Scientists* 31 (April 1975), 14–26, and *SIPRI, 1975*, chap. 11.

limitation of strategic armaments and how the parties might be able to assess their liberty of action in coming to accords that would protect their vital interests.

The Objective and the Nature of the Negotiations

Any agreement to negotiate the limitation of strategic arms will immediately raise many questions. Can one define which armaments are strategic? Are the limitations to apply to all armaments or only certain categories? Are defensive armaments on the same basis as offensive? Are the limitations to be on existing or on future weapons? Is absolute reciprocity demanded, or can a limitation in one category be equated to a corresponding limitation in another; if so, how is the correspondence to be established? How much freedom of choice is to be left within the terms of the agreement?

Attempts to define strategic arms have exposed some serious differences. The U.S.S.R. has a large number of IRBMs and MRBMs able to destroy almost any target in western Europe but incapable of reaching the United States.[5] The Americans have no weapons of this type, but they have a substantial force of nuclear-armed carrier-based aviation for which there is no Soviet counterpart. Both NATO and the WPO possess tactical aircraft able to reach any point in Europe with nuclear weapons, but in a bilateral negotiation the Soviets can claim that these weapons constitute a strategic threat to the homeland of the U.S.S.R. but not of the United States.

According to the joint Soviet-American communiqué of May 20, 1971,[6] it appeared that efforts were to be concentrated on the limitation of defensive armaments. This could well have been the result of failure to agree on the categories of offensive weapons to be considered as strategic and therefore candidates for negotiation. Fixed defensive weapons deployed in the two homelands clearly do fall within the category of strategic defensive systems, although there

[5] IRBMs or MRBMs in eastern Siberia could reach Alaska but no other state of the union.

[6] See *SIPRI, 1972*, p. 31.

is room for argument over the type of interceptor aircraft which could be used elsewhere in other roles, or over antisubmarine forces deployed in international waters and capable of other missions. However, in the end it did prove possible to include long-range offensive weapons in the first accord.

There is another route which could lead to agreed reductions in the number of offensive weapons, both missiles and aircraft, based in Europe. If they cannot be discussed under the heading of strategic arms at the SALT, perhaps they can be included in negotiations for mutual and balanced force reductions (MBFR) in Europe. These latter negotiations would, of course, include the allies of the two superpowers. But there must be a very close linkage between the bilateral SALT discussions and any multilateral or NATO/WPO approaches to MBFR. A weapon system excluded from one set of negotiations might be introduced into the other.

Pandora's Box

There are two versions of the Greek legend of Pandora's box. Pandora, the first woman, was sent from heaven and arrived on earth with a box. According to one version, the box contained all kinds of misery and evil, which subsequently escaped to spread everywhere when the box was opened. The lid was closed in time to imprison only Hope. In the other version the box contained not evils but blessings, which would have been preserved for the human race had they not been lost through man's opening the box, out of insatiable curiosity.

Opinions regarding strategic armaments correspond to both versions of the legend. Perhaps strategic weapons are unmitigated evils, released for the destruction of mankind, who would have been better off had they been imprisoned in their box forever. Or perhaps they have brought us the blessing of mutual stable deterrence, and we would be better to let well enough alone rather than lose their benefit through curiosity and tampering.

The reader can choose his legend according to his preference. However, we have been incautious enough to portray in Figure 44

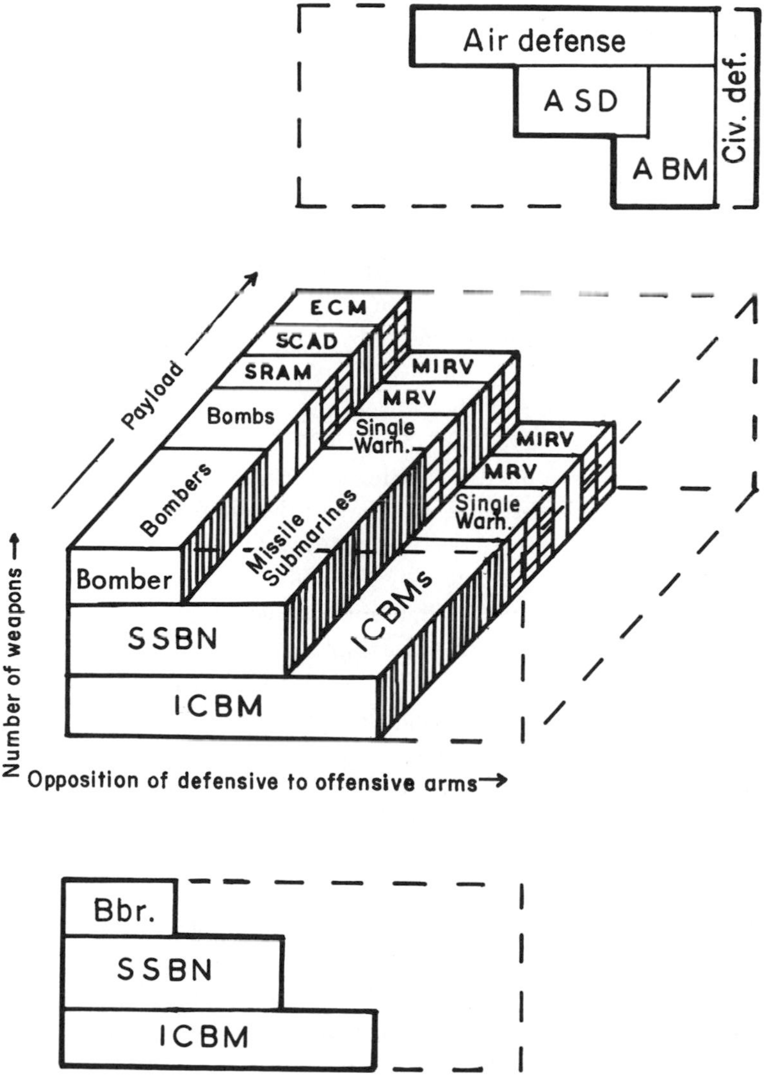

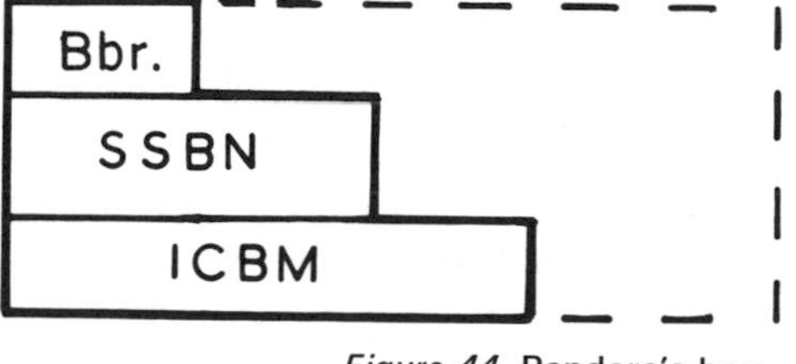

Figure 44. Pandora's box

the contents of Pandora's box. The box has three dimensions, which could be interpreted as dimensions in which arms limitations could be negotiated. They are numbers of weapons (the vertical depth of the box), opposition between defensive and offensive systems (width from left to right), and payload carried by offensive weapon carriers (length of box looking into the paper). Inside the box are the main offensive weapon carriers (bombers, ballistic-missile submarines, and ICBMs) and the various loads they can transport (bombers with bombs, short-range attack missiles, subsonic cruise armed decoys, and electronic countermeasures; submarines and ICBMs, able to deliver single warheads, MRVs, or MIRVs). One could add other penetration aids such as missile decoys.

Consider the vertical dimension first, representing number of weapons. In the case of the Soviets the total number of weapon carriers has been increasing, for ICBMs and SSBNs if not for bombers.[7] For the United States the numbers of ICBMs and SSBNs has remained constant since 1967, while the number of long-range bombers has been slowly decreasing (from 697 in 1967 to 432 in 1975, according to statements by the current secretary of defense). Perhaps the simplest type of limitation would be on the number of weapon carriers—that is, on the depth of the box.

For each offensive system there are offsetting defensive systems. These can be considered to occupy the righthand portion of Pandora's box, in the same horizontal layer as the corresponding offensive system. The two cross sections of the ends of the box show the three offensive systems (on the bottom cross section) and the four defensive systems (on the top one). Note that the air defense opposes bombers only, antisubmarine defense opposes submarines only, ABM opposes both ICBMs and SLBMs, and civil defense opposes all three offensive systems. An agreement to limit offensive weapons only could be followed by a rapid and expensive buildup in the offsetting defensive systems, producing a corresponding reduction in the effective strength of the offensive systems. More dangerously, such developments

[7] See Figures 41 and 42.

could jeopardize stability, or even deterrence, and eventually return the strategic situation to the prenuclear era where power would lie with the large armies. The alternative is to apply limitations to defensive as well as offensive systems—in other words, to limit the width of the box.

Finally, the length of the box takes account of the increased effectiveness that can be obtained from a given number of carrier vehicles if the payload is increased or otherwise improved. In this dimension the United States has made the same number of bombers and submarines considerably more effective, through changes such as the improvement of bomber weapons, replacement of Polaris by Poseidon, and the fitting of MIRV. If a limitation were on numbers of weapon carriers only, a feverish competition could develop in the various types of payload such as SRAM, SCAD, ECM, MIRV, and MARV,[8] perhaps accompanied by increased lifting capacity of the carriers.

Possible Types of Limitation

There are a large number of permutations and combinations of possible formulas for limitation.[9] Four basic formulas are

(1) a freeze at the present situation;
(2) separate quantitative limitations for each type of weapon (both offensive and defensive);
(3) an overall quantitative limitation on total strength, with freedom to alter the distribution within the agreed total;
(4) qualitative limitations on certain varieties of weapons, accessories, or possibly on development or testing of specific weapons.

The quantitative limitations could be on numbers of weapons, or numbers of weapon carriers. However, since size and payload are important measures of strength, the limitation could be set by over-

[8] See the article by G. W. Rathjens and G. B. Kistiakowski, "The Limitation of Strategic Arms," *Scientific American* 222 (January 1970), 19–29.

[9] An excellent article on this subject is by Herbert Scoville, Jr., "The Limitation of Offensive Weapons," *Scientific American* 224 (January 1971), 15–25.

all weight or by total payload rather than numbers.[10] This can be applied to bombers as well as missiles. When applied to missiles one encounters terms such as "all-up weight" for the gross weight on the launching pad and "throw-weight" for the total mass that can be delivered over the target, whether explosive warhead or penetration aid. Weight is certainly related to effectiveness for offensive weapons, but it does not have the same significance for the defense.

A simple form of arms control would be to freeze deployments at their present level. However, unless near parity existed, either side could complain that inequalities were being perpetuated. In fact, the scores are unequal in every category.[11]

The Soviets lead in both numbers and throw-weight[12] of ICBMs but the Americans have the advantage in long-range bombers. The Soviet momentum in their buildup of SSBNs will soon be matched, qualitatively if not quantitatively, by the American Trident program, and it is the United States which has the momentum in the deployment of MIRV. If a freeze included defensive weapons, neither power would have a significant level of BMD, the Soviets would have the stronger air and civil defense, and the Americans the better antisubmarine defense.

Separate quantitative limits on the various types of weapons could permit an approach towards parity; they could also be used to prevent the nullification of offense by defense.

A limitation of the total number of weapons in several categories can allow freedom to interchange between types as long as the total

[10] There is a precedent for this in the naval disarmament treaties between the wars. For example, the Washington Treaty of 1922 set a maximum permitted displacement for battleships at 35,000 tons, as well as a maximum permitted caliber of guns (16 inches). The London Naval Treaty set total tonnage limits on cruisers, destroyers, and submarines. Philip Noel-Baker, *The Arms Race* (London: Atlantic Books, 1958), pp. 444–451.

[11] The reader is referred to Table 2 (p. 53), Table 3 (p. 55), and Table 5 (p. 118), for comparisons.

[12] *Strategic Survey, 1974,* p. 48, puts the Soviet advantage in overall payload at over 4:1, and contrasts the throw-weight of 16–20,000 lb. for SS-18 and 4500–6000 lb. for SS-19 with 2000 lb. for Minuteman 3. Expected Soviet replacements will give them 10 million pounds as compared to 2 million for the U.S. Michael Nacht, "The Vladivostok

is not exceeded. It could, for example, allow the total phasing out of bomber aircraft or of land-based missiles, with a compensating increase in a sea-based force, which might be regarded by both sides as a guarantee of retaliation without any threat of increased first-strike potential.

Even if the significant goal is to maintain mutual stable deterrence rather than precise "parity" in each category, factors of psychology and prestige can be very important in determining which type of agreement may prove acceptable. The least objection would seem to attach to an accord for equal numerical ceilings for each side in each category of weapons. However, this would allow a "qualitative arms race" as improved designs were achieved. Under the third type of limitation in which the proportions of weapons of different types could be altered as long as the total stayed within the limit, there is even more room for qualitative competition. If, for example, a "technological breakthrough" offered the opportunity to improve overall strength by increasing the number of weapons of one type with corresponding reduction elsewhere, great programs to produce the improved type of weapon could follow on both sides.

Important Considerations for the United States and the U.S.S.R.

The principal concern of each of the parties, with or without an agreement, is that his opponent should not be attempting to acquire a first-strike capability. Defensive as well as offensive improvements could indicate such an attempt, although an ABM system sited only for the protection of missile silos should not give rise to fears of intentions to strike first. There would be little point in defending empty silos after the missiles had been launched.[13] But antisubmarine defense and air defense, which cannot be identified with protection of cities only or weapons only, and ABM defense of cities would form a necessary part of the arsenal of a country planning a first strike, so that a substantial strengthening of these systems could be

Accord and American Technological Options," *Survival* 17 (May/June 1975), 108.

[13] See W. K. H. Panofsky, "Roots of the Strategic Arms Race: Ambiguity and Ignorance," *Bulletin of the Atomic Scientists* 27 (June 1971), 20.

interpreted as a preparation so to do. However, as we have already seen, the antisubmarine units of NATO are part of naval forces with roles other than strategic defense against the SSBN, and the air defense forces of the Soviet Union oppose bombers based in Europe as well as in the United States, so that the considerations regarding their limitation or reduction would go beyond the domain of SALT. Moreover, while the United States and the Soviet Union may feel that they have sufficient offensive strength to deter each other and China too, they may be unwilling to weaken their defensive strength against the appearance of Chinese strategic offensive weapons.[14] This would also apply to Soviet defense against bombers and missiles of less than intercontinental range.

In the realm of strategic offensive weapons the most vital and difficult negotiations are likely to center on MIRV—unless, of course, the subject proves too delicate for discussion. These multiple warheads are currently moving through the stages of development, test, evaluation, and deployment. It is already too late to prevent the deployment, but because of the vital significance of accuracy, which can be improved only through further research, development, and testing, a suspension of these activities could prevent an important increase in the destabilizing counterforce capability of MIRV.

The United States is well in the lead with multiple-warhead technology and is completing its program to put MIRV into Minuteman 3 and Poseidon. However, it has made clear public statements that these weapons are for counter-city retaliation and not counterforce first strike. For example, in December 1969 President Nixon said there was no current United States program to develop a hard-target MIRV capability.[15] And in June 1970, in a hearing before the subcommittee on Arms Control, International Law and Organization of the Committee on Foreign Relations of the U.S. Senate, Dr. John S. Foster, Jr., Director of Defense Research and Engineering, participated in the following exchange:

[14] Harry Gelber, "China and SALT," *Survival* 12 (April 1970), 122–126.

[15] *SIPRI, 1969/70*, p. 56.

SENATOR COOPER: I understand the defense which has been made both for the deployment of MIRV and the ABM. But you are assuming, of course, that the Soviets will believe that our intentions are perfect. I would just ask you this question. Isn't it possible for the United States with all its technology to develop an accuracy, better accuracy, both in our Minuteman, Polaris, and Poseidon missiles? We have that capability, do we not?

DR. FOSTER: Senator Cooper, we do not have that capability, not in being; but it is technologically feasible, in my opinion, for the United States to develop sufficient accuracy that with multiple vehicles sometime in the future we would be able to attack silos in the Soviet Union.

However, we had a program of investigation along these lines and last year I canceled it. My purpose was to make it absolutely clear to the Congress and, hopefully, to the Soviet Union, that it is not the policy of the United States to deny the Soviet Union their deterrent capability.

SENATOR COOPER: But you say we could develop the accuracy and if that accuracy could be developed it could be a threat to their intercontinental ballistic missile too.

DR. FOSTER: Yes, sir, that is correct. It would be some time in the future, but I believe it is possible.[16]

Against these statements one can contrast two by General John D. Ryan, Chief of Staff of the U.S. Air Force. He told a congressional committee in October 1969 that "We have a program we are pushing to increase the yield of our warheads and decrease the circular error probable so that we have what we call a hard-target killer, which we do not have in the inventory at the present time." This may have been the program canceled by Dr. Foster. But in 1970 General Ryan said of the new MIRV warheads being introduced into Minuteman: "This missile with a multiple independently targetable reentry

[16] *Hearings on ABM, MIRV, SALT, and the Nuclear Arms Race*, 1970, pp. 509–510.

vehicle will be our best means of destroying time-urgent targets like the long-range weapons of the enemy."[17]

We saw in Chapter II how sensitive was the probability of destruction of a small hard target to the accuracy of the warhead. To return for a moment to Figure 8, assume that the yield of one warhead will be less than 200 KT and that a probability of destruction above 80 percent is required. It is evident that a CEP of 0.2 nm is quite inadequate, whereas a CEP of 0.1 nm would suffice for yields above 100 KT, and precision only a little better than 0.1 nm would make yields well below 50 KT sufficient.

The accumulated knowledge regarding nuclear bombs is almost certainly adequate to allow design, fabrication, and deployment of warheads of yields anywhere in the range from 1 to 200 KT without the need for testing. But it seems likely that the improvement of accuracy to a degree approaching 0.1 nm would represent an advance beyond present capabilities as well as an extensive program of testing and evaluation prior to deployment.

The U.S.S.R. has developed MIRV for at least three ICBMs.[18] However, theirs is almost certainly less advanced than the American program, so that the U.S.S.R. would feel at a disadvantage if a freeze included development and testing. The U.S.S.R. does hold one great advantage, however, in the form of 313 silos for heavy launchers, mostly occupied by SS-9 missiles but now receiving SS-18s.[19]

[17] Panofsky, *op. cit.*, p. 19. On the other hand, Dr. Schlesinger stated that "This improved Minuteman 3 system would be heavily dependent upon accuracy for its hard-target kill capability. Consequently, even a small degradation in accuracy would greatly reduce its effectiveness in that role. The Minuteman 3, therefore, is not a system that we would pursue if we were interested in developing a disarming first-strike capability." *Statement of Secretary Schlesinger, 1975*, pp. II–20–21.

[18] These are SS-17 (with 4 MIRV), one version of SS-18 (with 6 or 8), and SS-19 (with 6). *Statement of Secretary Schlesinger, 1975*, pp. II–12–15. Dr. Schlesinger ascribes three main objectives to this "most impressive Soviet ICBM program"—expanded target coverage (with MIRVs), improved pre-launch survivability (with new hard-silo designs), and the attainment of a significant hard-target kill capability. He says that the attainment of the last objective would depend upon the accuracy achievable with the SS-18 and the SS-19, and believes that the CEPs of both could be improved significantly.

[19] At a Pentagon news conference on June 20, 1975, Dr. Schlesinger announced that

If one assumes that research, development, and testing to improve accuracy will proceed in the absence of a formal agreement to desist, then the threat to stability will increase with time, since it is probably true that the accuracy of multiple warheads is not sufficient to constitute a serious counterforce threat today.

Multiple warheads of comparatively low accuracy (including MRV) can even be regarded as having a stabilizing influence. To quote Secretary Laird:

> We are continuing the program to deploy MIRVs in our Minuteman and Poseidon missiles. We consider this program essential to preserve the credibility of U.S. deterrent forces when faced with the growing Soviet strategic threat. The MIRV program will provide a number of small, independently targetable warheads on a single missile. Should part of our missile force be unexpectedly and severely degraded by Soviet preemptive actions, the increased number of warheads provided by the remaining MIRV missiles will insure that we have enough warheads to attack the essential soft urban/industrial targets in the Soviet Union. At the same time, the MIRV program gives us increased confidence in our ability to penetrate Soviet ABM defenses, even if part of our missile force were destroyed.[20]

And Dr. Foster testified that the increased number of warheads, carrying a smaller total megatonnage, would not increase the effective military, industrial, and urban damage beyond the level that would be inflicted by single warheads in the absense of ABM defense.[16] In other words, MIRV is there to penetrate defenses rather than to increase damage.

Because it may be possible to avert the dangers of highly accurate MIRV by stopping the testing programs, many writers[21] have urged

10 SS-17s, 10 SS-18s, and 50 SS-19s were already deployed. It is likely that only SS-18 will need to be put in the "heavy launcher" silos.

[20] *Statement of Secretary Laird, 1971*, pp. 66–67.

[21] See, for example, Leo Sartori, "The Myth of MIRV," *Saturday Review* (New York), August 30, 1969, reprinted in *Survival* 11 (December 1969), 382–390; A. de Volpi, "MIRV—Gorgon Medusa of the Nuclear Age," *Bulletin of the*

that this be placed first on the agenda of SALT, and it was the subject of a resolution in the U.S. Senate in 1969.

In the case of the other offensive weapon carriers, bombers and submarines, obsolescence would be an important factor in national attitudes towards limitation. Both of the bomber forces are composed of very old aircraft. It is probable that if either country built a new heavy bomber, its cost and performance would exceed those of the older type by substantial margins, and replacement might be at a lower ratio than one-for-one, both by number and by total weight. Hence an agreement to remain at the present level would not constrain plans for qualitative improvement. In fact, an agreement to remain within a total overall level for offensive (or for all) weapons would allow some numerical strength to be converted away from the bomber order of battle, even if a new bomber were constructed.

With submarines it can almost be said that diesel-powered boats are obsolescent en masse. The Americans have ceased to build them. However, in 1975 the Soviets still had about 210 in service and the Americans eleven.[22] Consequently, an agreement to limit numbers of submarines would allow replacement of conventional boats by new nuclear-powered ones, and it is likely that each plans to do this anyway, probably at a ratio less than one-for-one. A limitation on total tonnage could be more constraining, since the nuclear submarines usually have several times the displacement of a diesel boat.[23] It is possible, of course, that a limit could be applied to types of

---

Atomic Scientists 26 (January 1970); Joshua Lederberg, "A Freeze on Missile Testing," *Bulletin of the Atomic Scientists* 27 (March 1971); and the papers already cited by Rathjens and Kistiakowsky, H. Scoville, Jr., and W. K. H. Panofsky.

[22] Down from 426 and 153 respectively in 1960. The 1975 figures are from *The Military Balance, 1975–76,* pp. 6, 9; 1960 figures are from *SIPRI, 1969/70,* p. 324.

[23] The Soviet Y-class SSBN displaces 7300 tons on the surface. The conventional W-class, the last of which was completed in 1958, displaces only 1100 tons. However, with 66 still in service, they represent a considerable total tonnage. See *Proceedings of the U.S. Naval Institute* 97 (August 1971), 64 and 78. Also, note that the Trident is expected to gross over twice the tonnage of the Polaris/Poseidon boats.

submarines, but arguments over strategic categories could prove difficult to solve. An SSBN is clearly for strategic offense, and an SSK, especially if nuclear-powered, is certainly well suited for defense against the SSBN. But the other types of submarines (SSGN, SSG, SS, ...) can be used in many ways. The most significant categories would be SSBNs or all nuclear-powered submarines, since these are by far both the most effective and the newest.

Possibilities of Verification

We have already discussed the importance and the difficulties of verifying that the terms of agreements are being kept. The means by which countries may be able to ascertain what others are doing can be categorized as open, such as legal visits, activities of newspaper and radio correspondents, exchanges through diplomatic channels, and so on, which require, if not the active cooperation, at least the acquiescence of the other party; international, such as the inspection of nuclear reactor installations by IAEA officials to ensure that fissile material is not being diverted to weapon production, which requires that two or more countries agree to an inspection procedure and allow it to be carried out; and national unilateral, feasible with or without the acquiescence of the party observed, which can be covert, such as espionage, decoding of cyphered radio messages, or illegal aerial photography, but can also include legal gathering of intelligence, such as scrutiny of published material or collection of air samples for the monitoring of radioactivity. Detection and localization of underground nuclear explosions is partly national and partly international, since the data obtained by national seismograph stations in many countries need to be combined in order to yield the most reliable information.

There is an asymmetry between East and West, since the more secretive East makes gathering of information difficult, whether by open or by secret means. And in the West today, with constant discussion and criticism of government programs and a strong anti-military faction, a national contravention of a publicly agreed arms control measure would almost certainly be detected and denounced by citizens of the country committing the breach.

Although much discussed in disarmament conferences, very little international inspection has ever been allowed, except by the powerless losers in the aftermath of a war.[24]

One extraordinary series of changes has occurred as a result of technical progress in reconnaissance vehicles and high-altitude photography. Because cameras are very light, specially designed high-altitude reconnaissance aircraft could usually climb above the maximum altitude attainable by armed fighter aircraft. Being small and flying far above the usual altitudes, they might even escape radar detection. Consequently, in wartime it became normal to expect excellent photo coverage of enemy territory, the main obstacle being the weather rather than the defenses. In peacetime, such activity constitutes an illegal trespass, since the airspace above a country is part of its sovereign territory. However, if the opponent is unable to detect the aircraft and cannot intercept it, it may be possible to continue the activity without punishment. We cannot know how much is still carried out today, but two spectacular examples which came to public knowledge were the American U-2, shot down over the Soviet Union in 1960 by a high-performance surface-to-air missile, and the American reconnaissance flights over Cuba in 1962, which revealed the buildup of Soviet IRBMs in that island. The American "Open Skies" proposal of 1955 would have permitted overflights for photography by international agreement, perhaps limited to certain areas, although the purpose in this case was to have been prevention of surprise attack rather than detection of violations of a disarmament treaty.

The development of earth satellites has altered the situation.[25] Since their minimum orbital altitude is about 100 nm, the quality of

[24] By the Treaty of Versailles the Western allies had a mission of 400 officers in Germany with wide powers to enforce the continuing disarmament of that country. See Philip Noel-Baker, *op. cit.*, pp. 534–537.

[25] See Philip J. Klass, *Secret Sentries in Space* (New York: Random House, 1971). Also Ted Greenwood, "Reconnaissance and Arms Control," *Scientific American* 228 (Feb. 1973), 14–25, *SIPRI, 1973,* pp. 60–75, and *SIPRI, 1975,* chap. 13.

their photographs cannot match the product of the best aircraft cameras at an altitude of 10 nm, and an aircraft is a much better platform for a powerful radar. But the area swept per hour by a satellite is greater by a factor of the order of several hundred, and its overflight of foreign territory contravenes no law.

Thus the situation today regarding verification of agreements concerning strategic weapons, which form a far less conspicuous force than armies or surface warships, is that open means are of uncertain value, probably of little value for observation of Eastern forces; national unilateral means are effective for some categories, especially those detectable by satellite photography; and international means have never really been tried.

The excavation of an underground missile silo represents a considerable project, and it seems that the process can be identified by satellite photography. However, the camera cannot see inside the silo, and the replacement of one missile by another, or of a single warhead by multiple warheads, would not be detected, unless, of course, the silo had to be reexcavated and rebuilt to accept a larger rocket. Even a visit into the silo would not reveal the number of warheads unless the cover of the nose cone was removed.

It is probable that satellite photography can yield considerable, but less than complete information regarding types and deployment of aircraft, both offensive and defensive, but virtually nothing regarding their armament. Better photographs of ships and submarines are likely to be obtained by aircraft than by satellites, although little can be learned about the armament of a submarine from an external photograph. Large fixed defensive installations such as radars, ABM, or SAM batteries, should be easily detectable by satellites.

Satellite detection suffers from the limitation that any one satellite without maneuvering capability and in low earth orbit cannot cross over a given point on the earth's surface more than twice a day,[26] and

[26] Except for points on the equator. In practice, it is unlikely to come closer than a few hundred miles from any given point in a temperate latitude, except on intermittent occasions several times a week.

the schedule cannot be altered once the satellite is launched. To get good pictures, the ground must be in clear sunlight. It follows that a series of photographs of a particular point (such as a missile complex or an air or a naval base) can be obtained at intervals, and a pattern of change or of routine activity determined. But the ability to count mobile objects could be very poor (except perhaps to establish that there were *some* of them in existence). This provides one good reason to agree on complete prohibition of mobile land-based ICBMs.

A very effective means of avoiding detection by overhead photography is simply to place the objects under a roof. Photography might allow an accurate count of the number of missile launchers, but any number of additional "refire" missiles, able to use the same launcher, could be stored nearby under cover.[27]

Four types of limitation have been discussed: numbers, gross weight, weight of payload, and type of payload. Satellite photography would best be able to verify numbers. It might be able to indicate a change of type, which could possibly be related to other information to make an estimate of a change in gross weight. Payload can be related to gross weight by the mathematics of rocket or aircraft design. If an agreement were to be made on gross weight or on payload, there would be greater need for verification by inspection than if the agreement were on numbers alone. But if the agreement were on types of payload (such as MIRV, or nuclear as opposed to conventional explosive), verification would require not simply external inspection but the right to look inside the weapons.

Certain kinds of weapons testing can be monitored by national unilateral means. This problem has been discussed in Chapter VIII in connection with nuclear test explosions. Endless negotiations have produced no agreement on a limited number of inspection visits, but

[27] Note the express prohibition in the ABM treaty against development, testing, or deployment of ABM launchers for launching more than one interceptor missile at a time, against provision of such a capability, and against development, test, and deployment of automatic, semiautomatic, or other similar systems for rapid reload of ABM launchers. Also the undertaking not to use deliberate concealment to impede verification.

it now seems that the only nuclear tests which might escape detection by the instruments of other nations would be very small underground explosions. However, in the case of SALT, the type of testing most likely to form the subject of negotiation would be flight trials of multiple warheads, almost certainly without nuclear explosions. If the trial is on a full-scale intercontinental range, it may be necessary to declare an impact area in the ocean and deploy a number of instrumented ships. In any case, there is a good opportunity for other countries to obtain partial information of the test by national means. If there were a treaty forbidding the testing of multiple warheads, the best way to allay suspicions of violations would be to cease all missile trials at intercontinental ranges, or, failing this, to give advance notice of coming trials and virtually invite monitoring by other countries in order that they satisfy themselves that no test of multiple warheads was involved. Even without any agreement, a country which was, in fact, not attempting to improve the accuracy of its missiles, whether with single or multiple warheads, or to introduce any other significant improvement, but which nevertheless wished to continue with firing trials (perhaps to check reliability of its standard missiles, or simply for training purposes), could greatly reduce the danger of misinterpretation and unnecessary reaction by giving other countries the opportunity to monitor the test.[28]

The First SALT Agreements on Nuclear Weapons

The first important agreements on the limitations of strategic nuclear weapons were signed in Moscow on May 26, 1972, near the end of President Nixon's visit to the U.S.S.R.[29] They were recorded in three separate documents:

(a) an interim executive agreement to limit offensive armaments,

[28] See Ted Greenwood, "Reconnaissance, Surveillance, and Arms Control," *Adelphi Paper No. 88* (London: The International Institute for Strategic Studies, 1972), pp. 20–23.

[29] The text is reproduced in *SALT: The Moscow Agreement and Beyond,* Mason Willrich and J. B. Rhinelander, eds. (New York: The Free Press, 1974).

(b) a protocol to (a),[30]
(c) a treaty to limit the deployment of ABM systems.

The Limitations on Offensive Weapons

The principal agreements were to limit ICBMs, SSBNs, and SLBMs to the numbers operational or under construction in mid-1972. It was a freeze on numbers, by category. However, modernization and replacement are permitted, as well as a certain freedom to convert from one type of weapon to another. MRBMs and IRBMs cannot be replaced by ICBMs or SLBMs, and the number of "heavy ICBMs" cannot be increased,[31] but older ICBMs such as Titan, SS-7, and SS-8, and SLBMs such as Serb on older submarines can be replaced by SLBMs.

The actual numbers involved are listed in the following table:

	ICBMs		Modern	SLBMs	
	Older	Modern	SSBNs	Replacement level	Maximum
U.S.A.	54	1000	44	656	710
U.S.S.R.	210	1408	62	740	950

The United States may add three Trident SSBNs to their present total of 41 Polaris/Poseidon boats, but to arm them with SLBMs and still retain the 656 Polaris/Poseidon missiles, they would need to dismantle Titan 2 ICBMs. Similarly, the Soviets can exceed 740 SLBMs only by scrapping some of their 210 SS-7 or SS-8 ICBMs.

No mention was made of mobile land-based launchers, the number of warheads, nor of bomber aircraft.

Verification is to be by "national technical means," and neither party is to interfere with the verification or to resort to measures of concealment.

30 A protocol adds precise interpretation rather than establishing principles.

31 The only modern launchers categorized as "heavy" are the Soviet SS-9s and new large silos, believed to total 313 in all. Presumably SS-18 will be heavy. No clear common definition was agreed.

The agreement was for a period of five years, unless superseded by a more comprehensive agreement, but either party can withdraw on six months' notice should it decide that its supreme interests are jeopardized by extraordinary events.

The Treaty on ABM Systems

Each party was permitted to deploy two ABM systems, contained within circular areas of radius 81 nm. One area was to contain the national capital and the other an area of ICBM deployment, the two to be separated by at least 700 nm. Each area could have 100 ABM launchers and 100 ABM interceptor missiles. In the capital area the number of radar complexes is limited to six, while in the ICBM area there can be only two large phased array ABM radars with a specified maximum potential [32] and eighteen smaller ABM radars.

Early-warning radars are allowed only at the periphery of national territory, facing outward, and other radars and missiles such as those designed for antibomber defense are not to be given ABM capabilities. Development, testing, and modernization of components of fixed land-based ABM systems are permitted, but development is prohibited of components of sea-based, air-based, space-based, or mobile land-based systems or of multiple ABM launchers. No deployment or transfer of ABM system components beyond national territory is allowed.

The provisions for verification are the same as for offensive weapons.

The treaty, which has already been ratified by both the U.S. and the U.S.S.R., is of unlimited duration but is subject to review at five-year intervals. Withdrawal is possible on the same terms as for the offensive weapons.

No mention is made of antibomber defense, antisubmarine defense, or civil defense.

[32] The "potential" of a radar, defined as the product of power × antenna area, measures its capability for the rapid detection of small distant targets.

The only known program which was under way but became prohibited by the SALT I agreements was the construction of two Safeguard ABM complexes around American Minuteman silos. The agreement permitted only one such complex. Since the construction at Grand Forks was much farther advanced than at Malmstrom, the latter was abandoned.

Negotiations Subsequent to SALT I

The SALT I agreements were ratified by the U.S. Congress during the summer of 1972, although with an amendment (initiated by Senator Jackson) that no future agreement should set lower force levels for the U.S. than for the U.S.S.R. The agreement and the treaty became effective in October 1972.

Although the agreement on offensive weapons was for five years and the treaty on ABM of indefinite duration, Strategic Arms Limitation Talks, now labeled "SALT II," resumed in November 1972, and have been held, at intervals, in Geneva since that date. In December 1972, a Standing Consultative Commission on Arms Limitation was established to facilitate discussion of differences and interpretation of ambiguities, and to implement provisions for replacement or destruction of weapons.

Not much progress was evident in 1973, but urgency was added by the knowledge of the Soviet testing of their new missiles with multiple warheads. The large superiority in total throw-weight, if exploited by accurate MIRV, would allow them to pose a serious counterforce threat soon after the expiration of the agreement in 1977.

The first concrete results of SALT II appeared in July 1974 at the conclusion of the Moscow summit meeting between President Nixon and Secretary Brezhnev. They did not face the most important questions, offensive weapons in general and MIRV in particular, but did reach accord on four subjects.[33] These were to limit the number of ABM complexes to one in each country, to prohibit underground testing of nuclear weapons above a threshold energy yield of 150 KT, to

[33] The texts of the joint Soviet-U.S. communiqué, of the Treaty on the Limitation of

seek a comprehensive SALT agreement that would extend to 1985, and to avoid the dangers of using techniques of environmental modification for military purposes.

After their meeting at Vladivostok in November 1974, President Ford and Secretary Brezhnev announced[34] the basis on which they hoped to conclude a new agreement on the limitation of strategic arms, an agreement intended to last through 1985. Although the details remained to be negotiated, the governing principle would be to set a common ceiling on the total number of strategic delivery vehicles, and another on the number which could carry multiple warheads.

In addition to these steps, the two superpowers have made some progress toward agreeing on methods of verification.

The 1974 Protocol to the 1972 ABM Treaty

The official communiqué following the 1974 Moscow summit meeting announced that both sides had "concluded a protocol providing for the limitation of each side to a single deployment area for ABM systems instead of two such areas as permitted to each side by the (ABM) Treaty." Although the text of the protocol was not released, many details were explained in Secretary Kissinger's subsequent press conference. The agreement was for five years, automatically renewable at five-year intervals if not abrogated by either party. While the U.S. has elected to place its ABM complex for the defense of a missile field, and the U.S.S.R. for the defense of its capital city, each will be allowed to change to the other option. However, if the change is made once, it cannot be reversed at a later time. It should be noted that both

---

Underground Nuclear Weapon Tests, of the protocol to that treaty, and of a joint statement on environmental modification techniques are reprinted in *Survival* 16 (September/October 1974), 232–238. Following this is the text of a significant press conference given by U.S. Secretary of State Henry Kissinger, *ibid.*, pp. 239–246, subsequently cited under the abbreviated title *Kissinger Press Conference 3 July 1974*.

[34] The text of the joint Soviet-American statement on Strategic Arms Limitation is reprinted in *Survival* 17 (January/February 1975), 32–33. Following is the press statement by U.S. Secretary of State Kissinger, *ibid.*, pp. 33–34, cited hereafter as *Kissinger Statement 24 November 1974*.

parties retain the right to replace their present ABM system by a new, improved version, provided that the old one is dismantled.

In his press conference,[35] Dr. Kissinger reminded his audience that the original impetus for developing and installing multiple warheads came from the requirement to be able to overcome ABM defenses. The hope that it may be possible to curtail the numbers of offensive warheads is clearly dependent on a strict limit to ABM defense. With ABM defense restricted, there is no need for very large numbers of offensive warheads in order to preserve stable deterrence.

The Limitation of Underground Nuclear Weapons Tests

The treaty on the limitation of underground weapons tests can be considered as an extension to the Partial Test Ban Treaty as well as an element in the Strategic Arms Limitation Talks.

As explained in Chapter VIII, the efforts to restrict the testing of nuclear weapons began in 1954, and produced, in 1963, a multilateral treaty to ban nuclear weapons tests in the atmosphere, in outer space, and under water. It did, however, allow testing to proceed if the explosion was conducted underground and did not vent radioactive material into the atmosphere and thence to other countries. Between the date that the Partial Test Ban entered into force and the end of 1974, the U.S. had conducted 285 underground tests, the U.S.S.R. 157, the UK 3, France 9, China 1, and India 1.[36]

The United Nations Conference of the Committee on Disarmament has sought to expand the treaty into a comprehensive test ban to prohibit weapon testing in any location, but permitting the detonation of nuclear explosions if they are for peaceful purposes. However, the only agreement to be finalized has been the U.S.-U.S.S.R. treaty of July 1974. In this bilateral pact, each party agreed not to conduct any underground nuclear weapons test having a yield exceeding 150 kilo-

[35] *Kissinger Press Conference 3 July 1974*, p. 240.

[36] *SIPRI, 1975*, p. 510. France and China are not parties to the Partial Test Ban Treaty, and have also conducted many atmospheric tests since 1963. See page 215.

tons at any place under its jurisdiction or control subsequent to March 31, 1976. They also undertook to limit the number of underground nuclear weapons tests to a minimum, and to continue their negotiations with a view toward achieving a solution to the problem of the cessation of all underground nuclear weapons tests.

The treaty remains in force for five years, with provision for extension in successive five-year periods, unless either party serves notice of termination, or unless it is replaced by a more comprehensive test ban.

It is instructive to examine the provisions for verification that the treaty is being honored. In the case of the Partial Test Ban Treaty, national means of detecting nuclear explosions in the atmosphere, in space, or under water were sufficiently sensitive and reliable in 1963 to ensure a high probability that a transgression would be discovered. This was fortified by the large number of countries which had an interest in facilitating observations. Twelve years later, the advances in the methods of seismic detection make it virtually certain that an underground explosion with a yield of more than 150 KT, detonated in the U.S. or U.S.S.R., would be detected in the other country. Moreover, considerable pains are being taken to ensure the reliability of verification by national means. Each party undertakes not to interfere with the national means of verification of the other party, and, in a protocol to the treaty, they agree to exchange information facilitating interpretation of the signals received by the seismic instruments. Among the data to be exchanged are the location and a description of the geology of the test areas, and the exact locations of test explosions, to be transmitted after the test. In addition, at each test area two test explosions are to be used for calibration purposes, with full disclosure of the time of the explosion, the depth, and the energy yield.

This treaty covers the testing of nuclear weapons, but not nuclear explosions for peaceful purposes. Another agreement is to be negotiated covering Peaceful Nuclear Explosions (PNEs). In the meantime, all nuclear explosions detonated in the specified test areas will be considered to be weapons tests, and subject to the treaty, while all explosions outside the test areas will be held to be PNEs, and consequently exempt. PNEs may be of large yield, and the geology of the surrounding area may not be well known. However, it is expected that the time and place of PNEs will be announced in advance and observers invited from the other nation.

There can be no doubt that the terms of this treaty were influenced by the strategic plans of the two powers concerned. The most recent American MIRVs are believed to have yields of 170 KT[37] for Minuteman 3 and 50 KT for Poseidon. Only one of the 18 American and only six of the 24 Soviet tests exploded subsequent to 1972 had a yield above 200 KT.[38] Examination of Figure 8 (on page 49) shows that if CEPs can be brought down to the vicinity of 0.1 nm there would be little need to exceed a yield of 150 KT even against a fairly hard target. Further testing of large warheads can be continued up to the end of March 1976.[39] Thus, it seems likely that neither party is giving up very much if it forgoes the testing of warheads of higher yield. It is true, though, that when Dr. Kissinger was asked whether the Soviets would be able to test MIRVs on the SS-9 under the 150-KT limitation, he announced that he believed that MIRVs would be carried by SS-18 rather than SS-9, that the early tests of the SS-18 MIRVs suggested that their yield would be considerably larger than 150 KT, and that if they could be reduced below 150 KT he "would consider it a considerable success."[40] Certainly, if a contest developed between very hard silos and very accurate warheads, a limit to the yield of the warheads would make it more difficult for the attacker to achieve an assured counterforce capability.

[37] *SIPRI, 1974,* p. 107, estimates 160 KT. The International Institute for Strategic Studies states that the U.S. is planning a new warhead (Mark 12A) for Minuteman with a yield of 340 KT in place of the present 170 KT and that there is the possibility of a later development in or above the 400 KT range. *Strategic Survey, 1974,* p. 48.

[38] William Epstein, "The Proliferation of Nuclear Weapons," *Scientific American* 232 (April 1975), 18–33.

[39] The *Statement of Secretary Schlesinger, 1975,* p. II–21, says that the test program for the new higher-yield warhead for Minuteman 3 has been accelerated so that it can be completed before the end of March 1976.

[40] *Kissinger Press Conference 3 July 1974,* p. 243.

It may be that this treaty represents a step toward complete cessation of testing of nuclear weapons, although it seems unlikely that the two superpowers would be prepared to stop unless the other major countries were similarly bound. The agreement certainly exhibits a new degree of cooperation in its provision for exchange of information and for permission to have observers attend PNEs.

The Vladivostok Agreements on the Limitation of Offensive Weapons

Between the Moscow meeting in July 1974 and the Vladivostok meeting in November there must have been considerable difficulty in finding a basis on which the interim agreement to limit offensive armaments could be extended without the danger of losing the degree of balance currently existing. The balance depended on a numerical superiority in Soviet launchers and in total throw-weight being offset by an American advantage in multiple warheads. Given time, the U.S.S.R. could install MIRVs and obtain a considerable advantage in all three categories. This could motivate the U.S. to make a compensating increase to their offensive strength, either in categories not limited (such as bombers) or in quantitative or qualitative improvements timed to follow closely on the expiration of the interim agreement in 1977.

After discussing these factors, Secretary Kissinger explained that "therefore the two leaders have decided that the principal focus on the discussion would not be on a brief extension of the interim agreement tied to some MIRV agreement, but to see whether the three factors, time, quantity of launchers, and quantity of warheads, cannot be related in a more constructive and stabilizing fashion over a longer period of time, that is to say, by 1985."[41]

The official text[42] of the joint statement issued at Vladivostok explained that the basis for the new agreement would be an incorporation of "the relevant provisions of the interim agreement of 26 May 1972, which will remain in force until October 1977," that the new agree-

[41] *Ibid.*, p. 241.

[42] *Survival* 17 (January/February 1975), 32–33.

ment will cover the period from October 1977 through December 31, 1985, and that, based on the principle of equality and equal security, both sides will be entitled to have a certain agreed aggregate number of strategic delivery vehicles and a certain agreed aggregate number of ICBMs and SLBMs equipped with MIRVs. It added that negotiations to complete this agreement would resume in 1975, and that a further set of negotiations would be undertaken, beginning no later than 1980 or 1981, to seek additional limitations and possible reductions subsequent to 1985.

The text did not say what the aggregate numbers would be, but President Ford revealed that ceilings of 2400 strategic delivery systems and 1320 launchers equipped with MIRV had been agreed.

Behind these rather broad statements there will need to be a great deal of detailed clarification of definitions and interpretation. It does appear from collateral statements that long-range bombers will be included as strategic delivery systems, although not as launchers of multiple warheads. Also included are to be "certain other categories of weapons that would have the characteristics of strategic weapons," but these are unspecified. American forward-based systems are not to be included. These are normally considered to embrace aircraft such as the F-111 and F-4 which do not have intercontinental ranges, but can carry nuclear weapons and can reach the Soviet Union from bases in Europe, and also carrier-based aircraft which could reach the U.S.S.R. from aircraft carriers operating in European waters. In some negotiations the Soviets have claimed that American SSBNs operating out of bases in Britain or Spain are also "forward-based systems," but these certainly are included in the Vladivostok ceiling. It is not known whether air-launched or sea-launched strategic cruise missiles are to be included.[43] There are also a number of undefined points in connection with the carryover of "the relevant provisions of the interim agree-

[43] These could have ranges of 1500 nm. See Kosta Tsipis, "The Long-Range Cruise Missile," *Bulletin of the Atomic Scientists* 31 (April 1975), 14–25. It has been suggested that SALT II may define a cruise missile to be a strategic weapon if its range exceeds 325 nm (600 km). Michael Nacht, "The Vladivostok Accord and American Technological Options," *Survival* 17 (May/June 1975), 106–113.

ment of 1972." The interim agreement placed certain limitations on the freedom to modernize and replace ballistic missiles and launchers, although it omitted any definition of what constituted a "light ICBM," a type not allowed to be converted into "land-based launchers for heavy ICBMs."[44] The Vladivostok agreement suggests complete "freedom to mix," that is, to convert any system into any other, so long as the total remains within the agreed aggregate ceiling.

If we add the 1000 modern ICBMs and 710 modern SLBMs representing the limit allowed to the U.S. under the interim agreement to their current level of 432 heavy bombers, the total of 2142 allows them another 258 weapons—enough for the SLBMs in 10 new Trident submarines, or for the provisional plan for 244 B1 bombers, for example—before they would have to take existing modern weapons out of their inventory. However, if we add 1409 modern Soviet ICBMs and 950 modern SLBMs to their 140 heavy bombers, the total of 2499 exceeds the limit, so that some reduction would be necessary to the program permitted by the interim agreement.[45]

As regards MIRV, the program for 550 Minuteman 3 and 496 Poseidon missiles would give the U.S. 1046 MIRVed launchers by 1977. If the 10 oldest Polaris-carrying SSBNs were replaced by 10 Trident submarines, the total number of MIRV launchers would be 1286. The U.S.S.R. are just beginning to deploy MIRV, and it has

[44] In a unilateral statement, the U.S. delegation to SALT I recorded that "the United States would consider any ICBM having a volume significantly greater than that of the largest light ICBM now operational on either side to be a heavy ICBM." See M. Willrich and J. B. Rhinelander, eds., *op. cit.*, pp. 303–307. There did, however, appear to be agreement that "in the process of modernization and replacement the dimensions of land-based ICBM silo launchers will not be significantly increased," and that "the term 'significantly increased' means that an increase will not be greater than 10–15 per cent of the present dimensions of land-based ICBM silo launchers."

[45] The interim agreement already allows the U.S. to dismantle up to 54 Titan ICBMs for replacement by modern SLBMs—more than enough for three Trident submarines, and the U.S.S.R. to dismantle up to 210 SS-7 and SS-8 ICBMs and 24 SS-N-5 in H-class SSBNs for replacement by modern SLBMs—enough for fourteen enlarged D-class submarines. To keep within the new overall limit of 2400, the Soviets could not exceed seven more enlarged D-class SSBNs without having to sacrifice some bombers or modern ICBMs.

been estimated[46] that it might take up to 1980 for them to have more than 1000 in the field. Consequently, the limit of 1320 does not appear to constrain present plans for the next few years.

In comparison with the 1972 agreement, the main difference is the establishment of a common ceiling for all strategic weapons, including bombers. The level of 2400 does stabilize the total numbers at close to the present values. The inclusion of MIRV at the high level of 1320 allows present programs to proceed but may be an impediment to later proliferation. Quantitative improvements are allowed, perhaps even stimulated, by the numerical ceiling.

The question of verification of MIRV installation has not been solved. It seems probable that association of MIRV with a particular type of launcher will be established through observation of test firings, and the assumption will be made that all deployed launchers of that type are armed with MIRV. This could form an impediment to the retrofitting of a portion of a large class of missiles hitherto armed with single warheads, such as Minuteman 2, since all of the class would be considered by the other party to count against the MIRV limit.

Neither was anything said about mobile land-based missiles. The objection to these is not on grounds of stability, since they should be less vulnerable than static missiles, but because the numbers deployed will be difficult to verify by national nonintrusive means.[47]

Although Pandora's Box has not been closed, Dr. Kissinger was able to say: "If [the negotiations are successful] it will mean that a cap has been put on the arms race for a period of ten years; that this cap is substantially below the capabilities of either side; that the element of insecurity, inherent in an arms race in which both sides are attempting to anticipate not only the actual programmes but the capabilities of the

[46] *Survival* 17 (January/February 1975), 33. But the announcement that 60 MIRV launchers are already deployed in two new ICBMs may shorten the estimate.

[47] In a unilateral statement at the SALT I meetings, the U.S. delegation indicated that it would withdraw its proposal that mobile land-based ICBM launchers be prohibited by the interim agreement, but that it wished to bring the matter up at subsequent negotiations, and "would consider the deployment of operational land-mobile ICBM launchers during the period of the Interim Agreement as inconsistent with the objectives of that Agreement." See M. Willrich and J. B. Rhinelander, *op. cit.*, p. 306.

other side, will be substantially reduced with levels achieved over a ten-year period by agreement.'' [48]

The 1974 Agreements on Verification Procedures

We have noted previously that most of the verification of arms-control agreements depends on nonintrusive national means, of which one very important element in the case of the two superpowers is high-resolution photography from satellites. However, there will be many circumstances in which national means may be insufficient to assure confidence.

In the case of the treaty to limit underground nuclear weapons testing, it is recognized that the best way to convince other countries that a nuclear explosion is really intended for peaceful purposes is to invite observers to be present at the event.

Some of the experimental installations made during development of the ABM systems are not permitted under the 1972 ABM treaty and must be dismantled. It will be important to convince the other party that this is being done, and a protocol has been drawn up by the Standing Consultative Commission establishing ''procedures governing the replacement, dismantling, or destruction and notification thereof for ABM systems and their components.''

Since the 1972 interim agreement for the limitation of offensive weapons allows ICBMs and older SLBMs to be dismantled in order to be replaced by an equal number of modern SLBMs, it will be important to provide verification of the dismantling to the other party. The Standing Consultative Committee has prepared a second protocol on ''procedures governing replacement, dismantling or destruction and notification thereof for strategic offensive arms.''

The terms of both of these protocols for the verification of the destruction of weapons have been kept secret at the request of the U.S.S.R., but they have been submitted to U.S. Congressional committees.[49]

Development of new approaches to the question of verification are

[48] *Kissinger Statement 24 November 1974,* p. 34.

[49] *Kissinger Press Conference 3 July 1974,* p. 240.

encouraging, since many of the attempts to achieve arms-control agreements have foundered on this subject.

Conclusions on SALT

There is no doubt that uncertainty regarding the future stability of the strategic balance must have weighed heavily in the considerations which persuaded the two superpowers to come to the negotiating table, to return for extended sessions until the first agreement was made, and to undertake to continue the process. The two possible developments which gave them the greatest concern were probably the large-scale introduction of MIRV and ABM. The other principal inducement to open discussions may well have been their common apprehension concerning the growing threat from China, which might motivate each to build an ABM system not, in fact, intended to destabilize the U.S.–U.S.S.R. balance but nevertheless open to such an interpretation. No doubt there are many other subjects on the agenda for discussion, but they would be of secondary significance.

The real issue at stake in the SALT series is the management and control of the strategic balance during the next ten years. It is most unlikely that the negotiations will end in a sudden and complete success. Far more probable is a continuing series of meetings lasting for years, with occasional agreements being announced, and with the possible establishment of a permanent conference.

Some important progress has been made already with the official recognition that the balance must be considered in its entirety—that strategic offensive forces and strategic defensive forces constitute the two faces of the same coin.

The first negotiated limitations have not reduced the strength of either party. The building of new weapons systems may continue, either to come up to limits not yet reached, or with compensating reductions in other systems to keep below agreed ceilings. But it is generally believed that it is better to compete within a set of accepted rules than to have no rules at all, and that the risk of dangerous destabilizing developments is decreased to the extent that rules and understandings have been discussed and agreed, and uncertainty, though by no means eliminated, at least reduced.

It cannot be said that SALT has actually brought about any degree at all of actual disarmament. It has not stopped the development of new types of weapons, caused the reduction of forces, or prevented the initiation of anything which either superpower wished to build. But an important factor which makes short-term agreements both difficult to establish and of limited usefulness is the very long lead-time (seven to ten years) that now elapses between the conception and the realization of a major weapons system. Neither party dares to be left even temporarily without a weapon possessed in strength by the other. This has been the story of BMD and of MIRV, and to some extent of the supersonic long-range bomber. But if SALT II can establish a basis of equality over a period of ten years, and if the fears of a counterforce disarming capability are allayed, it may be possible to maintain the balance of stable deterrence without continual additions to the weapons systems.

But it would be a mistake to assess SALT on the grounds of weapons and the strategic balance alone. Political and psychological considerations are of comparable importance. Are the negotiations no more than a ritual to pacify public criticism? Is it hopeless to expect the Russians to analyze problems on the same terms as the Americans, let alone accept the same criteria and derive the same conclusions? Before answering such questions in a pessimistic vein, one should recall that meetings have been held over a period of more than five years, without any of the publicity, leaks, polemics, accusations, or recriminations that accompany negotiations that have failed or that were undertaken for ends of propaganda rather than agreement. Three important accords have been reached. Furthermore, both partners have been prepared to bear political costs for SALT, in the form of apprehension and rebukes from allies who would prefer to see negotiations in a forum in which they had a voice themselves, and from many quarters which resent the dominant position of the two superpowers.

The first important accomplishment of SALT in the psychological sphere may well have been to convince the two parties that, in fact, neither is really seeking a first-strike capability, but that each puts as his first objective the maintenance of stable nuclear deterrence. Once this is genuinely believed on both sides, it is not too much to hope that sufficient restraint and cooperation will be exercised to keep the balance of deterrence both mutual and stable. At this point, the main efforts toward arms control could be diverted to a multinational forum for the limitation and reduction of conventionally armed forces. And, as is the case for strategic weapons, the primary goal must be to guarantee the stability of deterrence which is the best protection against the scourge of war.

APPENDIX A

Mathematical Analysis of Deterrence

Assumptions

A country X has N_x missiles.

A rival country Y has N_y missiles.[1]

X can tolerate the damage to his cities that could be caused by a number of Y's missiles up to the number of U_y.

Similarly, X will need to devote at least U_x of his missiles to the attack of Y's cities in order to inflict more damage than Y can bear.[2]

Each of X's missiles has n_x warheads.

Each of Y's missiles has n_y warheads.

If X attacks Y's missile silos, the probability that a given warhead hits a silo is C_x.

Conversely, the probability that any one of Y's warheads hits one of X's silos in a counterforce attack is C_y.[3]

[1] The point $P(N_x, N_y)$ can be plotted in cartesian coordinates as on Figure 28.

[2] The rectangle of dimensions $U_x . U_y$ marks the zone of "no deterrence" as in Figure 30.

[3] We assume that the silos are too far apart for one warhead to be able to destroy more than one silo. In a heavy attack, more than one warhead may be aimed at one silo. But even if it can be hit more than once, a silo can be destroyed only once. Thus "hits" should be interpreted as "destroys, unless it has been destroyed already" or "comes close enough to destroy."

The Case of Single Warheads

Consider the case of single warheads, where $n_x = n_y = 1$.

Deterrence of X by Y

If Y has only a very few missiles, $N_y < U_y$, his capability to damage X's cities will be insufficient to deter X.

If Y has a large number of missiles, more than $(N_x + U_y)$, X cannot reduce the number below U_y, and X is deterred.

The problem that requires further calculation is the intermediate case. Suppose that X keeps U_x of his N_x missiles in reserve, to retain the capacity to threaten unbearable destruction of Y's cities, and launches the remaining $(N_x - U_x)$ missiles in a counterforce first strike against the N_y missile silos of Y. What must be the size of N_y in order that exactly U_y silos survive the attack?

If N_y silos are attacked by $(N_x - U_x)$ missiles, each silo will be attacked by an average of $(N_x - U_x)/N_y$ missiles. Consider only the integral values $S = (N_x - U_x)/N_y$, so that each silo is attacked exactly S times.[4]

The probability that a silo escapes one attack is $(1 - C_x)$.

The probability that it escapes each of S attacks is $(1 - C_x)^S$.

Out of the N_y silos attacked, the expected number of survivors will be $N_y(1 - C_x)^S$.

The condition that the expected number of Y's missiles surviving should be just equal to the threshold for the deterrence of X is then

$$N_y(1 - C_x)^S = U_y \quad (1)$$

To make numerical calculations, one should choose integral values $S = 1, 2, 3, \ldots$ and then compute $N_y = U_y(1 - C_x)^{-S}$. Then, with the values of N_y known, compute

$$N_x = U_x + S . N_y \quad (2)$$

This gives one a series of separated points $P(N_x, N_y)$ on the curve marking the limit for the deterrence of X. To complete the curve, join separate neighboring points by straight line segments.

[4] It can be shown that this is the most efficient way of attacking N_y targets by SN_y missiles.

It can be shown that the slope of the curve is C_x for the first segment, beginning at $A(U_x, U_y)$, for which $S = 0$. This demonstrates why the zone of mutual deterrence is narrow for high counterforce effectiveness. For subsequent segments between the points S, $S + 1$, the slope is $C_x/(1 + S.C_x)$. This obviously decreases with increasing values of S, so that the zone of mutual deterrence widens out for large N_x.

Deterrence of Y by X

The same reasoning can be retraced with X and Y interchanged. Points on the curve marking the values of N_x such that a counterforce attack by $(N_y - U_y)$ missiles will leave exactly U_x surviving, and hence just adequate force to deter Y by counter-city retaliation, are given by the two equations

$$N_x(1 - C_y)^S = U_x \qquad (3)$$

$$N_y = U_y + S.N_x \qquad (4)$$

Numerical Example

To give a numerical example, take the case illustrated on Figure 41, where

$$n_x = n_y = 1$$

$$C_x = \tfrac{1}{2}, C_y = \tfrac{3}{4}$$

$$U_x = 100, U_y = 50$$

To compute the limit for the deterrence of X, substitute the numbers in the equations:

$$N_y(\tfrac{1}{2})^S = 50 \qquad (1)$$

$$N_y = 50.2^S$$

$$N_x = 100 + S.N_y \qquad (2)$$

S	2^S	$N_y = 50.2^S$	$S.N_y$	$N_x = 100+S.N_y$
1	2	100	100	200
2	4	200	400	500
3	8	400	1200	1300
4	16	800	3200	3300

The limiting boundary is then traced by joining up the points (100, 50), (200, 100), (500, 200), (1300, 400), and (3300, 800).

Similarly, for the limit to the deterrence of Y,

$$N_x = 100.4^S \tag{3}$$

$$N_y = 50 + S.N_x \tag{4}$$

S	4^S	N_x	$S.N_x$	N_y
1	4	400	400	450
2	16	1600	3200	3250

One then joins up the points (100, 50), (400, 450), and (1600, 3250).

The Case of Multiple Warheads

If each of X's missiles has n_x warheads, and each warhead has a probability of C_x of hitting[3] a silo, the equations can be reformulated. Now X can consider making a counterforce attack with $(N_x - U_x)\, n_x$ warheads. Consider the integral values of

$$S = (N_x - U_x)\, n_x/N_y$$

which represents the number of warheads aimed at each silo. The probability that a silo will survive the attack is $(1 - C_x)^S$, and the expected number surviving is $N_y(1 - C_x)^S$. The condition that this equals the threshold of deterrence for X is then $N_y(1 - C_x)^S = U_y$, equation (1). The only difference from the case of single warheads is that the former equation (2) becomes

$$N_x = U_x + S.N_y/n_x \tag{2'}$$

As before, the points representing integral values of S should be joined up by straight segments, whose slopes are given by

$$n_x C_x/(1 + S.C_x)$$

The limit for the deterrence of Y is given by equation (3) and by

$$N_y = U_y + S.N_x/n_y \tag{4'}$$

The Condition for the Existence of a Doubly Unstable Zone

The slope of the first segment of the curve marking the limit for the deterrence of X, which begins at the point $A(U_x, U_y)$, is $n_x C_x$. Analytical geometry tells us that the first segment of the curve marking the limit for the deterrence of Y, which also begins at A, has a slope of $1/n_y C_y$. If the first slope is less than the second, as is the case on Figure 33, for example, a zone of mutual deterrence opens out from point A. However, if the curve marking the limit for the deterrence of X should commence at A with a larger slope than the other curve (marking the limit for the deterrence of Y), as is the case on Figure 35 and Figure 38, then the two curves enclose a zone where neither X or Y is deterred, and where each has a first-strike capability. The mathematical condition for the existence of a doubly unstable zone is then

$$n_x C_x > 1/n_y C_y$$

or, in other words,

$$n_x C_x n_y C_y > 1$$

Since for widely spaced silos C_x and C_y cannot exceed 1, double instability can occur only if at least one of the antagonists has multiple warheads.

APPENDIX B

Principal Characteristics of the Multilateral Nuclear Arms Regulation Treaties

Table B-1. Dates, zones covered, objectives, duration

Treaty	Date signed	Date in force	Zone covered by the treaty	Objectives sought: Military	Objectives sought: Civilian	Duration
Partial Test-Ban Treaty	5 Aug 1963	10 Oct 1963	Earth's atmosphere Exo-atmospheric space Underwater	To prevent the proliferation of nuclear weapons and the development of new weapons	To prevent the radioactive pollution of the atmosphere	Unlimited
Nonproliferation Treaty	1 July 1968	5 Mar 1970	All nonnuclear weapon states	To prevent the direct or indirect dissemination of nuclear weapons	Development of nuclear energy for peaceful purposes	25 years, with the possibility of limited or unlimited renewal
Antarctic Treaty	1 Dec 1959	23 June 1961	Antarctic	Nuclear and conventional nonmilitarization	Utilization of the Antarctic for peaceful purposes	30 years
Outer Space Treaty	27 Jan 1967	10 Oct 1967	Exo-atmospheric space The moon Other celestial bodies	Nuclear nonmilitarization	Utilization of space for peaceful purposes	Unspecified
Latin American Nuclear-Free Zone Treaty	14 Feb 1967	22 Apr 1968	All Latin American states including all territory under their sovereignty	Nuclear nonmilitarization	Development of nuclear energy for peaceful purposes	Indefinite
Sea Bed Treaty	11 Feb 1971	18 May 1972	Sea bed, ocean floor, and subsoil thereof, except for the bed of the territorial sea of the coastal state out to 12 miles	Nuclear nonmilitarization of the sea bed	Exploitation of the sea bed for peaceful purposes	Unspecified

Table B-2. Eligible countries, provision for amendments and verification

Treaty	Eligible countries	Provision for amendments	Provision for verification
Partial Test-Ban	All	On approval by a majority of the contracting parties, including the votes of all of the original parties	Unspecified
Nonproliferation	All	By majority of all contracting parties, but subject to veto by nuclear weapon states or members of Board of Governors of IAEA	Conforming to the statutes of the IAEA
Antarctic	All members of the U.N.	At any time by unanimous agreement	Unilateral on notification
Outer Space	All	Takes effect for each party accepting the amendment, after approval by an overall majority	Unilateral, on notification, under conditions of reciprocity
Latin America (Tlatelolco)	All Latin American republics. All other sovereign states south of 35° N in the Western Hemisphere. States for whom additional Protocols I and II are open	Approval by two-thirds of contracting parties present and voting at the General Conference	By the IAEA, conforming to its statutes, by the council of OPANAL
Sea Bed	All	Takes effect for each party accepting the amendment after approval by an overall majority	Unilateral and multilateral

Table B-3. Provisions for revision, withdrawal, and recourse

Treaty	Provision for revision	Provision for withdrawal	Recourse in event of violation
Partial Test-Ban	Unspecified	By announcement, with three months notice	Unspecified
Nonproliferation	By conference of the contracting parties, five years after treaty enters into force	By announcement, with three months notice and justification	Unspecified
Antarctic	After thirty years, or on demand of a contracting party	According to provision of Article XII of treaty	Peaceful means. International Court of Justice
Outer Space	Unspecified	Possible one year after entry into force, but requires written notification to take effect one year after receipt	Unspecified
Latin America (Tlatelolco)	On demand of a signatory, or by decision of OPANAL	By announcement, with three months notice required except for states having waived requirement that all other eligible states must have signed	General Conference of OPANAL will inform U.N. Security Council, U.N. General Assembly, OAS, and IAEA
Sea Bed	A review conference will be held five years after treaty enters into force	By announcement, with three months notice, and justification	Reference to U.N. Security Council

Personal Name and Author Index

(Reference is to page number only. Name may be in text or footnote.)

Subject Index

(Reference is to page number only. Item may be in text, footnote, figure or table)